D1568188

Critical Essays on Ford Madox Ford

Critical Essays on Ford Madox Ford

Richard A. Cassell

G. K. Hall & Co. • Boston, Massachusetts

Library of Congress Cataloging in Publication Data

Critical essays on Ford Madox Ford.

   Critical essays on modern British literature)
   Includes index.
   1. Ford, Ford Madox, 1873–1939—Criticism and interpretation.
I. Cassell, Richard A., 1921– . II. Series.
PR6011.053Z586 1987   823'.912   86-25620
ISBN 0-8161-8761-4 (alk. paper)

This publication is printed on permanent/durable acid-free paper
MANUFACTURED IN THE UNITED STATES OF AMERICA

CRITICAL ESSAYS ON BRITISH LITERATURE

Richard A. Cassell's introduction and text are less concerned with the sensationalism of Ford's life than with his position in the literary canon. His exceptionally clear and well written essay clarifies the thesis of how criticism should not be solely an adjunct of personal history. At the same time Cassell provides a first-rate history of Ford criticism. The volume emphasizes *The Good Soldier* and *Parade's End* — with essays on early writing, literary associations, poetry, and social criticism, concluding with overviews of Ford's position in the entire literary canon.

Cassell's evaluations of individual critics and schools of Ford criticism are always balanced and perceptive, separating his works from the fabled life of this intriguing personality.

Zack Bowen, GENERAL EDITOR

University of Delaware

CONTENTS

INTRODUCTION

"Words mean more than we mean to express when we use them; so a whole book ought to mean a great deal more than the writer meant."

"*Do* we decide questions at all? We decide *answers*, no doubt, but surely the questions decide *us*."
— Lewis Carroll, *Alice's Adventures in Wonderland.*

By a curious paradox, not unusual when assessing a writer's critical reputation, Ford Madox Ford, as we learn more about his life, seems in process of being properly separated from it. We grow nearer to a clear view of what is relevant to his work in his life, character, and times.

Ford was a complex, enigmatic personality who baffled, fascinated, or irritated his contemporaries, from those he loved and knew well to those who only read him or heard the gossip. He was a realist, visionary, romantic, and fabricator of myths—about himself or those he knew or imagined. He was a writer of fairy tales, novelist, poet, biographer, art and literary critic, editor, memoirist, social philosopher. A learned man with a remarkable if often inaccurate memory, he distrusted facts, placed his faith in impressions, and perfected his impressions into fictions that captured substantive realities. He could be haughty, patronizing, or humble; he wavered between an exaggerated self-assurance and an almost paralyzing lack of it. He was incompetent in business and often in personal relationships, sometimes with disastrous results. Always he was a generous man totally devoted to the supremacy of the arts in a civilized society. He was admired, tolerated, vilified, ignored, and on occasion celebrated. He died poor.

Critical response to Ford's work can be divided into two stages: before and after his death in 1939. A full accounting of published criticism up to 1962 is available in David Dow Harvey's indispensable annotated bibliography of the works and criticism (1962) and in the representative reviews and essays reprinted in Frank MacShane's *Ford Madox Ford: The Critical Heritage* (1972).

For thirty-eight of his forty-eight years as a writer, Ford published at least one book a year and in some years five or six. Most evaluations of

Ford the writer before his death are anchored in the critic's judgment of Ford the man. Since he had so many voices and allegiances and refused to be labeled, he was at best thought of as a talented dilettante, a literary butterfly, especially by established academic reviewers. Some praised; some promised the reader would at least be entertained; a few provided insights, but all in all these captives of conventional preconceptions and deadlines were limited in their vision of what Ford was about.

He was better served by a few Edwardian and twentieth century British and American novelists and poets, even those he not always kindly disguised as characters in his novels, such as H. G. Wells. The niggling Mr. Pett in *The New Humpty-Dumpty* is modeled on Wells, who later ridiculed Ford in *Boon*. And, yet, though Wells resented Ford's ascribing to him words he never said and things he never did, and disassociated himself from Ford's and James's and Conrad's "endless chatterings" about technique, he thought Ford a "splendid," and "very great" poet, called *The Good Soldier* "a great book," and defended him, if only in letters to editors, against personal attacks in the press.[1]

In their 1915 reviews of *The Good Soldier*, a young British novelist and an older American one disagree but offer about the only criticism at the time transcending a gathering of adjectives. Rebecca West sees beyond "the wonder of its technique" to a "beauty and wisdom" and depth of subject sustained by "a force of passion," and unlike any critic of the time perceived the novel as being about the "spiritual life of Ashburnham." Theodore Dreiser admires the story, its truth, its "beautiful theme," its plot infused with the inevitability of Greek tragedy, but argues that the novel fails to realize its subject because of the "encrusting formalism" of its narrative method and Ford's "sniffy reverence for conventionalism" and "the moldy past."

Ford met Joseph Conrad in 1889 and Ezra Pound in 1909. The elder artisan in fiction and the youthful poet turned to Ford for help and counsel and offered him the two most important personal and literary relationships in his career. The intimacy of Ford and Conrad excited the imaginations and frayed the nerves of both; they were artistically, not temperamentally, compatible. Their creative work profited in different ways, and their nerves suffered breakdowns for somewhat different reasons. Ford rightfully resented the minimizing by reviewers of his role in the collaboration and the denigration of his character and artistic integrity. The true measure of the man stands firmly behind the thousands of words he was to write about Conrad. If Ford had public reservations about the formal structure of some of Conrad's novels, and if he must have privately regretted the fading of their intimacy and Conrad's public silence about his writing, he always honored him as a great and genuine artist and declared generously, if inaccurately, that everything he knew about literature he had learned from Conrad.[2]

Ford's most supportive friend was Ezra Pound. They taught and learned from each other from the time they met until Ford's death. They were intellectually and artistically (but not politically) compatible, understood each other's quirky temperaments, and were honest with each other without any of the public posings or private nervous tensions or intimate involvement in each other's private lives that plagued the Conrad-Ford association. They could jest and joust with each other in conversations, letters, and print. They satisfied each other's ego sufficiently to place their public masks aside and advertised each other in such a way to be both generous and self-serving. Pound seemed more willing to express his admiration publicly, naming Ford "the best critic in England" and praising him for "his insistence upon clarity and precision," for treating contemporary subjects in contemporary language, and for defining and inspiring the reform in poetic expression so dear to Pound and important to modern poetry.

Very few other American poets and critics took notice of Ford's poetry. Conrad Aiken in his appreciative review of *On Heaven and Poems Written on Active Service* (1918), takes issue with Ford's defense of free verse and the language of good prose to convey "more intimate moods" than "symmetrical or rhymed verse" can. Yet, he finds his poems, if sometimes discursive, compelling and unusually "tender" for a contemporary poet. A year later Harriet Monroe declared Ford a master poet who brings us "the white light of truth."[3] Further support came from the 1936 publication of his *Collected Poems* with its friendly introduction by William Rose Benét and from a review by John Peale Bishop, who recognizes Ford's progress from skillful poetizing in the manner of his prose to a distinctive poetic voice in the war poetry, most genuinely in "Antwerp." During the thirties Ford's poetry was rarely taken seriously, and even today the importance of his theory of poetic language is recognized more than his creditable successes in transforming his theory into poetic practice.

As a novelist, Ford fared less well in the England of the late 1920s than in the United States, where his popularity seemed assured by the interest in the Tietjens novels, but as early as 1930 Granville Hicks would subtitle his essay on Ford in the popular journal *Bookman* "A Neglected Contemporary." He offers the first intelligent general assessment of Ford's literary career by a critic who did not know him personally, yet took him seriously and judged him to be a major talent, especially in his fiction. Hicks's essay and twenty-three other personal and critical evaluations, all save one by American writers, were included in the 1942 *New Directions* "Homage" to Ford. They had more the effect of elegies than pleas for revival. Few listened.

Ford's rescue from the relative obscurity of the final decade of his life and the years that followed possibly began with Douglas Goldring, Ford's subeditor on the *English Review*. In 1943 he had published *South Lodge*, his reminiscences of Ford, Violet Hunt, and the *Review* circle, but it was not until the appearance of his appreciative biographical study *The Last Pre-Raphaelite* in 1948 that enough response was awakened to encourage Knopf to publish *Parade's End* in 1950, with a perceptive introduction by Robie Macauley, and *The Good Soldier* in 1951, with an introductory interpretation by Mark Schorer that initiated a vigorous critical debate still in progress. Since Goldring's biography, three full-length critical biographies have appeared, as well as Harvey's bibliography, Ford's selected letters, the letters and published writings of Ford and Pound to each other, and several reprints, some edited, of his fiction, criticism, and reminiscences. In addition, some twenty book-length critical studies, hundreds of essays and reviews, three collections of critical essays on Ford, and numerous dissertations have been written. More recently the diaries of Olive Garnett (not yet in print but made available to Thomas Moser) and of Violet Hunt for 1917 (edited by Marie and Robert Secor, who are in the process of editing her other diaries) have been published. And Ford has figured with increasing prominence in critical studies of his contemporaries and of the modern novel and literature.

Since Ford's death the major novels have created more critical interest than his other writings and literary activities. That Ford was a great editor with an uncanny eye for literary talent and genius in both established and unknown writers has never been challenged. Nor has his lifelong generosity to young writers who sought him out or to any writer whose work he believed deserved publication or was being unjustly neglected. But his own published work, when not neglected, makes clear that in death as well as in life he has been a prodigy of controversy.

A persistent point of issue concerning Ford's nonfiction writings has been that of their factual inaccuracies, although Ford always made clear he intentionally used in these texts all the wiles of the writer of fiction, who creates illusions of reality that discover truth. For those who can read these writings as Ford intended, he offers a bounty of revelations. His extensive writings about Conrad, and especially his elegiac memoir written immediately after Conrad's death, provoked the most formidable attacks. Yet, it is interesting that since G. Jean-Aubry in 1957 labeled Ford "a pathological liar,"[4] Conrad and Ford scholars have abandoned the epithet. Critics such as Jocelyn Baines, Frederick Karl, John Meixner, Moser, and Ian Watt among others, have come to understand that the collaboration was more an actual collaboration than once believed, and that the years of intimacy between these two men were vitally important to both, personally and creatively. In Ford's case, several critics have noted analogues to *The Nigger of the Narcissus*, *Lord Jim*, and *Heart of Darkness* in *The Good Soldier*, although apparently no one has noted that Marlow's realization in the heart of Africa that he must relinquish "principles" and seek safety in his "efficiency" and the work at hand is not unlike the realization and resolution Tietjens comes to on the battleground of Europe; one might say, Marlow's rivets become Tietjens's duty rosters.

Undergirding all Ford's nonfiction is his desire to educate his readers, to shock them intellectually into asking questions and developing a "critical attitude." He was a celebrator of art, literature, and the civilized mind, all of which he felt modern life was bound to stifle. "A hero of letters," Edward Crankshaw calls him, and William H. Pritchard recognizes "the humanity of Ford's imagination" which brings his subjects "to new life."[5] These two, along with MacShane in his introduction to Ford's critical writings, give us about the only perceptive extended assessments of Ford as a literary critic, but their judgments apply as well to all of Ford's nonfiction.

Although critical thought and rhetoric have been preoccupied with the content and artistry of *The Good Soldier* and the Tietjens tetralogy, many critics have dutifully examined the twenty-five assorted fairy tales, romances, and novels, including the three collaborations with Conrad, that preceded *The Good Soldier* for whatever clues they could find to explain Ford's lengthy apprenticeship and his reluctance to commit himself to the innovative theory he had mostly formulated during his years with Conrad. Many have recognized in the early fiction subjects, characters, narrative techniques, and sensitivities to be refined, integrated, and re-formed in the major fiction. For example, Caroline Gordon discovers in *The Young Lovell* a mythic key to Ford's fiction, and Ambrose Gordon, Jr., another not unrelated key in the fairy tales.[6] In fact, we now realize the early fiction is not all apprentice work. Alison Lurie believes *The Queen Who Flew* comparable to the contemporary fairy tales of Andrew Lang and Oscar Wilde.[7] Since Conrad's ambivalent, possibly misunderstood, response to the Fifth Queen novels as "the swan song of Historical Romance — and frankly I am glad to have heard it," many have found them admirable, including V.S. Pritchett, Graham Greene, Arthur Mizener, and recently William Gass, who defends them most eloquently of all.[8] Ann Barr Snitow more recently has dared suggest and support that Ford's freshman novel *The Shifting of the Fire* "already shows signs of being closer in temperament to the Joyce of *Ulysses* than he is to any Victorian novelistic tradition."[9]

The five novels Ford was able to publish after the Tietjens series (1928–1936) are, except for a lame reversion to the historical romance in *A Little Less Than Gods*, in part complex maneuverings of techniques he had mastered, in part experiments in narrative modes that could render the depraved materialistic values of the Depression years and still extricate his protagonists to place them in fairy-tale denouements. Paul L. Wiley (1962) speculates that Ford was seeking in them to create a contemporary myth, but most critics follow Mizener's judgment, reflecting Pound's of the early novels, that even with their ingenious scenes and evocations, the later fiction is fantastic and absurd.[10] More recently, reviewing the 1984 reprint of *The Rash Act* and the still out-of-print *Henry for Hugh*, Cornelia Cook dexterously argues these companion novels limp toward destroying the literary modernism that Ford himself was instrumental in initiating.

The drama of the extensive criticism on *The Good Soldier* and *Parade's End* since Ford's rescue from oblivion in the late 1940s had first to decide what kinds of novels they are. Although previous critics had tentatively approached defining a genre for *The Good Soldier*, it was not until Schorer's "Interpretation," a revision of a 1948 essay, which introduced the 1951 Vintage reprint, that the question made its dramatic entrance. He named it "an ironic comedy of humor, and the humor is phlegm." Even those who agreed it is an ironic comedy have suggested several other comic modes. In a 1980 virtuoso piece of critical synthesis, Avrom Fleishman expands upon Schorer's reductive classification and argues that several of the comic forms previously identified are subsumed in the broader scope of the novel that creates "the ironic world of low-mimetic realism," not unlike that of Shakespeare in the variety of its appeals. Further, he claims that Dowell becomes "one of the great comic characters of literature" and that the novel foresees the modern comic mode of an inquisitive "but inveterately self-defeating speculation."[11]

On the other side of the stage, Meixner in an important 1960 essay argues that *The Good Soldier*, which he ranks "among the more powerful novels that have been written," is "at its core, a tragedy" around which Ford has "placed a context of comic irony." His view has been supported, though based on other assumptions, by several others and most recently (1980) by Gordon Hartford. But unlike Meixner, who at one point evokes Aristotle, Hartford concludes a wide-ranging essay by suggesting, less convincingly, that the novel is a "premonition" of the social tragedy of Arthur Miller.[12]

The genre of *Parade's End* seems more identifiable with several fictional narratives from ancient epic to characteristic British novels from Richardson to Thackeray and Dickens. But, more significantly, it is an— possibly *the*—exemplar of a transitional novel. It is both a culmination and an innovation that spans the glorious panoramas of the Victorian novel and the tautly structured masterworks of twentieth-century fiction in English, principally engendered by James, Conrad, and Ford himself. George Core's comprehensive yet concise "Ordered Life and the Abysses of Chaos: *Parade's End*," included in this collection, defends the importance of this great, if flawed, work with an imaginative probe that transcends mere identification of its genre.

Another issue of critical judgments is concerned with Ford's pervasive presence in his novels. Ford used the novel as memoir and as an instrument of his personality by a process of autobiographical insemination, not unique to him, that conceives content and formal structure out of intimate relations, emotions, thoughts, and all the disjointed actualities of life. In doing so he appears to challenge his own demand for authorial objectivity, but he was aware the implied contradiction is only apparent. "The

Impressionist author," he writes in 1913, "is sedulous to avoid letting his personality appear in the course of his book. On the other hand, his whole book his whole poem is merely an expression of his personality."[13] The created illusion of "an affair in real life" must eschew judgment but cannot conceal the temperament of the creator. Few would disagree that Ford's novels seldom achieve such a delicate balance. Fortunately, since the appearance of MacShane's and Mizener's biographies and Moser's recent psychological study *The Life in the Fiction of Ford Madox Ford* (1980), we now know a good deal about Ford's life and how far he and those he knew are imaginatively transformed into his fiction. All three books are indispensable, and though Moser is more speculative and the Ford he creates admittedly "an abstraction," he allows us as revealing an inward view of the man and of the created projections of his experience and personality as is now possible from an outsider looking in.

Ford was an impressionist realist determined to leave an unbiased record of his own times, but his novels under the pressures of his temperament resolve reality into romance. In R.P. Blackmur's early and critically persistent phrase, Ford's fiction embodies a dedication "to lost causes known to be lost." Elliott Gose revealingly titles his 1956 study of *Parade's End* "From Reality to Romance," a shift in the novel's mode which he argues is a flaw that endangers Tietjens's "position as a symbolic ideal."[14] In the early 1960s some others, from somewhat different vantage points, observe a similar shift in Ford's novels, but Samuel Hynes believes that in his best novels Ford found a successful "structural use for his romancing habit of mind," and James Trammell Cox admires the "human" quality of Ford's romantic turn of mind, his "passion for Provence," that weakens the formal unity of *The Good Soldier* but raises it "above the level of the totally controlled work of art."[15]

Ford's reluctance to abandon romance reflects an ingrained trait that Pound understood, as did Morton Dauwen Zabel, who in the early 1930s recognized that Ford's "uncertainty of nature . . . may be traced at least partly to his inability to resolve and localize his aesthetic and civil morals." Twenty years later, discussing *The Good Soldier*, Hugh Kenner suggests that Dowell's bewilderment is Ford's. "The gap between presentation and 'values' is never bridged. Ford's presented values are those of the craftsman; the man Ford, most compassionate of novelists, is himself in an impasse, an impasse of sympathy for all sides."[16] One need add only the reader's and the critic's bewilderment, and not alone with Dowell's tale.

That enigmatic tale understandably has inspired more critical statement and counter-statement than any other novel of Ford. Schorer began the contest with his "Interpretation," and not only by calling it a comedy of humor or perceiving its "bewildering maze," but, more important, by his seeing Dowell as an unreliable, self-deceived narrator suffering from "the madness of moral inertia." But Schorer is certain Ford is not self-deceived, is rather the master ironist: ". . . the author, while speaking through his simple infatuated character, lets us know how to take his simplicity and his infatuation." Self-deception seems a corollary or, at least, a not unusual consequence, of bewilderment. The critical question has since become whose bewilderment, whose deception—Dowell's, Ford's, the critics', the general reader's, or all four? And if that can be determined, what is the meaning to be harvested?

Meixner in "The Saddest Story" was among the first to take a stand against Schorer's reading by affirming that if Dowell is incapable of acting, he does in retrospect feel deeply, and the apparent absurdity of a man long blind to what was happening around and to him evokes a tone of "grave sadness" making Dowell a "deeper, more human and sympathetic" character than Schorer's morally inert fool. Hence, Dowell is as reliable as "a psychic cripple" can humanly be. Hynes in his important 1961 "The Epistemology of *The Good Soldier*" looks elsewhere than Schorer's ascription of *accidia* to Dowell and asserts that "the narrator's fallibility *is* the norm," and that Dowell is able to share vicariously Ashburnham's suffering and finally to know what he cannot know.

Two later noteworthy essays focus on Ford's epistemology. William P. Pierce in "The Epistemological Style of Ford's *The Good Soldier*" (1975) equates Schorer's "technique as discovery" with "style as epistemology." Comparing the style of the first and final chapters, Pierce concludes that the first is designed to render Dowell's mind and involve the reader in his dilemma, the last to reveal how Dowell tries rhetorical strategies to order his experiences and assign meaning, but instead ironically renders "his complete withdrawal from life."[17] Drawing upon the phenomenology of Husserl and Merleau-Ponty with whom Ford's theory and practice have something in common, Paul B. Armstrong in "The Epistemology of Ford's Impressionism," written for this edition, clarifies the epistemological process Ford employs in both the first person narration of *The Good Soldier* and the omniscient third person narration of *Parade's End*.

As early as 1963 Joseph Wiesenfarth tried to redirect critical inquiry into *The Good Soldier* away from the dominating issue of Dowell's reliability. He boldly confronts nine interpretations and in a valuable, if not altogether accurate or complete, summary concludes that "the simple truth of logic remains that the greater probability of one opinion does not and cannot destroy the probability of its contrary." Directing critics to other dimensions of this complex novel, he suggests it is the failure of every character to communicate that leads to everyone's suffering, making the novel truly "a tale of passion," as the subtitle foretells it is.[18]

Not unexpectedly, critics have had more to say about Dowell's reliability. Walter G. Creed, for example, insists we do not have to go outside the novel to understand it because all the clues are there; if we would sort and assess them, we would discover Ford is not saying that to know and judge others is impossible. Rex Bishop defends Dowell, since he has the gift of imagination Ford considered necessary for passion and manages to give form to Ashburnham's passion and in a real way "immortalizes" him for an age that had ostracized him. Robert Micklus sees Dowell's narrative as his vengeance against those who have deceived him. Other critics are less certain, becoming Dowell-like, having to resort to his "I don't know," "God knows," "I leave it to you to make head or tail of it." The impasse crumbles as another tells us "it is better to stop looking for the key to a hidden coherence" and simply enjoy Ford's skillful game with traditional plots and genres.[19] Lawrence A. Thornton's "Escaping the Impasse" is included in this collection for its compact, closely argued objection to Schorer's "Interpretation" and its influence. By examining the title, subtitle, and epigraph, along with Ford's 1927 "Dedicatory Letter," which leads us to the true story by way of Maupassant's *Fort comme le mort*, Thornton claims the novel is "preeminently about suffering, suffering for love in particular, and suffering as the lot of man in general," a view consistent with Ford's experience and conviction.

A different focus emerges that reminds us that Ford in *The Good Soldier* is creating a fiction about Dowell creating a fiction. The source may well be Kenner's earlier perception that Ford writing "out of his capacity for compassion and worry" discovers in the narrator's bewilderment a "most serviceable device" to avoid resolution. Both Ford and Dowell are illusionists, both use the same impressionistic narrative techniques, and both in their ambiguous, ambivalent fictions by avoiding experience are protected from what they do not want to or cannot face. From this view, Dowell is not an inept narrator but, like Ford, a craftsman for whom "the truth of an event is always the accuracy of his perception of it."[20] Miriam Bailin convincingly argues Dowell consciously employs Fordian techniques, and by allowing his contradictions to stand he can both "blame and absolve" everyone, including himself, and, in effect, evade "the treacherous moral ambiguities of contemporary experience."

The most comprehensive synthesis to date of the presence of the irresolute romantic, temperamentally intrusive Ford in his fiction is Snitow's recent *Ford Madox Ford and the Voice of Uncertainty*. Drawing upon MacShane's and Mizener's biographies and apparently Moser's *Life in the Fiction*, though she makes no specific reference to it, she gives innovative readings of the never fully successful experiments with several generic forms in the early novels as Ford was learning to make "not knowing into an art." Success comes with *The Good Soldier*, which is "both an Edwardian and modernist masterpiece that displays Ford's own unmistakable blend of irony, absurdity, and deep feeling." His despairing elegy for a lost time shifts in tone from that of comic irony to romance as Ashburnham eventually assumes heroic proportions for Dowell. In the enlarged visionary landscape of *Parade's End* Ford's typical ironies and paradoxes "are bounded by a romantic, mythic frame." Tietjens is allowed to retreat into a comic, if sadly ironic, pastoral. "To study Ford," Snitow believes, "is to study the history of consciousness between 1898 and, say,

1928," since "the voice of uncertainty" is that of both Ford and modernism: "subjective, ironic, indirect, often ludicrous or comic."

A large share of Ford's genius was to innovate, share, support, and absorb the stimulating artistic activities and experiments of his time while simultaneously holding on to Edwardian ideals and the Pre-Raphaelite idealization of art and the artist. It is possible today to agree with Gass that "in an arrogant display of literary genius, Ford Madox Ford brought the nineteenth century novel, in each of its principal areas of excellence, to its final and most complete expression."[21] But Ford is also among those artists who, in Harry Levin's phrases, belonging to both Victorian and twentieth century worlds, were driven by the "metamorphic impulse" to work "experimental transformations in traditional continuities."[22]

Several Fordian critics have long recognized Ford as a pioneer of modernism. *The Good Soldier* has been viewed as the epitome "of the altered tragic vision of our modern sensibility" (Meixner); Dowell and Ashburnham "represent the tragic figure of modern man" (Todd K. Bender); the novel reveals "the spiritual void that is the fundamental reality of our age" (Robert J. Andreach); "Dowell is the perfect spokesman for the society he interprets" (Duncan Aswell).[23] Further, critics have seen alliances to Impressionistic painting, Imagism, Futurism, Vorticism, Cubism, Expressionism, and the Absurdists. *The Good Soldier* prefigures the despair of Beckett, Ionesco, Pinter (Lawrence W. Jones); *Parade's End* "should be placed alongside *Ulysses* and the major Lawrence" (Roger Sale).[24] Ford's presence is found in Pound, Hemingway, Fitzgerald, Greene, Waugh, and Durrell, among others. Not every critic or literary historian will accept these judgments of Ford the novelist, but few now question that Ford was a motivating force in shaping contemporary theories of artistic language and of poetry in particular; several have endorsed Pound's conviction that he was, recent among them D.I.B. Smith in "Ford Madox Ford and Modernism." In fact, Ford may prove to be the pioneer uneasily "groping" toward Post-modernism that Cook perceives in Ford's final novels of double identities. In them Ford questions even the fractured degree of conscious knowledge he once thought possible, since his epistemology no longer seems adequate to absorb the 1930s. In these novels he parodies his own methods, subverts his own text, and in effect denies any assurance except that of absurdity, including the hero's escape at the end of *Henry for Hugh* into moneyed happiness. A weary, ever-seeking Ford finally opened hesitantly the window in his house of fiction that looked out through a morning haze to a vision of the post-modern conscious denial of conscious knowing.

Ford sincerely meant it when he requested of his heirs that no biography be written, since he had long insisted that the critic's subject is not a writer's private life, but his work, which, after all, reveals his genuine biography. We can now, when we wish, see and document in Ford's work a reflected image of Ford the living man as he emerges from the memoirs of his contemporaries and the scholarly biographies. We need insights of critical wisdom, but the surer test as the man slips further into history will be his works that survive. Those that do will have to be greater than the man who lived.[25]

I am grateful for the counsel and good will of many, but especially Professor John Meixner, Rice University; Professor Sondra J. Stang, Washington University; Professor Frank MacShane, Columbia University; and Butler University for awarding me a Butler University Fellowship to work on this book.

RICHARD A. CASSELL

Butler University

Notes

1. See H.G. Wells, *Boon* (London: T. Fisher Unwin, 1920), 124. Cited in David Dow Harvey, *Ford Madox Ford 1873–1939: A Bibliography of Works and Criticism* (Princeton: Princeton University Press, 1962), 600; H.G. Wells, "A Footnote to Hueffer," *English Review* 31 (August 1920): 178–79; reprinted in *Ford Madox Ford: The Critical Heritage*, ed. Frank MacShane (London: Routledge and Kegan Paul, 1972), 128–29.

2. Ford Madox Ford, "To Herbert Read," 19 September 1920, *Letters of Ford Madox Ford*, ed. Richard M. Ludwig (Princeton: Princeton University Press, 1965), 127.

3. Harriet Monroe, "Great Poetry," *Poetry* 13 (January 1919):219; reprinted in MacShane, *Critical Heritage*, 75–78.

4. G. Jean-Aubry, *The Sea-Dreamer: A Definitive Biography of Joseph Conrad*, trans. Helen Sebba (Garden City, N.Y.: Doubleday, 1957), 232.

5. Edward Crankshaw, "Afterword," and William A. Pritchard, "Fabulous Monster: Ford as Literary Critic" in *The Presence of Ford Madox Ford*, ed. Sondra J. Stang (Philadelphia: University of Pennsylvania Press, 1981), 236–39; 115–29.

6. Caroline Gordon, *A Good Soldier, Chapbook Number 1* (Davis: University of California Library, 1963); Ambrose Gordon, Jr., "*Parade's End*: Where War Was Fairy Tale," *Texas Studies in Literature and Language* 5 (Spring 1963):25–41.

7. Alison Lurie, "Ford Madox Ford's Fairy Tales for Children" in Stang, *Presence*, 130–42.

8. William Gass, "The Neglect of *The Fifth Queen*" in Stang, *Presence*, 25–43.

9. Ann Barr Snitow, *Ford Madox Ford and the Voice of Uncertainty* (Baton Rouge: Louisiana State University Press, 1984), 29–30.

10. Paul L. Wiley, *Novelist of Three Worlds: Ford Madox Ford* (Syracuse: Syracuse University Press, 1962), 248–92; Arthur Mizener, *The Saddest Story: A Biography of Ford Madox Ford* (New York: World, 1971), 515–23.

11. Avrom Fleishman, "The Genre of *The Good Soldier*: Ford's Comic Mastery," *Studies in the Literary Imagination* 13 (1980):31–42.

12. John A. Meixner, "The Saddest Story," *Kenyon Review* 22 (Spring 1960):234–64; Gordon Hartford, "Ford and *The Good Soldier*: A Bid for Tragedy," *English Studies in Africa: A Journal of the Humanities* 23 (1980):93–102.

13. Ford Madox Ford, "On Impressionism," *Poetry and Drama* 1 (1914):323.

14. Elliott Gose, "From Reality to Romance," *College English* 17 (1956):445–50.

15. Samuel Hynes, "Ford and the Spirit of Romance," *Modern Fiction Studies* 9 (1963):17–24; James Trammell Cox, "Ford's 'Passion for Provence,' " *ELH* 28 (1961):383–98.

16. Morton D. Zabel, review of *Return to Yesterday, Nation* 134 (6 April 1932):403–4; Hugh Kenner, "Conrad and Ford," *Shenandoah* 3 (Summer 1952):50–55.

17. William P. Pierce, "The Epistemological Style of Ford's *The Good Soldier*," *Language and Style* 8 (1975):34–46.

18. Joseph Wiesenfarth, "Criticism and the Semiosis of *The Good Soldier*," *Modern Fiction Studies* 9 (1963):39–49.

19. Walter G. Creed, "*The Good Soldier*: Knowing and Judging," *English Literature in Transition: 1880–1920* 23 (1980):215–30; Rex Bishop, "Passion in *The Good Soldier*: Ford's Tale and its Teller Re-examined," *English Studies in Canada* 4 (1978):60–68; Robert Micklus, "Dowell's Passion in *The Good Soldier*," *English Literature in Transition: 1880–1920* 22 (1979):281–92; David Eggenschwiler, "Very Like a Whale: The Comical-Tragical Illusions of *The Good Soldier*," *Genre* 12 (1979):401–14.

20. The phrase is Denis Donoghue's in "Listening to the Saddest Story" in Stang, *Presence*, 49.

21. Gass, "The Neglect of *The Fifth Queen*," 35.

22. Harry Levin, *Refractions* (New York: Oxford University Press, 1966), 287. Quoted in D. I. B. Smith, "Ford Madox Ford and Modernism," *University of Toronto Quarterly* 51 (1981):62, 63.

23. Todd K. Bender, "The Sad Tale of Dowell: Ford Madox Ford's *The Good Soldier*," *Criticism* 4 (1962):353–68; Robert J. Andreach, "Ford's *The Good Soldier*: The Quest for Permanence and Stability," *Tennessee Studies in Literature* 10 (1965):81–92; Duncan Aswell, "The Saddest Story-Teller in Ford's *The Good Soldier*," *College Language Association Journal* 14 (1970):187–96.

24. Lawrence W. Jones, "The Quality of Sadness in Ford's *The Good Soldier*," *English Literature in Transition: 1880–1920* 13 (1970):296–302; Roger Sale, "Ford's Coming of Age: *The Good Soldier* and *Parade's End*," in Stang, *Presence*, 55–76.

25. See also *Antaeus*, no. 56 (Spring 1986), ed. by Sondra J. Stang, for several more recent critical essays on Ford and his works, published since this book went to press.

The Young Writer, Collaborator, Editor

Ford and Conrad

John A. Meixner*

The 1950s were a breeding time of many changes in our understanding of the relationship between Joseph Conrad and Ford Madox Ford. Conrad's reputation was building rapidly throughout the decade, to culminate in Albert Guerard's *Conrad the Novelist* (1958). And the publication of Goldring's biography of Ford in 1948, followed by Knopf's reissuing of the Tietjens tetralogy and *The Good Soldier* in 1950 and 1951, stimulated a new awareness of a previously neglected figure. Simply by presentation these novels established, at least for a substantial body of readers, that Ford had written major, distinguished, even great works of fiction. Thereafter it was inevitable that the relationship between Ford and Conrad would be looked at more closely. And it was extremely valuable that it was now considered by people who were uncaught up in the various contentions and impassioned irrelevancies of those who had known both.

By and large, these explorers of Ford during the fifties — there were, it turned out, at least a baker's dozen of us — worked separately. Some exchange of correspondence went on. But inevitably the complexities and puzzlements of the problems presented had to be wrestled with independently, in the usual solitariness of authorship. There were all those volumes by Ford to work one's way through — in fact even to get hold of. All those books to read by authors Ford had known, and by progenitors he admired. All those anecdotes and passages about the man to be tracked down in a far-flung, disparate mass of memoir books and articles. As E. M. Forster has tidily lamented: "Books have to be read (worse luck, for it takes a long time)."[1] And — more to our present point — there were all those puzzling blanks in the Conrad scholarship: the curious silences about Ford; the brief, implied dismissals — as epitomized best perhaps in the insistence most writers on Conrad in referring to Ford as Hueffer. (That Guerard referred to Ford as Ford seemed only one more sign of his larger good sense.) Among the negative Conrad material Ford researchers had to contend with were, to begin with, the vehement attacks on Ford by Jessie

*From *Conradiana* 6 (1974):157–69. Reprinted by permission of the journal.

Conrad, in her two books about her husband and in articles and letters to the press. (For, after all, who would know better the truth of such matters than a man's very own wife, who must assuredly had been there?) We were conscious too of Conrad's own highly critical tone toward his collaborator and his talent on several occasions, especially in a letter to Edward Garnett concerning *The Inheritors:*

> There is not a chapter I haven't made him write twice — Most of them three times over. . . . I've been fiendish. I've been rude to him; if I've not called him names I've *implied* in my remarks and the course of our discussions the most opprobrious epithets. . . . And there's no doubt that in the course of that agony I have been ready to weep more than once. Yet not for him. Not for him. You'll have to burn this letter — but I shall say no more. Someday we shall meet and then — ![2]

Of particular perplexity also was the minuscule place Ford occupied in Jean-Aubry's large two-volume *Life and Letters* (1927), with almost nothing in the biographical section, and only a mere six letters included — of which at least half were either hostile or cool. (The much reprinted hostile letter of 31 July 1909, in which Conrad refused to write any further installments of *Some Reminiscences* for *The English Review*, may not even have been sent.)[3] And, of course, from the start, each Ford investigator was compelled to come to grips with the numerous stern assertions, from nearly every side, that Ford's voluminous biographical reports of himself and others were simply not to be credited. Jean-Aubry even went so far as to say, in print, that Ford was "a pathological liar."[4]

By 1950 there were only two voices of consequence to contest any of this. Ford himself, in his *Joseph Conrad: A Personal Remembrance* and a variety of articles — clearly a self-serving witness. And Douglas Goldring, in his biography *Trained for Genius* (in England, *The Last Pre-Raphaelite*). Goldring's scholarship was of course incomplete, as he himself acknowledged. Certainly his enterprise was conducted — as was to be Frank MacShane's later — against a formidable non-cooperation from Ford's literary executrix. Still, for all that, there it was. Goldring, after all, had worked with Ford on *The English Review*, had witnessed Conrad and Ford in action, and was himself someone with an experienced insider's grasp of the realities and miseries of the literary life. More crucial still, Goldring put into print for the first time a substantial number of letters from Conrad to Ford which seemed to run directly against the view set forth by Jessie Conrad and the others in the Conrad circle. Letters whose salutations moved from "Dear Mr. Hueffer" (before the collaboration began) to "My dear Ford" to "Dearest Ford" to "My Dearest Ford," and which closed "Yours affectionately," "With love ever yours," "With our love, Always yours," "Jessie and Borys, your great friends, send their love. As to mine it is always with you. Yours ever." And letters that in their body included such statements as: "it is a fact I work better in your home in touch with your sympathy." "I miss collaboration in a most ridiculous manner. I hope you don't intend dropping me altogether. . . . *Mon cher*, I appreciate your regard for my wretched affairs." And that referred to "our theory of *welded* collaboration."[5] And which, in general, seemed to reveal a good deal of intimacy between the two households — a partnership of spirit and the affections, as well as professionally.

My own investigations of Ford — to be personal for a moment — were concentrated directly in the middle of the decade, in the years 1954 through 1956. During this period I became totally absorbed by the man and his work — read, thought, ate, discussed, and slept nothing but Ford — trying to make sense of his peculiar personality, character and career. Gradually, however, during the course of these thirty-six months of sorting out and formulating, I did arrive at a goodly number of conclusions on a diversity of points, which were distilled into my book on Ford's novels: a work completed in early 1957, but not published until 1962, in a shortened version. Most of my conclusions — including those on Ford and Conrad, which total about twenty-five pages — still seem to me sound. But two further conclusions, I did not set down, because I knew I could not even begin to prove them — though I think the first at least strongly informed what I did say. Namely that the more I fitted together what I knew of Ford, the more I came to trust his statements. However casual they may have been in literal fact, in their essential meaning, that is, in what really counted, they seemed to my judgment irresistibly to be true. The other conclusion was that Ford had been done a serious injustice by people of the Conrad persuasion.

Therefore, when at the end of the decade, in 1960, there at last appeared the statement which has been made the centerpiece of this occasion, from Jocelyn Baines' biography of Conrad — that the meeting with Ford was "the most important event in Conrad's literary career"[6] — I hardly had reason for surprise. (However shocked I assume some Conradians may have been.) Nor do I expect there was much astonishment from the other explorers into Ford who had labored during the 50's: Richard A. Cassell, David Dow Harvey, Frank MacShane, Richard Ludwig, Paul L. Wiley, Thomas Moser, Samuel Hynes, Elliott Gose, R. W. Lid, Ambrose Gordon, Jr. And least of all would there have been incredulity from Richard Herndon and John Hope Morey, each of whom had already prepared dissertations (the first in 1957, the second in 1960) which unlike the others had concentrated directly on the relationship of Ford and Conrad.

It think it is fair to say that Baines in his biography does not himself make his own case. (His remark is not the thesis sentence for a chapter, for example, but rather an observation made in passing as part of his narrative.) Nevertheless, when the new documentation supplied in the biography is supplemented by the factual and interpretive evidence presented by other students (especially by Herndon and Morey, and with his own emphasis by

Bernard C. Meyer), the essential thrust of Baines' statement — that Conrad's relationship with Ford was the most useful, the most seminal, and the most important of connections — seems unassailable.

Obviously the argument in support of such a proposition cannot be made adequately in brief space. Herndon's dissertation alone is more than 400 pages.[7] Still, the chief points can be run over; and in the process may even accumulate a certain conviction — enough perhaps to throw into some doubt the claims of such alternative vessels of light as Garnett, Galsworthy, or Richard Curle.

II

The case for the importance of Ford to Conrad can probably best begin with the, in one sense, littler things: the numerous practical ways in which the younger man was useful to Conrad and his work. When Ford published his *Personal Remembrances* in 1924 there were numerous outcries against his claim to have given such aid. But research during and since the fifties has pretty much shown that most of his statements are essentially correct. For example, neither of Conrad's two books of personal biography — *The Mirror of the Sea* or *A Personal Record* — would have been written without Ford's enterprise. The older man's rootedly evasive nature had very much to be prodded to write them at all — Ford constantly jogging Conrad's memory against Conrad's despair that he had nothing to say, and copying down the resultant words in his own form of shorthand. Even Jessie Conrad has conceded that *"The Mirror of the Sea* owes a great deal to his ready and patient assistance — not perhaps to the actual writing, but that book would never have come into being if Joseph Conrad had had no intelligent person with whom to talk over these intimate reminiscences."[8] (Arthur Mizener more recently has offered a fair show of evidence that, contrary to Jessie, Ford did considerable "actual writing" on the *Mirror*, and received part of its royalties.)[9] A similar process was followed, at least in the early stages, with *A Personal Record* — again promoted by Ford, this time to provide his friend with a substantial (and very much needed) income from their serialization in *The English Review*.

Few can now dispute either that Conrad took from Ford the basic situation of his short story, "Amy Foster." In *A Personal Remembrance*, Ford made the remark that Conrad had taken a short story he had written and made it his own. Later, following the protest of Jessie, the account was altered to say that Ford had told Conrad the narrative.[10] Whether Ford wrote such a story isn't known: one suspects not. However, it does seem reasonable that Ford as an author making a living by his pen did intend to use the anecdote at some time. And the indisputable fact is that the heart of "Amy Foster" can be found, in a fairly full paragraph, in Ford's *The Cinque Ports* — copies of which became available a month before Conrad began to write his story.[11]

Again, Ford supplied the central situation—the essential germ—of *The Secret Agent*—a debt which Conrad himself all but acknowledged later on, in his "Author's Note," in which he remarks that his special angle on the materials of the Greenwich bombing had crystallized when a friend, "in his characteristically casual and omniscient manner," had observed: "Oh, that fellow was half an idiot. His sister committed suicide afterwards." Neither here nor elsewhere, however, does Conrad go as far as to credit Ford by name.

As to Ford's help to Conrad in his actual writing (though it seems naive to think ideas, conceptions, and situations are of little consequence compared to the glow of words), not a little evidence points to an active role on several occasions. Two instances never came to much. Ford rearranged the manuscript of *The Rescue* for Conrad, to try to help him out of a structural problem. And Ford extracted the dialogue from Conrad's story, "To-morrow" (and it would appear contributed a good deal else)[12] to convert it into a play (*One Day More*)—again with the hope of bringing in some money for Conrad. More well known is the help Ford supplied when Conrad's desk lamp exploded, and a sizable segment of "The End of the Tether," which was already being serialized, went up in flames.[13] Indeed, it seems highly probable that Ford closely went over everything Conrad wrote before it went off to the postman. In an unpublished passage from *A Personal Remembrance* for example, Ford made the following interesting claim: "The m.s. and proofs of Heart of Darkness were the first literary works of Conrad's that the writer worked over minutely and with attention. . . . He worked minutely and with attention over every one of Conrad's books between that date and the publication of Nostromo." In Morey's view, Ford is "obviously overstating his case." But only in the sense, I think, that "worked over" implies an authority more final than was probably so. Otherwise, the passage seems completely in keeping with a major preoccupation of Ford at the time— the *mot juste*—as well as with one of Conrad's chief acknowledged reasons, his idiomatic insecurity in English, for collaboration. As to *Heart of Darkness*, Morey has assembled a persuasive case that Ford probably did work on its famous closing section, in proof stage—trying to get the absolutely right words and cadences.[14]

The most substantial piece of writing that Ford did for Conrad, however, was a section of *Nostromo*: a scene of rather intensely quiet passion between Martin Decoud and Antonia Avellanos in Chapter 5 of Part II, "the Isabels." That Ford wrote this section has not been proved beyond the shadow of any doubt, but the argument is very strong. It rests 1) on Ford's own assertion that he did; 2) on the existence in the Yale library of the manuscript of the section written in Ford's hand; 3) on a variety of facts and circumstances that support Ford's account (for which see the very full analysis in Morey's dissertation,[15] including the arguments against the section being taken down by dictation); and 4) on a letter by

Conrad to Pinker (22 August 1903), in which he assures his agent that he would be able to meet the deadlines for the serialization of *Nostromo* (which appeared in *T. P.'s Weekly* from 29 January 1904 to 7 October 1904): "If people want to begin printing (serial) say in Sept. you may let them safely—for you know that, at the very worst, H. stands in the background (quite confidentially you understand)." (It is of note—and one assumes instructive—that in Jean-Aubry's *Life and Letters*, the initial "H", which can only mean Hueffer, appeared instead as "M".)[16]

And, lastly, of course, Ford's aid to Conrad meant backing him with money as well. In 1901 he loaned Conrad £100, and as time went on Conrad owed Ford as much as £200, including the arrears in rent payment on the Pent. Morey prints a long letter from Conrad to Ford, written on 27 March 1913, in which we see that Conrad still owed the £100 capital loan plus £40 interest, and asks to be pressed for no more than the £40 over the next twelve months. (It is clear that Ford would not have troubled Conrad on this if Marwood had not suddenly turned the screw on Ford himself.) In late 1921, another letter from Conrad shows that he still owed Ford a substantial sum—at a time when in fact Conrad had decidedly begun to prosper.[17]

<h2 style="text-align:center">III</h2>

When we turn to the collaborations—works whose conceptions began in the mind of the younger man—the value of Ford for Conrad is seen even more clearly. Not so much, of course, for their own intrinsic importance, as for the territory they helped the older writer to open up. For following each novel written in partnership, Conrad's own independent writing advanced into new domains of subject matter and setting similar to those of the collaborations. Conrad's experience in the writing of *Romance*, for example, was to have at least three important consequences for his later fiction, especially for the very next novel he wrote, *Nostromo*—as Richard Herndon trenchantly points out.[18] To begin with, the materials of *Seraphina* (together with the Hispano-American writings of W. H. Hudson and R. B. Cunninghame Graham) stimulated Conrad to a further examination of the Caribbean-Central American region and its revolutionary history. Then, too, while preparing *Romance* Conrad discovered the value of using old memoirs, newspaper accounts, books of travel, and of history. As Herndon remarks, there is no conclusive evidence of Conrad's having resorted to research before he met the younger man. But Ford had already used its methods in his biography of Ford Madox Brown, in developing his first draft of *Seraphina*, and later in preparing his history of the Cinque Ports, and in his researches into the life of Henry VIII, which eventually became the basis of the *Fifth Queen* novels. Without similar historical delvings, Conrad could scarcely have composed *Nostromo* or "Gaspar Ruiz," or have contemplated in 1906 writing a novel about

Napoleon's later career. A final result of his writing of *Romance* was that for the first time Conrad was able to use in fiction his early adventures in Marseilles, including his experiences with Dominic Cervoni, material he was to exploit again in *Nostromo* — in which the character of Manuel del Populo in *Romance* becomes split into Nostromo (note the names) and Col. Sotillo — and still later in *The Arrow of Gold*, *The Rover*, and *Suspense.*

So, too, with *Inheritors.* Ford is probably correct in saying that by 1889 Conrad was regarded as a continuer of the Stevenson tradition, and that Henley had convinced him (probably with Garnett's assent) that his only chance to make a living lay in writing about the sea. With *The Nigger of the "Narcissus"* and "Youth," the sea and the exotic East were certainly the subjects around which his reputation was already growing. Thus, *The Inheritors* had the important, fortunate consequence of pushing Conrad in a quite different, and deeply congenial, direction: the exploration of political and revolutionary subjects — which was to be carried forward in the writing of "The Informer," *The Secret Agent* and *Under Western Eyes* — and *Nostromo* as well.

Even *The Nature of a Crime* can be seen to be a precursor for Conrad — particularly of *Chance.* "Both works contain as principal characters dishonest financiers, who plan to commit suicide by means of concealed poison if their loves become unbearable for them; and both depict love relationships left unconsummated because of the lover's chivalrous scruples." Herndon notes as well a number of interesting parallels of language and of strategies of sententiousness between the two works, "which suggest that Conrad either wrote more of *The Nature of a Crime* than critics have supposed or that he remembered phrases and subtle juxtapositions of circumstances and included them in *Chance*."[19]

IV

All of this already adds up to a great deal of benefit to Conrad. But still fails to touch the heart of things: the artistic, moral, and spiritual support (choose one or all) that Ford provided. On the title page of the first novel Conrad wrote after beginning to work with the younger man, he placed the following quotation (from Novalis): "It is certain my conviction gains infinitely, the moment another soul will believe in it." The epigraph neatly applies to the tale of Jim and Marlow and Stein. But it is difficult to think that in Conrad's thoughts the problems of artistic creation were not also very much involved. Or that his young friend himself did not recognize what Conrad seemed to be saying. Indeed, as late as 1916 near Christmas (always a time of festivity between the two families during the collaborations) we find Ford, in a long somewhat dispirited letter from a Rouen hospital, in which he makes several allusions to their past association, writing: "However, perhaps all this does not interest you: I can't tell. Since I have been out here this time I have not had one letter from one living soul. So one's conviction does not get much from wh. to gain anything!"[20]

No one would deny that of the two Conrad was by far the more formidable. By the time of their collaboration he had already written *The Nigger of the "Narcissus"* and its remarkable Preface — with its magnificently self-confident projection of his own mission in art. The force of Conrad's character, his intellectual strength, and his command of psychological and physical reality were far more powerful than Ford's. But anyone acquainted with the wretchedness of Conrad's childhood experiences, and his many years in political and cultural exile, must recognize that Conrad bore within himself a deeply vulnerable and almost desperately lonely personality. His confidence in his creative powers — even though he so often forged on to display them — was continually beset by doubts, fears, and collapses, as his letters and Jessie's memoirs amply show. His deference to the opinion of Edward Garnett is well known, and his prolonged difficulties with *The Rescue* and "The Return" in 1897 and most of 1898, probably can be directly attributed to a breakdown of morale before Garnett's adverse criticisms — made still worse by the crippling burdens of already spent publisher's advances. In brief, Conrad very much needed psychological support, specifically of a knowledgable kind — very much needed to break out of his own intellectual loneliness. It has not often been noted that before Conrad suggested to Ford in late 1898 that they collaborate on *Seraphina*, he had already sought to work in partnership with at least two other authors — with his "aunt" Marguerite Poradowska, and with Stephen Crane. Collaborations at that period of course were not altogether unknown, and Ford's already first-drafted manuscript, with its potential for becoming another money-making *Treasure Island*, doubtless justified Conrad further. But it seems difficult to down the conclusion that the persistent wish to work with a collaborator was part of a deeper need.

To urge the creative importance of Ford to Conrad is not to maintain that the younger writer, who was not yet twenty-five when the collaboration began, was already a novelist of high attainments. Though Ford did in fact have a good deal to say, his expressive powers were still faint and thin. The talent of the two was clearly Conrad's — a fact that emerged quickly for both as they began to work on *Seraphina* — and which could hardly have come as a surprise to the older writer (who had read both the original draft and *The Shifting of the Fire*). It is no wonder then that Conrad, with debt piling up around him, and wanting desperately to turn out productive work, should on occasion have grown frustrated by Ford's vaguer, less dramatic and dominating skills — as in his "burn this" letter to Garnett and elsewhere. Nevertheless, the telling fact is that despite such outbursts of irritation, Conrad continued to work with Ford. The reasons seem apparent enough. A thinness of creative power by no means signifies the lack of critical perception, taste, or sensibility. Despite his youth Ford had thought much about writing. (His articulateness on literary problems and his well worked out conceptions of the high business of the novel are on record as early as October, 1900, in a lengthy analysis of Galsworthy's *Villa Rubein*.)[21] That the two men were not equals is undeniable—no more than the wife or mistress of many a distinguished and famous man has been his "equal." And yet, as we know from experience and history, without that wife, or mistress, or friend, that distinguished mind might well have run to silence or the second-rate. In gaining the partnership of a personality as sympathetic and generous as Ford's, Conrad was as lucky for his own work (and surely he knew it) as, say, Virginia Woolf was when she married Leonard. With Ford's arrival on the scene, things fell into place for him. Suddenly he began to write *Heart of Darkness* and *Lord Jim*, and imaginatively to surge.

V

In time, as we know, the two fell apart, after eleven years of close association. Even today the reasons for this break are not definitive. But we can see a conjunction of forces.

Starting in 1904 one basic condition of the relationship was beginning to alter. Before then, the pair had lived close to one another, by the South Downs, in continuous, often daily exchange. But thereafter the younger man began to show an increased preference for town. The dullness of rural life had begun to wear on him—not to mention the strains of his failing marriage with Elsie, who was very much a country person. Though Ford retained his base in Winchelsea (with visits on weekends) and his proximity to Conrad, more and more his life was spent in London. He also made several lenghty trips abroad, to Germany (for his health) and the United States (on business)—as at other times the Conrads were to go to Capri or Montpellier. In addition, in September 1907 the Conrads were themselves to move from the Pent to Bedfordshire. Throughout this period, however, the bond between the two men remained strong. Both worked closely together during the summers of 1905 (preparing the production *One Day More*) and of 1906 (on *The Secret Agent* and *The Nature of a Crime*). They frequently met, and at times shared households. And during the latter part of 1908, they were particularly close, as together they planned with excitement the early stages and first numbers of *The English Review*. Nevertheless, the cement of propinquity had been loosened.

Then, there was the angry antipathy of Mrs. Conrad. At bottom (how can we escape the recognition?) Ford was a rival—someone far more intimate with the essential life of Conrad's spirit than Jessie could ever be. Undoubtedly she could single out many objective reasons for complaint, but personal dislike and resentment, as her books reveal, were the heart of it. And how long can any husband and father of two sons hold out against such a campaign — especially when that husband is approaching his middle fifties, is still not financially solvent, and can use all the peace and quiet he can get? Jessie did not prevail at once — Conrad was not so foolish — but when Ford gave her an opening through which to move, one may be sure that the ground had long since been prepared.

And the opening that Ford gave Jessie was spectacular. In no sense could he have less strengthened Conrad's position in relation to him than by the distraught, inconsistent, foolish, and socially destructive course he conducted not only in the affairs of *The English Review* but even more in his relationship with Violet Hunt — as can be seen in its full fantastical messiness in Arthur Mizener's biography.[22] Ford's course — no little assisted by the explosive hysteria of Elsie[23] — all but guaranteed a general ostracizing among his literary peers, certainly at that period in English social history.

The received view still persists in being — Arthur Mizener has regrettably become the latest Malvolio in a series[24] — that Conrad's breach with Ford was a triumph of responsible merit over pretension and folly, rather like the victory of Henry IV and Prince Hal over Falstaff. For Conrad, a freeing from a self-seeking hanger-on; and for Madox Hueffer, the casting-out of an impossibly vain, swell-headed egomaniac. But such a position is simplistic and superficial. Indeed, if anything, the meaningful defeat in this division was the older man's. The break was deeply regretted by Ford, naturally enough, and on a number of occasions he sought to repair it, but it was not a disaster. Ford did go on, after all, to write all of his best work — *The Good Soldier*, *Some Do Not* and the other Tietjens novels, his brilliant memoir books, some of his most interesting poems; and — from the time of "Les Jeunes" and Pound before the War, through the twenties in Paris and America, and on into the thirties — to form a whole variety of remarkable new friends and connections.

For Conrad, however, the break was calamitous. By permitting himself to be separated by pressures conjugal and social from the one person who, through a long tally of supportive actions, had proved to be his single most valuable friend, Conrad was to let go an indispensible life-pump for his spirit. It may be argued that Ford's behavior gave Conrad no real alternative, or that the relationship had anyway run its route, as relationships will. But the more likely truth is that some crucial part of Conrad's spirit had grown too weary to fight, on deeper levels, any longer. That he simply made do. It is extremely intriguing that almost immediately following his breach with Ford, Conrad began to write "The Secret Sharer," one of his most profound and mysterious works. Early in that astonishing tale — is Leggatt somehow Hueffer? — there occurs an imaginatively striking but seemingly irrelevant passage, concerning the chief mate, who "liked to account to himself" for everything that came his way — "down to a miserable scorpion he had found in his cabin a week before." "The why and the wherefore of that scorpion — how it got on board and came to select his room rather than the pantry (which was a dark place and more what a scorpion would be partial to), and how on earth it managed to drown itself in the inkwell of his writing-desk — had exercised him infinitely." Unfortunately, however, the fact would seem to be that the scorpion in Conrad's mind was not to be "drowned" by such a means. For on finishing this tale and then making his final effort to complete *Under Western Eyes* (the major part of which had been left on his desk for more than a year), Conrad underwent an extraordinary nervous collapse, from which he was not to recover for perhaps as much as seven months.[25]

Bernard C. Meyer, in his psychoanalytic biography of Conrad, attributes a crucial cause of this mental breakdown to the rupture with Ford. During the preceding year and a half, he argues, Conrad had been feeling a growing inner strain in his relation with his younger friend — a sense of psychological abandonment as a result of Ford's developing attachment to Violet Hunt. Conrad's sudden attacks on Ford and his "vanity" during the second half of 1909 are, in Meyer's view, the reactions of a man deeply dismayed by a psychic rejection — responses not unlike those of a spurned lover. The argument has the ring of psychological truth. For, as Meyer points out, Ford's vanity and egotism after eleven years of intimacy would scarcely have become an issue to Conrad unless deeper resentments were at work. If taken as the entire explanation of the breakdown, such an interpretation would clearly be reductive and over-drawn. Conrad, after all, was far too shrewd about himself to have risked his ties with Ford for such a natural enough displacement alone. But joined with the other pressures at work, Meyer's analysis may explain not a little of the ferocity of Conrad's attack — as well as subsequent (doubtless ambivalent) indications that his deeper, outlaw's self may well have wished the association to continue.[26]

But whatever the reasons for either the break or the breakdown, these twelve months of Conrad's life — from mid-1909 to mid-1910 — mark a decisive turning point in his career. In the books that came from his pen thereafter, the heroic psychological probings and vital interior tensions that are the constituent powers of his best fiction have largely vanished, to be replaced by conventional story-telling values. Few serious Conrad critics have maintained that even the most effective of Conrad's post-1910 writings — works like *Chance*, *Victory*, or the artistically more subtle *The Shadow-Line* — are of equal stature with his earlier fiction. That Conrad continued to need moral backing is evident from his taking up of Richard Curle in 1912. But Curle was no Hueffer. Adulation he could supply in abundance, but not the natural rapport or gifts, the critical discernment, the passion for literature, or the generosity of personality, which Conrad needed to flourish in.

The central truth about the relationship between Ford and Conrad is lodged in dates. Between late 1898 and late 1909, Conrad began to move, with a new sudden freedom, not only to write *Heart of Darkness* and *Lord*

Jim, but also to push steadily onward to create *Typhoon*, Part IV of *Romance*, *Nostromo*, *The Secret Agent*, *The Mirror of the Sea* and *A Personal Record*, *Under Western Eyes*, and, as the last "ripe" fruit of his genius, "The Secret Sharer." To put the matter thriftily, the time of Ford Madox Ford in Joseph Conrad's life was the time of Conrad's greatness.

Notes

1. *Aspects of the Novel* (New York: Harcourt Brace, 1927), p. 13.

2. Jocelyn Baines, *Joseph Conrad: A Critical Biography* (London: Weidenfeld and Nicolson, 1960), p. 239; 26 March 1900.

3. Richard J. Herndon, "The Collaboration of Joseph Conrad with Ford Madox Ford," Diss. Stanford 1957, p. 318.

4. G. Jean-Aubry, *The Sea Dreamer* (New York: Doubleday, 1957), p. 232.

5. *Trained for Genius: The Life and Writings of Ford Madox Ford* (New York: Dutton, 1949), pp. 68–80; 124–28.

6. Baines, pp. 214–15.

7. All in all, this intelligent work is the most valuable piece of writing on the relationship, despite its 1957 date.

8. *Joseph Conrad and His Circle* (New York: Dutton, 1935), p. 87.

9. Arthur Mizener, *The Saddest Story: A Biography of Ford Madox Ford* (New York: World, 1971), pp. 88–89.

10. Ford Madox Ford, *Joseph Conrad: A Personal Remembrance* (Boston: Little Brown, 1924), pp. 127, 139–40: Jessie Conrad, *Joseph Conrad As I Knew Him* (London: Heinemann, 1926), pp. 117–18; Ford Madox Ford, *Return to Yesterday* (New York: Liveright, 1932), pp. 166, 190.

11. *Cinque Ports* (London: Blackwood, 1900), pp. 162–63; see also Herndon, pp. 158–60; and John Hope Morey, "Joseph Conrad and Ford Madox Ford: A Study in Collaboration," Diss. Cornell, 1960, pp. 52–56.

12. Morey, pp. 44–46, Mizener, pp. 107–09.

13. Baines, pp. 278–79; Mizener, p. 79.

14. Morey, pp. 207–20; 107–16.

15. Morey, pp. 117–49; 228–311. In addition, in its rendering of an emotional exchange between a man and a woman, the passage seems far more characteristic of Ford than Conrad.

16. G. Jean-Aubry, *Joseph Conrad: Life and Letters* (New York: Doubleday, 1927), I, 316. See also Baines, pp. 291–292, and Morey, p. 131 n.

17. Mizener, p. 96; Morey, pp. 47–49; 51–52, 6 December 1921.

18. Herndon, pp. 245–51; 395–400.

19. Herndon, pp. 287–88.

20. Richard M. Ludwig, ed., *Letters of Ford Madox Ford* (Princeton: Princeton Univ. Press, 1965), p. 80.

21. Ludwig, *Letters*, pp. 10–14.

22. Mizener, pp. 175–234, passim.

23. Mizener, pp. 180–86; Bernard C. Meyer, *Joseph Conrad: A Psychoanalytic Biography* (Princeton: Princeton Univ. Press, 1967), p. 205, 210; and Frederick R. Karl, "Conrad, Ford, and the Novel," *Midway*, 10 (Autumn 1969), 30–31.

24. Mizener, p. 187; and passim.

25. Baines, pp. 372–73; and especially Meyer, pp. 205–07, 210–11, who draws more fully than Baines on material from Jessie Conrad.

26. See, for example, Meyer, p. 149r, 210, 228e; and Karl, p. 32: (Conrad letter to Ford, 21 December 1911: "These old days may not have been such very 'good old days' as they should have been—but to me my dear Ford they are a very precious possession. In fact I have nothing else that I can call my own.").

The *English Review*   Frank MacShane*

In December of 1908 there appeared for the first time one of the most extraordinary literary magazines ever to be published in England. Edited by a young man of thirty-five who, except for a few months' employment as a literary columnist, was wholly inexperienced in English journalism, this magazine more than any other introduced contemporary literature to the world. The name of the magazine was the *English Review*, and its editor was Ford Madox Ford (né Hueffer).

In his early literary career, Ford had been something of a dilettante. He had written several books but was better known as a poet than as a novelist. In the few years prior to the establishment of the *Review*, however, he had collaborated with Joseph Conrad in a number of novels. None of these works was of great importance, but through the experience of working with Conrad, a man whose literary point of view was similar to his own, Ford had come to realize the importance of being a conscious craftsman and of writing with an awareness of technique as against writing in an unreliably inspired manner. But he also realized that such an ambition rarely paid commercially: indeed he knew only too well that the writers he most admired—men like Conrad and James—had considerable difficulty in placing their work with much hope of remuneration in the literary magazines of London. Ford's purpose in founding the *English Review* was therefore to give these writers and others like them a forum, and through the joint publication of their work to bring about a reform in English letters.

Even while still engaged in the Conrad collaboration, Ford had approached his friend, Edward Garnett, then a London publisher's reader, with the suggestion that a series of books be published ". . . conceived on the broad general idea of making manifest, to the most unintelligent, how great writers *get their effects*. As distinct from the general line of tub-thumping about moral purposes, the number of feet in a verse, or the noble and amiable ideas entertained, by said Great Writers, of Elevating and of making the world a better place. . . . Why couldn't

*From *South Atlantic Quarterly* 60 (1961):311–20. Reprinted by permission of the author.

one make some sort of nucleus, just some little attempt at forming a small heap on which people could stand and get a point of view with their heads a few inches above the moral atmosphere of these Islands."[1]

Garnett was not, as Ford suspected, interested in the scheme, but a few years later, after Ford had gained a certain amount of experience as columnist for the book supplement of Northcliffe's *Daily Mail*, the opportunity finally arose for the establishment of a periodical in which these and other ideas could be intelligently propagated. By January of 1908, Ford and his friend H. G. Wells had begun to discuss the possibility of starting a review that would publish Wells's new novel, *Tono-Bungay*. Ford was full of high hopes, but during the course of the year Wells procrastinated and the scheme was delayed. Finally, when he realized that he could not depend on Wells, Ford approached a friend of his from Winchelsea, a man by the name of Arthur Marwood whom he later used as a model for Christopher Tietjens in the *Parade's End* tetralogy. Marwood came from an old Yorkshire family and had been educated at Clifton and Cambridge, where he had read mathematics. He was also interested in the arts and in worthy projects, however, and was therefore sympathetic towards the proposed review. According to Ford, this general interest was converted into action when one day Marwood came to his house with the news that every review in London had rejected a new poem by Thomas Hardy called "A Sunday Morning Tragedy." This fact so shocked him, apparently, that he was determined then and there to start a review so that this poem and others like it might be published. While perhaps apocryphal, the story is symbolically true, for soon afterwards the two men pooled their resources and undertook the proprietorship of a new literary magazine.

From the beginning, Ford wanted the *Review* to serve as a rostrum for a new literary movement: he continually consulted friends like Wells and Galsworthy, and the whole first number of the magazine was put together one night at Conrad's house in the country. Premises were procured in a somewhat dingy but colorful sector of London, over a fishmonger's in Holland Park Avenue. There Ford himself lived and managed the business of the *Review*. He contrived to give an aura of tradition to the place by lining the stairs with Pre-Raphaelite engravings by Madox Brown and Rossetti and with drawings of Conrad and others by Rothenstein, and by the door he placed a gilt plaque which read "English Review, Ltd." Despite its strange location and the frequency with which it was assailed by beggars, thieves, and refugees from the Czarist secret police, it soon became one of the literary salons of London, as much at home to Thomas Hardy and Arnold Bennett as to Ezra Pound and W. B. Yeats.

The first thick number of the *Review*, bound with heavy blue covers, was published in December of 1908 and sold for half a crown. Unlike many magazines which after an exciting opening number tend to peter out in subsequent issues, the *English Review* published in its first issue a selection of writings that was to be typical of its first year. Its table of contents is therefore worth quoting in its entirety. The *Review* opened with Hardy's poem, "A Sunday Morning Tragedy," and this was followed by Henry James's story, "A Jolly Corner." Then came the first portion of Joseph Conrad's *Some Reminiscences*, Galsworthy's short story, "A Fisher of Men," a travel article on Stonehenge by W. H. Hudson, a translation by Constance Garnett of Tolstoi's "The Raid," and the opening chapters of Wells's *Tono-Bungay*. The remaining section of the magazine included a critical essay on Henry James; articles on social questions by Cunninghame Graham, W. H. Davies, Arthur Marwood, H. W. Nevinson; and a few reviews, including one by Conrad of Anatole France's *Ile des Pingouins*.

Later numbers maintained this high standard. Number Three, for example, contained contributions by Gerhart Hauptmann, W. B. Yeats, Walter de la Mare, R. H. Mottram, John Galsworthy, Norman Douglas, Granville Barker, Joseph Conrad, Vernon Lee, H. G. Wells, the Ali Khan, R. A. Scott-James, and F. E. Green; while Number Seven included Galsworthy, Gerald Gould, Eden Philpotts, Ezra Pound, Ella D'Arcy, Wyndham Lewis, Conrad, H. M. Tomlinson, Stephen Reynolds, Hilaire Belloc, and Edward Thomas.

So long as Ford remained in complete control of the magazine, imaginative literature occupied most of its pages, and only a small number were devoted to reviews, criticism, and general articles. Later on, under new proprietors, Ford was forced to enlarge the section containing "serious literature," but his first policy was clear: since there were already plenty of heavy quarterlies full of articles on economics and politics, the *English Review* was to be a truly literary magazine. Each issue normally opened with a selection of verse by two or three different poets, because, as Ford later explained, "we acknowledged that verse writing was the Senior Service."[2] These poems would be followed by an essay or travel article, which in turn would be followed by a short story and a portion of the serial then being run: in the first numbers it was Conrad's *Some Reminiscences*. Ford realized that nobody liked serials but thought the publicity the author received made up for the disability. The magazine would then close with more short stories, perhaps another serialized book like Wells's *Tono-Bungay*, and a few short articles. This method of alternating types seems deceptively simple, but in his letters to Edward Garnett and Arnold Bennett, Ford showed that he had a carefully worked-out plan, whose purpose was to introduce a slight shock to the reader's interest so that he would approach each piece in a fresh frame of mind.

Ezra Pound has written that one reason for the success of the *English Review* was the existence of a group of capable writers upon whom Ford could depend to keep the standard high. More important, however, was the editor's instinctive eye for good writing. In her book of memoirs, Violet Hunt recalls the first time she brought a sheaf of her manuscripts to the editorial office. Ford sat with them, opening and shutting them and glancing at a page here and there, without reading any of them straight through. Then he suddenly made his selection. At other times he would go with his sub-editor, Douglas Goldring, to the nearby Empire Theatre, where, during the duller turns, he would make his choices from the manuscripts Goldring had brought along. While such methods of editing seem haphazard and irresponsible, Ford has explained his peculiar ability to choose quickly. In an article on D. H. Lawrence, he describes how he chose the short story *Odour of Chrysanthemums*. If, he writes, the first few sentences show that the author's subject is to be a clear and careful projection of life as it is, and if the opening words set the tone of the story and give enough information, then you needn't read further: "You can pitch the story straight away into your wicker tray with the few accepted manuscripts. . . . Because this man knows. He knows how to open a story with a sentence of the right cadence for holding the attention. He knows how to construct a paragraph. He knows the life he is writing about in a landscape just sufficiently constructed with a casual word here and there. You can trust him for the rest."[3]

This method might not work for other editors, but it certainly worked for Ford and the *English Review*, since, in terms of literary history, the magazine is probably most famous for the "discoveries" it made. Of the hitherto unknown writers whose first work was published in the *Review*, the appearance of D. H. Lawrence was probably the most important, while that of Wyndham Lewis was the most spectacular.

In 1909 Lawrence was an assistant master at a board school in Croydon. He had submitted some of his poems to the Nottingham University *Magazine*, but when they were rejected, Mrs. Lawrence sent them to the new *English Review*. When the poems arrived at Holland Park Avenue, they caused a great stir. Asked by his secretary, "You've got another genius?" Ford replied, "It's a big one this time."[4] According to Violet Hunt, Ford was "beside himself with his pleasure at his discovery," and the poems, written very close and in pencil, went in "in chunks," appearing as the first item in the November, 1909, issue.[5] Although Lawrence and Ford were never particularly friendly, Lawrence has recorded his debt to Ford for printing his first work, describing him as the first man he had ever met "who had a real and true feeling for literature."[6]

Another of the "discoveries" appeared in an extremely mysterious manner. One day in the spring of 1909, while Ford and Marwood sat together despairing over the quality of the May number, to their consternation a weirdly-clad figure entered the office. He was dressed in a long black coat and did not speak. Ford took him to be a Russian anarchist and exclaimed that the *Review* was not interested in publishing accounts of the secret police. But the silent visitor merely drew from his voluminous pockets several bundles of manuscripts. These he presented to the editor and silently withdrew.

When he had recovered from his surprise, Ford began to look at the manuscripts and then with joy realized that the success of the May number was assured. Thus Wyndham Lewis was introduced to the world with the publication of his short piece, "The Pole." In later years Lewis, who was never one to praise without reason, wrote that he thought Ford "as good an editor as could be found for an English literary review. He had by birth artistic associations and could write himself much better than most editors."[7]

Other writers whose first work was published in the *English Review* included H. M. Tomlinson and Norman Douglas, whose appearance was typical of that of many young men, "les Jeunes" as Ford used to call them, who, hearing of the new magazine and immediately recognizing its quality, sent their manuscripts to it and contributed so much to making it a success. Naturally Ford balanced his support of the young by securing contributions from such "world figures," as he termed them, as President Taft and Anatole France, and he also printed the poetical "remains" of Swinburne and Rossetti. Yet his real interest was with the young — so much so that, with Lawrence and Pound and Lewis and Cannan, the *English Review* really became the center of a revival in English letters. While consolidating and confirming the reputations of older writers, it also inspired new movements among the younger writers and was ultimately responsible for Imagism and Vorticism.

But despite its literary success, the *Review* was an economic failure. Part of the fault must be attributed to Ford, who badly neglected the business details of his enterprise. Although admittedly inexperienced in financial matters, he tried to look after circulation and advertising himself. Then realizing after some months that he did not have the time to devote to them, he tried to find a business manager, but instead of securing an expert, he engaged another writer, Stephen Reynolds, whose real occupation was that of fisherman. Ford had also realized that his plan to run the magazine on a profit-sharing basis would cause quarrels and recriminations, but, as he wrote to Edward Garnett, "in some things I am an idealist and my ideal is to run the 'English Review' as far as possible as a socialistic undertaking. The kicks I shall get will be the price I shall pay for indulging my idealism and these I trust to bear with equanimity."[8] Soon enough Ford became involved in wrangles with his contributors. He quarreled with Arnold Bennett, for example, because Bennett had submitted his "Matador of the Five Towns" through an agent, an action Ford considered insulting to his personal friendship with Bennett. These rows made for bad blood and acted as a tremendous nervous strain on Ford.

By August of 1909, his idealism had taken its toll: the £5000 put up by Marwood and himself was exhausted, and Ford decided to suspend operations. At this juncture, his brother-in-law, David Soskice, undertook to form a syndicate that promised to continue the *Review* without interfering with the editorial policy, and at the same time to pay Ford a salary as editor. To these arrangements Ford naturally agreed, because he still hoped the magazine would be able to provide space for distinguished writing. Soon, however, the arrangement became unsatisfactory. Ford discovered he was to be paid nothing for his services, and once, after returning from a brief journey, he found Galsworthy installed in his editorial chair. Galsworthy left, and there was no ill-feeling between the two men, but Ford soon realized that the syndicate wished to use the *Review* for political purposes, and he was forced to turn over space that had formerly been given to imaginative literature to articles of propaganda for the Liberal party.

Finally, in a desperate attempt to save the magazine, Violet Hunt persuaded Lady Mond, the wife of the munitions magnate, to buy it. The inner story of this manipulation is complex and involves highly personal matters, but the upshot was that the Monds bought the magazine and then, contrary to Miss Hunt's intention, discharged Ford and installed Austin Harrison as the new editor. For a while, thanks to Ford's decency in helping Harrison, the *Review* maintained respectable standards, but soon it began to deteriorate. By 1912, according to Sir Compton Mackenzie, it had sunk "to the bottom of mediocrity,"[9] and by 1913, D. H. Lawrence sadly noted how "piffling" it had become.[10]

However convenient it would be to blame the collapse of Ford's Review on financial mismanagement, it would be an oversimplification of London literary life to do so. What happened was that many of the old guard, finding their positions under attack by the young, adopted a hostile attitude towards the *Review*, while the incompetents clubbed together to cry it down. For when the *English Review* first appeared, it was clear that it had standards and as a result it made a definite impression. In his book on the Georgians, Frank Swinnerton has described the excitement with which it was read. For the first time in many years, he writes, English literature was treated as something that was as important and exciting as politics and sports. The *review* was therefore a threat to the established journals and, to save themselves, their proprietors reacted as expected. With characteristic vigor, Ezra Pound summed up the situation by comparing Ford with T. E. Hulme. "Hulme wasn't hated and loathed by the ole bastards," he wrote, "because they didn't know he was there. The man who did the *work* for English writing was Ford Madox Hueffer (now Ford). The old crusted lice and advocates of corpse language knew that the *English Review* existed."[11]

What did they do? Some of the older men who were not asked to write for the review were so insulted that they denigrated the *Review* and attacked Ford's character in private. The younger critics, on the other hand, submitted their manuscripts with the expectation that they would be printed. At this point they encountered Ford's standards, which were, as Wyndham Lewis said. ". . . too exacting for latter-day England."[12] The consequences, here described by Edgar Jepson, were inevitable: "Ford demanded a quality of writing in that review such as no review had demanded before, or has since, and it was by that demand that he so hindered the recognition and advancement of his novels. As editor he rejected the work of so many critics. For the life of me I do not see what else he could have done; there was his standard of writing, and they could not reach it. I felt sorry for them, for they tried so hard to write. But after all it is hardly fair to expect a man, who makes it his business to teach other people to write, to be able to write himself."[13] Many of these disappointed critics, of whom several were men of power and influence in the literary life of London, took their revenge by crying down both Ford and his review.

Yet the collapse of the *Review* cannot wholly be attributed to the revenge of critics, and there is no question that Ford engaged in a number of costly squabbles. Literary friendships are of course frequently marred by flare-ups, but Ford and his friends seemed especially given to temperamental excesses. Ford himself, for example, tended to approach people in a roundabout manner instead of directly. His intention was not to be devious or dishonest; he was merely succumbing to a temperamental predilection. Nevertheless, this mannerism irritated his friends and contributed to a growing distrust between Ford's *English Review* associates and himself.

On the whole, however, despite the complexity of human relationships, the failure of the *English Review* must, as Richard Aldington has said, "be laid to the stupidity and genuine hatred of culture displayed by our countrymen."[14] For petty squabbles cannot explain why the circulation of the *Review* hardly ever rose above 1000 copies a month.

Yet for all its ups and downs, Ford was not — at least in later years — dissatisfied with the result of his editorial labors. "To some extent that undertaking had justified its existence for me," he wrote. "It had got together, at any rate between two covers, a great many — the majority of the distinguished writers of imaginative literature in England of that day and a great many foreign writers of eminence."[15] What more a magazine should do is hard to guess, and Arnold Bennett was certainly right in noting at the time that "In fifteen months Mr. Hueffer has managed to publish more genuine literature than was ever, I think, got into fifteen numbers of a monthly review before. . . . As a haven for literature the 'English Review' has been unique, absolutely."[16]

Notes

    1. Ford Madox Hueffer to Edward Garnett, dated by Mr. Garnett 1901–1904. In the possession of Mr. David Garnett.

    2. Ford Madox Ford, Introduction to *The English Review Book of Short Stories*, ed. Horace Shipp (London, n. d.).

    3. Ford Madox Ford, *Mightier than the Sword* (London, 1938), pp. 100–103.

    4. *Ibid.*, pp. 98–99.

5. Violet Hunt, *The Flurried Years* (London [1926]), p. 47.

6. D. H. Lawrence, *Phoenix* (London, 1936), p. 253.

7. Wyndham Lewis, *Rude Assignment* (London, 1947), p. 122.

8. Ford Madox Hueffer to Edward Garnett, 17 October, 1908. In the possession of Mr. David Garnett.

9. Sir Compton Mackenzie, *Literature in My Time* (London, 1933), p. 182.

10. D. H. Lawrence to Edward Garnett, 11 June, 1913, in *The Letters of D. H. Lawrence*, ed. Aldous Huxley (London, 1932), p. 125.

11. Ezra Pound to Michael Roberts, July 1937, in *The Letters of Ezra Pound*, ed. D. D. Paige (New York, 1950), p. 296.

12. Wyndham Lewis, *Rude Assignment*, p. 122.

13. Edgar Jepson, *Memories of an Edwardian* (London, 1937), p. 149.

14. Richard Aldington to the writer, 17 May 1954.

15. Ford Madox Ford, *Return to Yesterday* (London, 1931), pp. 411–412.

16. "Jacob Tonson" (Arnold Bennett), "Books and Persons," *The New Age*, VII (27 January, 1910), 305.

[The Historical Novels and Romances of Ford Madox Ford]   Grover Smith*

Apart from the millennialistic yet Wellsian fantasy *Mr. Apollo* (1908) and the Jamesian psychological experiment *A Call* (1910), the backbone of Ford's work between 1905 and the appearance of *The Good Soldier* ten years later was historical fiction. Some critics look down on his romances, the Conrad-James association being more congenial academically; but, along with *The Good Soldier* and of course the Tietjens novels, those maintain in surest balance the elements of good art and good *Fordian* art. At the same time a very clear exception must be admitted for *The Benefactor*. *A Call* has been extravagantly praised; but to some tastes it may seem too much like parody. Besides the *Fifth Queen* trilogy, the novels *The "Half Moon"* (1909), *The Portrait* (1910), *Ladies Whose Bright Eyes* (1911), and *The Young Lovell* (1913) all belong to the historical class; and all except *The Portrait* have distinct merit. Ford's theory of historical fiction included the postulate that it might be *romance*; in other words, that it was consistent with the presentation of invented along with actual personages and events, as in Scott. This is normal enough. Ford had no objection to the characters' being legendary to the point of the mythological, and the machinery might comprise paranormal or miraculous happenings. At the same time it is necessary to keep in mind certain

*From "Ford Madox Ford" in *Six Modern British Novelists*, edited by George Stade (New York: Columbia University Press, 1974), 104–11. © 1974 by Columbia University Press. Reprinted by permission of the publisher.

gradations. The *Fifth Queen* trilogy is most properly historical in the sense of Shakespeare's history plays; the main characters are historical, though all the fine detail is supplied. *The "Half Moon"* has an invented hero whose destiny, though ruled by witchcraft, is bound up with a historical voyage, and so the structure is reminiscent of the plot-levels in Restoration heroical drama; the main character is on the romance level. *Ladies Whose Bright Eyes* is a *déjà-vu* fantasy with a historical setting; that is, its protagonist relives the actions of a fourteenth-century counterpart who, like himself, is unhistorical. *The Young Lovell* is a romance set at the end of the fifteenth century — so far analogus to *The "Half Moon"* — but the tale involves a psycho-supernatural element, something either less than or more than necromancy, and this parallels the Tannhäuser form of the *belle dame sans merci* legend; the story ends with the hero split into two people, though not quite like Sorrell in *Ladies Whose Bright Eyes*. (Sorrell is one man in two places; young Lovell is two *beings*, at least, in two places.) Clearly the *Fifth Queen* trilogy belongs to the genre of the historical novel; *The "Half Moon"* and, much later, *A Little Less Than Gods* (1928), Ford's Napoleonic tale, are romances. The others may be called romances, too; but they are more or less fantasies, with *Ladies Whose Bright Eyes* vastly the stronger in circumstantial realism. All have indeed the stamp of past time. But verisimilitude is a perishable commodity: suit one generation and you are derided by another. Nowhere is this fact more true than in historical fiction, where the apparent past has to be built up detail by detail out of the notions and values of the author's contemporaries; it need not be, and preferably should not be, dealt with in the idiom familiar to these, but it must be dealt with in an ideologically translatable idiom. And that is something which all of Ford's historical tales do manage.

T. S. Eliot, in his Introduction to Charlotte Eliot's historical drama *Savonarola* (1926), talked about *Ladies Whose Bright Eyes* as a romance which filtered the fourteenth century through Ford's own time, and revealed the latter. Although one must always suspect feline intention in the Cat That Walked by Himself, his point was interesting; it was a point dear to Eliot as essential to his theory of tradition. He said that "the past is in perpetual flux," because every age reviews and revises it. In our own time we can usefully "supplement our direct knowledge of a period, by contrasting its view of a third, more remote period with our own views of this third period." His primary idea was an off-shoot of the Idealistic argument of his old teacher Josiah Royce that reality is a *community of interpretation*. The supplementary refinement, about making a contrast, seems to have been his own. But it was inappropriate of him to suggest that a romance by Ford would have much evidential value for the purpose indicated. *Ladies Whose Bright Eyes* embodies neither a popular view of the fourteenth century nor a scientific view originating with a scholar historian. On the contrary, it does not embody a "view" of the fourteenth century at all. Ford, quite as much as Eliot, could *see through* history. He understood that seeing is now, that the impressionist's "past" is bathed in the time of his viewing. *Ladies Whose Bright Eyes* is essentially about the world of 1911. Any value it might have according to the scheme described by Eliot dissolves in the fact that, though a romance, it is more contemporary than historical. It has already, as it were, absorbed the scheme.

Ford's 1935 version of the novel, in which after a quarter of a century the 1911 scene is brought up to date, shows where the emphasis should fall. Ford was concerned with modern life. His chief character, Sorrell, "sees" the fourteenth century, but only as a refraction of his own time. The changes between the two versions are almost all for the sake of clarifying the modern, though some have the connected function of stressing the purely dreamlike character of the fourteenth-century world — the world of comparative health for the man who, in the twentieth century, is undergoing surgery for hurts with a twentieth-century cause. It may be argued that *Ladies Whose Bright Eyes* is not the *Fifth Queen* trilogy, and that this, a more sedate and a tragic work, clearly not a fantasy, obeys a different law from a dream vision, an allegory; it may be argued that the *Fifth Queen* trilogy really attempts to reveal a historical epoch, that of Henry VIII, by analyzing the modes of thought and feeling which governed the lives of Queen Katharine Howard and the King. But such an argument will not stand up. Not only is the proceeding impossible, it is profoundly un-Fordian. Ford as an artist knew one way to deal with facts, and that was to substitute meaning for them; as an impressionist he knew one way to fabricate meaning, and that was to mold it out of interpretations. "Historical" or "contemporary" — the words designate fancy dress and thees and thous and yea forsooths and evanescent slang; they have nothing to do with how Ford made fictions out of the timeless urges and checks of desire, memory, ought and ought not.

Even witchcraft as he instances it is a psychological fancy dress. It is true that fancy dress and archaic speech, along with the profusion of circumstantial antiquities crowding Ford's historical romances, were all chosen according to the needs of the time setting; but they do not in themselves compose a historical period or, indeed, serve for more than ornament. It is character that makes a novel; if the ornamental details do their best work, they serve character. In Ford's romances they often do precisely this, by having psychological value; and so the romances in effect are metamorphosed back into novels truly. This is the same, exactly, as to say that in Ford the "past" always zeroes in on the present. Modernity of motive and sensibility populates his historical fiction with human characters belonging recognizably to his century. The "time-travel" device in *Ladies Whose Bright Eyes* forces us to notice the modern cast of values there; but the psychology (again, not just the fancy dress of the mind, consisting of science and superstition, but the laws of behavior itself) is equally slanted toward the modern in the other romances, where time is not shown as a double layer.

It is always important in reading Ford to keep in mind the implied authorial presence, which hovers offstage, beaming value judgments by stylistic telepathy. Part of its message in such a context amounts to a help in translation, as if to say: "This character has done such and such, and you can understand why, because I am here to remind you. He is one of us, though in his speech and system of beliefs the meaning of his acts must assume a different form; all you need to do is reflect a moment, and you will see in him the same human machinery as in yourself." Ford in *The Young Lovell* seems to hint at a classic sort of mental aberration, perhaps schizophrenia, when he represents his goddess-infatuated hero as carried in spirit to the paradise of Venus while his body lives in a hermit's bricked-up cell. And what happens in the fifteenth-century world of young Lovell is an index to the operations of human passion in the time world we know.

Ford's own either-or description of what the historical novelist can do is too general and rough, but it provides Ford with an allegiance and explains his *donnée*. He said:

> The business of all novelists is to trick you into believing you have taken part in the scenes that they render. But the historical novelist is on the horns of a dilemma: he must either present you with the superficial view of history given by the serious and scientific Historian than whom no one is more misleading, or diving deeper he must present you with the mendacities in which mankind perforce indulges when treating of contemporary events or its immediate fellows. For who are we to know the truth?

This comes from the epistle prefatory to *A Little Less Than Gods*, his last historical romance. He concluded that "the worst historical novelist is better for giving you a vicarious sense of existence than the most industrious of compilers of scientific evidence. And the novelist is there to give you a sense of vicarious experience."

The techniques, in his case, were always those which Ford was currently using in his other novels. The *Fifth Queen* trilogy uses a dense texture of snapshot impressions, exterior and interior from multiple points of view, and profuse dialogue often illustrating the principle, which he was later to describe, that people converse along parallel or diverging or criss-crossing lines, but not along the same line. The effect of this style is what Graham Greene calls "the sense of saturation." It is equally characteristic of the whole period from *Romance* to *The Young Lovell* and of Ford's modern as well as historical fiction. But the techniques evolve, so that in successive novels the saturation changes its composition. Throughout the trilogy the impressions have immediacy and depend on concreteness. As Meixner observes, Ford's early impressionism is of an objective type. It involves things and experiences of them. The linear order of the details is different from the free-ranging order possible when, later, Ford used time-shift. The details are different, too, at least in feeling, from those which the stream-of-consciousness writer would convey. They do not seem, as details, to be altered by passage through the mind: they are not blurred, commingled, or confused. Stream-of-consciousness and free-association effects (the latter in Proust, for example) emerge in a *damaged* condition; the mind has done violence to the things which have passed through it from outside, and to time by melting and blending it. The temporal reality shown by Ford is revealed as quantum impulses, not waves of energy. His reality resembles a shooting gallery, not an aquarium: the senses are not soaked but bombarded. No Bergsonian flux here, no *durée*, no Heraclitus. The Proustian dissolving views and magic-lantern projections were still to be made known when *The Fifth Queen* was written; they never held much interest for Ford. When he came to use the time-shift, he still avoided aimless subjectivities. Really, *congestion* is a better word for his effect than *saturation:* he leaves space between the units.

Of course the congestion can be subjective in composition; the details can crowd in from memory and yet be impressionistically rendered. As Ford's work went on, external details tended more and more to be mixed with internal reflections. In the second and third chapters of *The Young Lovell*, which depict the company at table in Lord Lovell's castle, Ford uses as a matter of course the method of exposition by reminiscence (third person), telling, with impressionistic effects, what each of several charac-ters thinks about present matters in light of experience. In particular the section concerned with the Bishop Palatine makes a curious blend of omniscient narration and third-person interior monologue — though not of a free-association sort: it hangs together logically, and time is kept under rule, with pluperfect verb tenses abounding. The general effect is not unlike the time-shift technique; those two chapters move about in time in a manner new to Ford's novels. *The Young Lovell*, preceding *The Good Soldier* by two years, marked the emergence of the "Marlow" type of unchronological narration in Ford's work.

[Foreword to Stories from *Zeppelin Nights*]

Richard Foster*

Ford's wish, late in life, that *Zeppelin Nights* (1916) might be republished after more than twenty years would go a long way toward justifying republication of parts of it here. Furthermore, though the book was copyrighted in this country by John Lane, it seems never to have been actually published in the United States. And now that the long-overdue revival of interest in Ford's writing seems healthily under way, it would be less than historical justice if in the course of that revival his late wishes were not decently honored. But there are other justifications: *Zeppelin Nights* is simply a good book — charming, intelligent, delicately complex, often movingly humane. It is a minor masterpiece by a major writer, and we should not deprive ourselves of it.

Zeppelin Nights is a rather old-fashioned book in its form. It is a conscious parallel to the *Decameron:* twenty-four tales, timeless in import, set down in a sharply contemporaneous setting of war. It is London of 1914–15 — zeppelins and German bombs coming over in the night, and the life of London haunted by the "Night Hag" of the dread of sudden death. Viola Candour's soirées, consisting of bridge, whiskey, sandwiches, and her lover Serapion's stories, serve to keep the Night Hag at bay by cheering simple human courage. As they accumulate, Serapion's stories, read at first for the distraction of Viola's guests and later for the benefit of war relief causes, seem to be showing Englishmen why they are where they are in history and what history demands of them now. The stories begin with an anecdote of the Battle of Marathon in 490 B.C. and end with an evocative impression of the coronation of George V in 1910.

Ford published *Zeppelin Nights* with Violet Hunt, and although the book carries no indication of how the responsibilities were divided, evidence unearthed by Mr. David Harvey in an as yet unpublished bibliographical study of Ford's career indicates that while Violet Hunt was largely responsible for the connective material the tales were exclusively Ford's. A few of the stories — and they tend to be explicitly "historical" ones — are less than Ford at his best, being a bit too conventionally romantic in feeling, or too melodramatic, or too heavily gilded with the "quaint." But most of them, certainly all those printed here, represent Ford at his delicately minor, yet delicately profound best. They have Ford's rich implicativeness. Mere anecdotes — Ford is one of the great anecdotists

*From the *Minnesota Review* 2 (1962):465–67. Reprinted by permission of the journal. The stories included are "The Battle of Portus Lemanis: Oct. 24th, A.D. 421," "Bertram De Born: May 26th, 1180," "Ladies at the Mayoring: 1453," "Modernism: September 11th, 1520," "Clubs: 15th September, 1644," "The Crowning Mercy: Sept. 3rd, 1658," "No Popery: June 7, 1780," "A Closing Show: Oct. 31st-Nov. 1st, 1792," "The Death of a Hero: May 3rd to 9th, 1821," "Contact with History: Oct. 12th, 1899."

of our literature — become bathed in metaphysical lights, as in the superb little tale "Modernism." They also show his way of compacting his materials — the quality of near discontinuity and unfinishedness which he sometimes called "impressionism," and which becomes, as in the tender "A Closing Show," a way of opening-out and revealing vistas of significance. And they also have, as a strengthening counterpoint to Ford's familiar note of elegiac nostalgia and compassion, his characteristically tough and bouyant humor. Surely "No Popery" and "Ladies at the Mayoring" are perfect examples of Ford's magnificently spirited comic sense. And the style is Ford's everywhere. Its variety and suppleness, its magical capacity to express the stages of history and the strata of class without effort or obviousness or triteness, shows that the subtlety of his ear is finer even than James', perhaps second in subtlety only to Joyce's.

But the *whole* of the book is finally Ford's, too, whatever Violet Hunt's incidental contributions to it may have been. The idea of it, or rather the *feeling* pervading the whole is unmistakably Ford's. One recognizes the typically Fordian sense of the human condition as a tragic history of persistent and miraculous realizations of human value that are doomed at birth by the destructive compulsions of the fathering human heart itself. But one also recognizes Ford's faith in the individual human integrity created by the loves that can transcend hatreds and the consciences that can transcend even the precious selves that love itself creates. The great persons in Ford's fiction save themselves always in the renunciation of self. They do it, too, in Ford's special way — not by withdrawing from life, but by entering it more fully. They take the full burden of their human natures by accepting the great moral fact of human complicity. They enter the stream of human history — immerse themselves in it — not with any rash confidence that they will not go under, much less that they can turn its course, but rather because, doomed to being better than most men they decline to be luckier.

These are Ford's themes, from the early Tudor novels to the now classic Tietjens tetralogy to the late great books of reflection and prophecy, *Great Trade Route* and *Provence*. They may be described in different words, as when R. P. Blackmur writes of Ford's characteristic theme of "devotion to lost causes known to be lost." But they are Ford's themes everywhere in his books. They were the themes even of Ford's own life. And they are the themes that create the special poignancy of the little book *Zeppelin Nights*.

The Good Soldier

[Review of *The Good Soldier*]

Rebecca West*

Mr. Ford Madox Hueffer is the Scholar Gipsy of English letters: he is the author who is recognised only as he disappears round the corner. It is impossible for anybody with any kind of sense about writing to miss some sort of distant apprehension of the magnificence of his work: but unfortunately this apprehension usually takes the form of enthusiastic but belated discoveries of work that he left on the doorstep ten years ago.

The Good Soldier will put an end to any such sequestration of Mr. Hueffer's wealth. For it is as impossible to miss the light of its extreme beauty and wisdom as it would be to miss the full moon on a clear night. Its first claim on the attention is the obvious loveliness of the colour and cadence of its language: and it is also clever as the novels of Mr. Henry James are clever, with all sorts of acute discoveries about human nature, and at times it is radiantly witty. And behind these things there is the delight of a noble and ambitious design, and behind that, again, there is the thing we call inspiration — a force of passion which so sustains the story in its flight that never once does it appear as the work of a man's invention. It is because of that union of inspiration and the finest technique that this story, this close and relentless recital of how the good soldier struggled from the mere clean innocence which was the most his class could expect of him to the knowledge of love, can bear up under the vastness of its subject. For the subject is, one realises when one has come to the end of this saddest story, much vaster than one had imagined that any story about well-bred people, who live in sunny houses, with deer in the park, and play polo, and go to Nauheim for the cure, could possibly contain.

It is the record of the spiritual life of Edward Ashburnham, who was a large, fair person of the governing class, with an entirely deceptive appearance of being just the kind of person he looked. It was his misfortune that he had brought to the business of landowning a fatal touch of imagination which made him believe it his duty to be "an overlord doing his best by his dependents, the dependents meanwhile

*–From the *Daily News*, 2 April 1915, p. 6. Reprinted by permission of A. D. Peters & Co., Ltd.

39

doing their best by the overlord"; to make life splendid and noble and easier for everybody by his government. And since this ideal meant that he became in his way a creative artist, he began to feel the desire to go to some woman for "moral support, the encouragement, the relief from the sense of loneliness, the assurance of his own worth." And although Leonora, his wife, was fine and proud, a Northern light among women, she simply could not understand that marriage meant anything but an appearance of loyalty before the world and the efficient management of one's husband's estate. She "had a vague sort of idea that, to a man, all women are the same after three weeks of close intercourse. She thought that the kindness should no longer appeal, the soft and mournful voice no longer thrill, the tall darkness no longer give a man the illusion that he was going into the depths of an unexplored wood." And so poor Edward walked the world starved.

His starvation leads him into any number of gentle, innocent, sentimental passions: it delivers him over as the prey of a terrible and wholly credible American, a cold and controlled egoist who reads like the real truth about an Anne Douglas Sedgwick or Edith Wharton heroine. And meanwhile his wife becomes so embittered by what she considers as an insane, and possibly rather nasty, obsession, that she loses her pride and her nobility and becomes, in that last hour when Edward has found a real passion, so darkly, subtly treacherous that he and the quite innocent young girl whom he loves are precipitated down into the blackest tragedy. All three are lost: and perhaps Leonora, robbed of her fineness, is most lost of all.

And when one has come to the end of this beautiful and moving story it is worth while reading the book over again simply to observe the wonders of its technique. Mr. Hueffer has used the device, invented and used successfully by Mr. Henry James, and used not nearly so credibly by Mr. Conrad, of presenting the story not as it appeared to a divine and omnipresent intelligence, but as it was observed by some intervener not too intimately concerned in the plot. It is a device that always breaks down at the great moment, when the revelatory detail must be given; but it has the great advantage of setting the tone of the prose from the beginning to the end. And out of the leisured colloquialism of the gentle American who tells the story Mr. Hueffer has made a prose that falls on the page like sunlight. It has the supreme triumph of art, that effect of effortlessness and inevitableness, which Mengs described when he said that one of Velasquez's pictures seemed to be painted not by the hand but by pure thought. Indeed, this is a much, much better book than any of us deserve.

The Saddest Story [Review of
The Good Soldier]

Theodore Dreiser*

Captain Edward Ashburnham, heir of a wealthy British family, is wedded for reasons of family courtesy to Leonora Powys, the daughter of a financially embarrassed Irish landlord. The Captain is a sentimentalist, his wife a practical-minded moralist. Uninterested and unhappy in his wedded state he approaches or takes up with (1) La Dolciquita, a Spanish coquette, (2) Mrs. Basil, wife of a British Major in India, (3) Maisie Maidan, wife of another British officer, (4) Florence Dowell, wife of an American globe-trotter who is the friend of the Ashburnhams, who tells the story, and (5) Nancy Rufford, a ward. Both her religious training and her social code compel Mrs. Ashburnham to keep up all those appearances which she deems that these and her dignity and social rights demand. She devotes her life to the task of standing by, saving, and reforming her husband. This results in her supervision of both his finances and his love affairs, to the end that her own soul is tortured while she tortures his. The minor characters suffer also, and in the end the Captain kills himself, his last love goes mad, and Leonora accomplishes her ideal, a happy marriage. Previous to this, one flame has died, another committed suicide, and the wise Spaniard has milked the Captain to the tune of twenty thousand pounds.

> I have, I am aware, told this story in a very rambling way, so that it may be difficult for any one to find their path through what may be a sort of maze. I cannot help it. I have stuck to my idea of being in a country cottage with a silent listener, hearing between the gust of the wind and amidst the noises of the distant sea, the story as it comes. And, when one discusses an affair — a long, sad affair — one goes back, one goes forward. One remembers points that one has forgotten, and one explains them all the more minutely since one recognizes that one has forgotten to mention them in their proper places, and that one may have given, by omitting them, a false impression. I console myself with thinking that this is a real story, and that, after all, real stories are best told in the way that a person telling a story would tell them. They will then seem most real.

Thus Mr. Hueffer in explanation of his style; a good explanation of a bad method.

In this story, as has been said, the author makes Dowell, Florence's husband, the narrator, and it is he who dubs it the "saddest one." This is rather a large order when one thinks of all the sad stories that have been told of this mad old world. Nevertheless it is a sad story, and a splendid one from a psychological point of view; but Mr. Hueffer, in spite of the care he

*Reprinted from *New Republic* 3 (12 June 1915):155–56.

has bestowed upon it, has not made it splendid in the telling. In the main he has only suggested its splendor, quite as the paragraph above suggests, and for the reasons it suggests. One half suspects that since Mr. Hueffer shared with Mr. Conrad in the writing of *Romance*, the intricate weavings to and fro of that literary colorist have, to a certain extent, influenced him in the spoiling of this story. For it is spoiled to the extent that you are compelled to say, "Well, this is too bad. This is quite a wonderful thing, but it is not well done." Personally I would have suggested to Mr. Hueffer, if I might have, that he begin at the beginning, which is where Colonel Powys wishes to marry off his daughters—not at the beginning as some tertiary or quadrutiary character in the book sees it, since it really concerns Ashburnham and his wife. This is neither here nor there, however, a mere suggestion. A story may begin in many ways.

Of far more importance is it that, once begun, it should go forward in a more or less direct line, or at least that it should retain one's uninterrupted interest. This is not the case in this book. The interlacings, the cross references, the re-re-references to all sort of things which subsequently are told somewhere in full, irritate one to the point of one's laying down the book. As a matter of fact, except for the perception that will come to any man, that here is a real statement of fact picked up from somewhere and related by the author as best he could, I doubt whether even the lover of naturalism—entirely free of conventional prejudice—would go on.

As for those dreary minds who find life morally ordered and the universe murmurous of divine law—they would run from it as from the plague. For, with all its faults of telling, it is an honest story, and there is no blinking of the commonplaces of our existence which so many find immoral and make such a valiant effort to conceal. One of the most irritating difficulties of the tale is that Dowell, the American husband who tells the story, is described as, first, that amazingly tame thing, an Englishman's conception of an American husband; second, as a profound psychologist able to follow out to the last detail the morbid minutiae of this tragedy, and to philosophize on them as only a deeply thinking and observing man could; and lastly as one who is as blind as a bat, as dull as a mallet, and as weak as any sentimentalist ever. The combination proves a little trying before one is done with it.

This story has been called immoral. One can predict such a charge today in the case of any book, play, or picture which refuses to concern itself with the high-school ideal of what life should be. It is immoral apparently to do anything except dress well and talk platitudes. But it is interesting to find this English author (German by extraction, I believe) and presumably, from all accounts, in revolt against these sickening strictures, dotting his book with apologies for this, that, and another condition not in line with this high-school standard (albeit it is the wretched American who speaks) and actually smacking his lips over the stated order that damns his book. And worse yet, Dowell is no American. He is that literary packhorse or scapegoat on whom the native Englishman loads all his contempt for

Americans. And Captain and Mrs. Ashburnham, whom he so soulfully lauds for their love of English pretence and order, are two who would have promptly pitched his book out of doors, I can tell him. Yet he babbles of the fineness of their point of view. As a matter of fact their point of view is that same accursed thing which has been handed on to America as "good form," and which we are now asked to sustain by force of arms as representing civilization.

After all, I have no real quarrel with the English as such. It is against smug conventionalism wherever found, too dull to perceive the import of anything except money and social precedence, that I uncap my fountain pen. It is this condition which makes difficult — one might almost fear impossible at times — the production of any great work of art, be it picture, play, philosophy, or novel. It is the Leonoras, the Dowells, and the Nancys that make life safe, stale, and impossible. They represent that thickness of wit which prospers impossible religions, and moral codes, and causes the mob to look askance at those finer flowers of fancy which are all the world has to show for its power to think in the drift of circumstance. All the rest is formalism and parade, and "go thou and do likewise." We all, to such a horrible extent, go and do likewise.

But you may well suspect that there is a good story here and that it is well worth your reading. But suppositions are true. In the hands of a better writer this jointure of events might well have articulated into one of the finest pictures in any language. Its facts are true, in the main. Its theme beautiful. It is tragic in the best sense that the Greeks knew tragedy, that tragedy for which there is no solution. But to achieve a high result in any book its component characters must of necessity stand forth unmistakeable in their moods and characteristics. In this one they do not. Every scene of any importance has been blinked or passed over with a few words or cross references. I am not now referring to any moral fact. Every conversation which should have appeared, every storm which should have contained revealing flashes, making clear the minds, the hearts, and the agonies of those concerned, has been avoided. There are no paragraphs or pages of which you can say "This is a truly moving description," or "This is a brilliant vital interpretation." You are never really stirred. You are never hurt. You are merely told and referred. It is all cold narrative, never truly poignant.

This is a pity. This book had the making of a fine story. I half suspect that its failure is due to the author's formal British leanings, whatever his birth — that leaning which Mr. Dowell seems to think so important, which will not let him loosen up and sing. The whole book is indeed fairly representative of that encrusting formalism which, barnacle-wise, is apparently overtaking and destroying all that is best in English life. The arts will surely die unless formalism is destroyed. And when you find a great theme marred by a sniffy reverence for conventionalism and the glories of a fixed condition it is a thing for tears. I would almost commend Mr. Hueffer to the futurists, or to anyone that has the strength to scorn the moldy past, in the hope that he might develop a method entirely different from that which is here employed, if I did not know that at bottom the great artist is never to be commended. Rather from his brain, as Athena from that of Zeus, spring flawless and shining all those art forms which the world adores and preserves.

The Good Soldier:
An Interpretation
Mark Schorer*

Learning to read novels, we slowly learn to read ourselves. A few years ago, writing of Ford Madox Ford, Herbert Gorman said: "If he enlarged upon himself he was quite justified in doing so and it seems to me that the time has come now for somebody to enlarge upon him." I translate this remark to mean that the good novelist sees himself as the source of a subject that, when it has taken its form in his work, we may profitably examine because our analysis will bring it back to ourselves, perhaps to kiss us, more likely to slap us in the face — either way, to tell us where *we* are. These are the fruits of criticism.

The time had indeed come, and today we are hearing again about Ford Madox Ford in a way that we have not heard of him for twenty years — for until recently he has had to survive as best he could in the person of Conrad's collaborator and of that brilliant editor who said to the young D. H. Lawrence that his first novel had "every fault that the English novel can have" and that his second was "a rotten work of genius." The always present friend of all the great, the abettor of all the promising young, Ford was great in his own right, and now Time indeed seems ready at last, as Herbert Gorman predicted that it would, to "weed out his own accomplishments."

He began work on *The Good Soldier* on his fortieth birthday — the 17th of December in 1913 — and he himself thought that it was his first really serious effort in the novel. "I had never really tried to put into any novel of mine *all* that I knew about writing. I had written rather desultorily a number of books — a great number — but they had all been in the nature of *pastiches*, of pieces of rather precious writing, or of *tours de force*." This was to be the real thing, and it was; many years later he remarked of it that it was his "best book technically, unless you read the Tietjens books as one novel, in which case the whole design appears. But I think the Tietjens books will probably 'date' a good deal, whereas the other may — and indeed need — not." It need not have; it did not.

As in most great works of comic irony, the mechanical structure of

*From Ford Madox Ford, *The Good Soldier* (New York: Knopf, 1951). Reprinted by permission of Ruth Page Schorer.

The Good Soldier is controlled to a degree nothing less than taut, while the structure of meaning is almost blandly open, capable of limitless refractions. One may go further, perhaps, and say that the novel renews a major lesson of all classic art: from the very delimitation of form arises the exfoliation of theme. This, at any rate, is the fact about *The Good Soldier* that gives point to John Rodker's quip that "it is the finest French novel in the English language," which is to say that it has perfect clarity of surface and nearly mathematical poise, and — as an admirer would wish to extend the remark — a substance at once exact and richly enigmatic. As a novel, *The Good Soldier* is like a hall of mirrors, so constructed that, while one is always looking straight ahead at a perfectly solid surface, one is made to contemplate not the bright surface itself, but the bewildering maze, of past circumstances and future consequence that — somewhat falsely — it contains. Or it is like some structure all of glass and brilliantly illuminated, from which one looks out upon a sable jungle and ragged darkness.

The Good Soldier carries the subtitle "A Tale of Passion," and the book's controlling irony lies in the fact that passionate situations are related by a narrator who is himself incapable of passion, sexual and moral alike. His is the true *accidia*, and so, from his opening absurdity: "This is the saddest story I have ever heard," on to the end and at every point, we are forced to ask: "How can we believe *him*? His must be exactly the *wrong* view." The fracture between the character of the event as we feel it to be and the character of the narrator as he reports the event to us is the essential irony, yet it is not in any way a simple one; for the narrator's view as we soon discover, is not so much the wrong view as merely *a* view, although a special one. No simple inversion of statement can yield up the truth, for the truth is the maze, and, as we learn from what is perhaps the major theme of the book, appearances have their reality.

First of all, this novel is about the difference between convention and fact. The story consists of the narrator's attempt to adjust his reason to the shattering discovery that, in his most intimate relationships, he has, for nine years, mistaken the conventions of social behavior for the actual human fact. That he did not want it otherwise, that the deception was in effect self-induced, that he could not have lived at all with the actuality, is, for the moment, beside our point, although ultimately, for the attitude and the architecture of the novel, it is the whole point.

The narrator and his wife, Florence, are wealthy Americans; the friends with whom they are intimately concerned, Edward and Leonora Ashburnham, are wealthy English people. Together, these four seem to be the very bloom of international society; they are all, as the narrator repeatedly tells us, "good people," and the Ashburnhams are even that special kind of good people, "good county people." Florence is a little pathetic, because she suffers from heart trouble and must be protected against every shock and exposure. Leonora is perhaps a little strong-willed in the management of her domestic affairs, but these have been very trying and in their cause she has been altogether splendid and self-sacrificing, a noblewoman. Edward is nearly flawless: "the fine soldier, the excellent landlord, the extraordinarily kind, careful, and industrious magistrate, the upright, honest, fair-dealing, fair-thinking, public character . . . the model of humanity, the hero, the athlete, the father of his country, the law-giver." For nine years these four have enjoyed an apparently placid and civilized friendship, visiting back and forth, meeting annually at Nauheim, where they take the seasonal hypochondriac baths, sharing in one another's interests and affairs. Then comes the tremendous, the stunning reversal: when illness proves to be a lusterless debauchery; domestic competence the maniacal will of the tigress, the egoistic composure of the serpent; heroic masculinity the most sentimental libertinism. And the narrator, charged at the end with the responsibility of caring for a little mad girl, Edward's last love, is left to relate his new knowledge of an exposed reality to his long untroubled faith in its appearance. Which he is not able to do, of course; as which of us could?

But are not these "realities," in effect, "appearances"? Are not the "facts" that the narrator discovers in themselves "conventions" of a sort? We are forced, at every point, to look back at this narrator, to scan his beguiling surprise, to measure the angle of refraction at which that veiled glance penetrates experience. He himself suggests that we are looking at events here as one looks at the image of a mirror in a mirror, at the box within the box, the arch beyond the arch beyond the arch. All on one page we find these reversals: "Upon my word, yes, our intimacy was like a minuet. . . . No, by God, it is false! It wasn't a minuet that we stepped; it was a prison—a prison full of screaming hysterics. . . . And yet I swear by the sacred name of my creator that it was true. It was true sunshine; the true music; the true plash of the fountains from the mouths of stone dolphins. For, if for me we were four people with the same tastes, with the same desires, acting—or, no, not acting—sitting here and there unanimously, isn't that the truth?" The appearance had its reality. How, then, does the "reality" suggest that it is something less—or more?

Why is Florence always "poor Florence" or "that poor wretch" or "that poor cuckoo"? Why the persistent denigration of tone? Why can Florence not be charged with something less trivial and vulgar than "making eyes at Edward"? The narrator has something to gain in Florence's loss, and that is a fragment of self-esteem. If Florence is a harlot, she is so, in part, because of her husband's fantastic failure, but if we can be persuaded of her calculated vice and of her nearly monstrous malice, her husband appears before us as the pathetic victim of life's ironic circumstance. What, again, is the meaning of the narrator's nearly phobic concern with Catholicism, or of the way in which his slurs at Leonora are justified by her attachment to that persuasion? This is a mind not quite in balance. And again, Leonora's loss is Edward's gain, and Edward's gain at last is the narrator's gain. For why are Florence's indiscretions crimes, and

Edward's, with Florence, follies at worst, and at best true goodnesses of heart? Why, after his degradation, is Edward still "a fine fellow"? In every case, the "fact" is somewhere between the mere social convention and that different order of convention which the distorted understanding of the narrator imposes upon them.

Yet the good novelist does not let us rest here. These distortions are further revelations. Mirror illumines mirror, each arch marks farther distances. Ford tells us that he suggested the title, *The Good Soldier*, "in hasty irony," when the publisher's objections to *The Saddest Story* became imperative; and while, under the circumstances of 1915, the new title must have seemed, for this novel and for this real soldier, Ford, peculiarly inappropriate, certainly uncongenial enough to cause the author under-standable "horror," it is nevertheless very useful to readers today, so accustomed to war that the word "soldier" no longer carries its special force. The novel designates Edward as the good soldier, as Edward has seen Imperial service in India. For Edward the narrator has the strongest affection and his only forgiveness. Of him, he says: "I guess that I myself, in my fainter way, come into the category of the passionate, of the headstrong, and the too-truthful. [This is his weirdest absurdity, the final, total blindness of infatuation and self-infatuation.] For I can't conceal from myself the fact that I loved Edward Ashburnham — and that I love him because he was just myself. If I had had the courage and the virility and possibly also the physique of Edward Ashburnham I should, I fancy, have done much what he did. He seems to me like a large elder brother who took me out on several excursions and did many dashing things whilst I just watched him robbing the orchards, from a distance. And, you see, I am just as much of a sentimentalist as he was. . . ." Niggardly, niggardly half-truth! — for observe the impossible exceptions: courage, virility, phy-sique! What sane man could expect them? The narrator aspires to be "the good soldier," the conventionally fine fellow, yet has no expectation of ever being in the least like him in any but his most passive features, and these working not at the level of sexuality, as with Edward, but of malformed friendship. To understand the exact significance here, we must turn, perhaps, to another book.

In his dedicatory epistle in the 1927 edition Ford says that he hoped *The Good Soldier* would do in English something of the sort that Maupassant's *Fort comme la Mort* did in French. The remark is suggestive in the structural terms that Ford must have had in mind; I wish, however, to call attention to what may be the most accidental connection of theme. Of one of his characters Maupassant says: "He was an old intellectual who might have been, perhaps, a good soldier, and who could never console himself for what he had not been."

The vicious consolations of failure form our narrator. "Men," said D. H. Lawrence, "men can suck the heady juice of exalted self-importance from the bitter weed of failure — failures are usually the most conceited of men." Thus at the end of the novel we have forgotten the named good soldier, and we look instead at the nominated one, the narrator himself. His consolations are small: attendance upon the ill, "seeing them through"—for twelve years his wife, for the rest of his life the mad girl whom he fancies he might have loved; yet they give him a function, at least. This is the bitter, paltry destiny that, he thinks, life has forced upon him; thus he need never see himself as bitter or as paltry—or, indeed, as even telling a story.

And thus we come to the final circles of meaning, and these, like ripples round a stone tossed into a pool, never stop. For, finally, *The Good Soldier* describes a world that is without moral point, a narrator who suffers from the madness of moral inertia. "You ask how it feels to be a deceived husband. Just heavens, I do not know. It feels just nothing at all. It is not hell, certainly it is not necessarily heaven. So I suppose it is the intermediate stage. What do they call it? Limbo." *Accidia!* It is the dull hysteria of sloth that besets him, the sluggish insanity of defective love. "And, yes, from that day forward she always treated me and not Florence as if I were the invalid." "Why, even to me she had the air of being submissive—to me that not the youngest child ever pay heed to. Yes, this is the saddest story. . . ." The saddest story? One may say this another way, and say the same thing. *The Good Soldier* is a comedy of humor, and the humor is phlegm.

It is in the comedy that Ford displays his great art. Irony, which makes no absolute commitments and can thus enjoy the advantage of many ambiguities of meaning and endless complexities of situation, is at the same time an evaluative mood, and, in a master, a sharp one. Perhaps the most astonishing achievement in this astonishing novel is the manner in which the author, while speaking through his simple, infatuated character, lets us know how to take his simplicity and his infatuation. This is comic genius. It shows, for example, in the characteristic figures, the rather simple-minded and, at the same time, grotesquely comic metaphors: a girl in a white dress in the dark is "like a phosphorescent fish in a cupboard"; Leonora glances at the narrator, and he feels "as if for a moment a lighthouse had looked at me"; Leonora, boxing the ears of one of Edward's little mistresses, "was just striking the face of an intolerable universe." Figures such as these, and they occur in abundance, are the main ingredient in Ford's tone, and they are the subtle supports of such broader statements as this: "I should marry Nancy if her reason were ever sufficiently restored to let her appreciate the meaning of the Anglican marriage service. But it is probable that her reason will never be sufficiently restored to let her appreciate the meaning of the Anglican marriage service. Therefore I cannot marry her, according to the law of the land." This is a mode of comic revelation and evaluation less difficult, perhaps, than that which is evident in Ford's figures of speech, but to sustain it as he does, with never a rupture of intent, is the highest art.

Then there are the wonderfully comic events—little Mrs Maidan dead in a trunk with her feet sticking out, as though a crocodile had caught her in its giant jaws, or the poor little mad girl saying to the narrator after weeks of silence: "Shuttlecocks!" There are the frequent moments when the author leads his characters to the most absurd anti-climaxes (as when, at the end of the fourth chapter, Leonora, in a frenzy of self-important drama, demands: "Don't you know that I'm an Irish Catholic?"), and then, with superb composure, Ford leads his *work* away from the pit of bathos into which his people have fallen. There is the incessant wit, of style and statement, the wittier for its deceptive clothing of pathos. And, most important in this catalogue of comic devices, there is the covering symbolism of illness: characters who fancy that they suffer from "hearts," who do suffer defective hearts not, as they would have us believe, in the physiological but in the moral sense, and who are told about by a character who has no heart at all, and hence no mind. "I never," he tells us with his habitually comic solemnity, "I never was a patient anywhere." To which we may add: only always, in the madhouse of the world.

Is *The Good Soldier*, perhaps, a novelist's novel? Ford thought that it was his best work, and his judgment was always the judgment of the craftsman. Certainly it can tell us more about the nature of the novel than most novels or books about them: the material under perfect control, the control resulting in the maximum meaning, the style precisely evaluating that meaning. But if it is a kind of archetype of the processes of fiction, if, that is to say, it can demonstrate his craft to the craftsman, then it can also help all of us to read. And is it not true that, once we learn how to read, even if then we do not live more wisely, we can at least begin to be aware of why we have not? *The Good Soldier* like all great works, has the gift and power of remorse.

The Epistemology of
The Good Soldier
Samuel Hynes*

The problems involved in the interpretation of *The Good Soldier* all stem from one question: What are we to make of the novel's narrator? Or, to put it a bit more formally, what authority should we allow to the version of events which he narrates? The question is not, of course, particular to this novel; it raises a point of critical theory touching every novel which employs a limited mode of narration.

The point is really an epistemological one; for a novel is a version of the ways in which a man can know reality, as well as a version of reality

*From *Sewanee Review* 49 (1961):225–35. Reprinted by permission of the author.

itself. The techniques by which a novelist controls our contact with his fictional world, and particularly his choice of point of view and his treatment of time, combine to create a model of a theory of knowledge. Thus the narrative technique of Fielding, with the author omniscient and all consciousness equally open to him, implies eighteenth-century ideas of Reason, Order, and General Nature, while the modern inclination toward a restricted and subjective narrative mode implies a more limited and tentative conception of the way man knows.

When we speak of a limited-point-of-view novel, then, we are talking about a novel which implies a limited theory of knowledge. In this kind of novel, the reality that a man can know is two-fold; the external world exists as discrete, observed phenomena, and the individual consciousness exists. That is, a man is given what his senses tell him, and what he thinks. "The central intelligence" is a narrow room, from which we the readers look out at the disorderly phenomena of experience. We do not *know* (as we know in Fielding) that what we see has meaning; if it has, it is an order which the narrator imposes upon phenomena, not one which is inherent there. And we can know only one consciousness — the one we are in. Other human beings are simply other events outside.

This seems to be equally true of first- and third-person narration in this mode; it is difficult to see an epistemological difference between, say, *The Ambassadors* and *The Aspern Papers.* James, however, favored the third-person method, and used it in all his major novels. He did so, I think, because it enabled him to take for granted, "by the general law of nature," as he put it, "a primary author"; it allowed him, that is to say, to retain a vestige of authority, even though that authority "works upon us most in fact by making us forget him." In fact, though the "primary author" of James's novels is a rather retiring figure, we do not forget him, and from time to time he comes forward to realign us with the truth, to tell us what we know.

In the first-person novel, on the other hand, it is at least possible to eliminate authority altogether, and to devise a narrative which raises uncertainty about the nature of truth and reality to the level of a structural principle. A classic example is the one before us, and it is in these terms that I will examine Ford's narrative techniques.

The Good Soldier is "A Tale of Passion," a story of seduction, adultery, and suicide told by a deceived husband. These are melodramatic materials; yet the novel is not a melodrama, because the action of which it is an imitation is not the sequence of passionate gestures which in another novel we would call the plot, but rather the action of the narrator's mind as it gropes for the meaning, the reality of what has occurred. It is an interior action, taking its order from the processes of a puzzled mind rather than from the external forms of chronology and causation. This point is clear enough if one considers the way in which Ford treats the violent events which would, in a true melodrama, be climactic — the deaths of Maisie

Maidan, Florence, and Ashburnham. All these climaxes are, dramatically speaking, "thrown away," anticipated in casual remarks as to deprive them of melodramatic force, and treated, when they do occur, almost as afterthoughts. (Ashburnham's death is literally an afterthought: Dowell says on the last page but one, "It suddenly occurs to me that I have forgotten to say how Edward met his death," and even then he does not give us an account of the actual suicide.)

The narrative technique of *The Good Soldier* is a formal model of this interior action. We are entirely restricted to what Dowell perceives, and the order in which we receive his perceptions is the order of his thought; we never know more than he knows about his "saddest story," and we must accept his contradictions and uncertainties as stages in our own progress toward knowledge. At first glance, Dowell seems peculiarly ill-equipped to tell this story, because he is ill-equipped to *know* a tale of passion. He is a kind of eunuch, a married virgin, a cuckold. He has apparently never felt passion — certainly he has never acted passionately. He is a stranger to human affairs; he tells his wife's aunts that he does nothing because he has never seen any call to. And he is an American, a stranger to the society in which his story takes place.

But more than all this, Dowell would seem to be disqualified as the narrator of *any* story by the doubt and uncertainty which are the defining characters of his mind. One phrase runs through his narrative, from the first pages to the last: "I don't know"; and again and again he raises questions of knowledge, only to leave them unanswered: "What does one know and why is one here?" "Who in this world can know anything of any other heart — or of his own?"

The patent inadequacies of Dowell as a narrator have led critics of the novel to dismiss his version of the meaning of the events, and to look elsewhere for authority. Mark Schorer speaks of Dowell's "distorted understanding," and James Hafley of his "incoherent vision," and both look outside the narrator himself for objective truths to justify their judgments. But the point of technique here is simply that the factors which seem to disqualify Dowell — his ignorance, his inability to act, his profound doubt — are not seen in relation to any norm; there is neither a "primary author" nor a "knower" (of the kind of James's Fanny Assingham or Conrad's Marlow) in terms of which we can get a true perspective of either Dowell or the events of the novel. There is only Dowell, sitting down "to puzzle out what I know." The world of the novel is his world, in which "It is all a darkness"; there is no knowledge offered, or even implied, which is superior to his own.

In a novel which postulates such severe limits to human knowledge — a novel of doubt, that is, in which the narrator's fallibility *is* the norm — the problem of authority cannot be settled directly, because the question which authority answers: "How can we know what is true?" is itself what the novel is about. There are, however, two indirect ways in which a sense of the truth can be introduced into such a novel without violating its formal (which is to say epistemological) limitations: either through ironic tone, which will act to discredit the narrator's version of events and to imply the correctness of some alternative version, or through the development of the narrator toward some partial knowledge, if only of his own fallibility (and indeed in an extreme case this may be the only kind of knowledge possible for him). Glenway Wescott's *The Pilgrim Hawk* and Eudora Welty's "Why I Live at the P.O." are examples of the first device; each offers a sequence of events which are in themselves clear enough to the reader, and the irony lies in the disparity which we feel between the way the narrator understands these events and the way we understand them. The point made is thus a point of character, the revelation of a personal failure of perception.

The Great Gatsby is a fair example of the other sort. Fitzgerald's Nick Carraway learns as the action moves, and though he misunderstands and is surrounded by misunderstanding, in the end he knows something about himself, and about Gatsby, and about the world. The point made is a point of knowledge.

It has generally been assumed by Ford's commentators that *The Good Soldier* belongs to the class of *The Pilgrim Hawk*; but in fact it is closer to *Gatsby*. Ford's novel is, to be sure, as ironic as Wescott's, but with this difference; that Ford's narrator is conscious of the irony, and consciously turns it upon himself. When he describes his own inactions, or ventures an analysis of his own character—when he says "I appeared to be like a woman or a solicitor," and describes himself as "just as much of a sentimentalist" as Ashburnham—he is consciously self-deprecating, and thus blocks, as any conscious ironist does, the possibility of being charged with self-delusion. Schorer errs on this crucial point when he says that "the author, while speaking through his simple, infatuated character, lets us know how to take his simplicity and his infatuation." For the author does not speak—the novel has no "primary author"; it is Dowell himself who says, in effect, "I am simple and infatuated" (though there is irony in this, too; he is not all *that* simple).

The case for reading the novel as Schorer does, as a comedy of humor, is based on the enormity of Dowell's inadequacies. There are two arguments to be raised against this reading. First, Dowell's failures—his failure to act, his failure to understand the people around him, his failure to "connect"—are shared by all the other characters in the novel, and thus would seem to constitute a generalization about the human condition rather than a moral state peculiar to him. Alienation, silence, loneliness, repression—these describe Ashburnham and Leonora and Nancy, and even "poor Florence" as well as they describe Dowell. Each character confronts his destiny alone.

Second, Dowell does have certain positive qualities which perhaps, in the light of recent criticism of the novel, require some rehabilitation. For instance, if his moral doubt prevents positive action, it also restrains him from passing judgment, even on those who have most wronged him. "But what were they?" he asks. "The just? The unjust? God knows! I think that the pair of them were only poor wretches creeping over this earth in the shadow of an eternal wrath. It is very terrible." And though he doubts judgment—doubts, that is, the existence of moral absolutes—he is filled with a desire to know, a compelling need for the truth to sustain him in the ruin of his life. In the action of the novel, the doubt and the need to know are equally real, though they deny each other.

Dowell has one other quality, and it is his finest and most saving attribute—his capacity for love; for ironically, it is he, the eunuch, who is the Lover. Florence and Ashburnham and Maisie Maidan suffer from "hearts," but Dowell is sound, and able, after his fashion, to love—to love Ashburnham and Nancy, and even Leonora. It is he who performs the two acts of wholly unselfish love in the book—he crosses the Atlantic in answer to Ashburnham's plea for help, and he travels to Ceylon to bring back the mad Nancy, when Leonora will not. And he can forgive, as no other character can.

This is the character, then, through whom Ford chooses to tell this "saddest story." He is a limited, fallible man, but the novel is not a study of his particular limitations; it is rather a study of the difficulties which man's nature and the world's put in the way of his will to know. Absolute truth and objective judgment are not possible; experience is a darkness, and other hearts are closed to us. If man nevertheless desires to know, and he does, then he will have to do the best he can with the shabby equipment which life offers him, and to be content with small and tentative achievements.

Dowell's account of this affair is told, as all first-person narratives must be, in retrospect, but the technique is in some ways unusual. We know the physical, melodramatic world only at one remove, so that the real events of the novel are Dowell's thoughts about what has happened, and not the happenings themselves. We are never thrown back into the stream of events, as we are, for example, in the narratives of Conrad's Marlow; dramatic scenes are rare, and tend to be told in scattered fragments, as Dowell reverts to them in his thoughts. We are always with Dowell, after the event.

Yet though we are constantly reminded that all the events are over and done, we are also reminded that time passes during the telling (two years in all). The point of this device is the clear distinction that the novel makes between events and meaning, between what we witnessed and what we know. All the returns are in, but their meaning can only be discovered (if at all) in time, by re-examination of the data, by reflection, and ultimately by love. And so Dowell tells his story as a puzzled man thinks—not in chronological order, but compulsively, going over the ground in circles, returning to crucial points, like someone looking for a lost object in a dim light. What he is looking for is the meaning of his experience.

Since the action of the novel is Dowell's struggle to understand, the events are ordered in relation to his developing knowledge, and are given importance in relation to what he learns from them. Thus we know in the first chapter that Dowell's wife, Florence, is dead, hear in the second chapter of Part II Dowell's account of that death (which he believes to be a heart attack), and only in Part III learn, through Dowell's account of Leonora's version of the event, that it was in fact suicide. We move among the events of the affair, to stand with Dowell for a moment behind Ashburnham, then to Leonora, to Nancy, and back to Ashburnham, getting in each case an account, colored always by Dowell's compassionate doubt, of the individual's version of events. The effect of this ordering is not that we finally see one version as right and another as wrong, but that we recognize an irresolvable pluralism of truths, in a world that remains essentially dark.

There are, as I have said, certain crucial points in the narrative to which Dowell returns, or around which the narrative hovers. These are the points at which the two conflicting principles of the novel — Convention and Passion — intersect. The most important of these is the "Protest" scene, in which Florence shows Ashburnham the Protestant document, signed by Luther, Bucer and Zwingli, which has made him what he is — "honest, sober, industrious, provident, and clean-lived." Leonora's reaction to this typical tourist scene strikes Dowell as a bit extravagant: " 'Don't you see,' she said, with a really horrible bitterness, with a really horrible lamentation in her voice, 'Don't you see that that's the cause of the whole miserable affair; of the whole sorrow of the world? And of the eternal damnation of you and me and them. . . .' " He is relieved when she tells him that she is a Roman Catholic because it seems to provide an explanation of her outburst; and later his discovery that Florence was Ashburnham's mistress offers another, and more credible explanation. But neither explanation is really adequate. For Leonora is not simply reacting either to Protestantism or to adultery; she is reacting, in the name of a rigid conventionalism, to the destructive power of passion, which may equally well take the form of religious protest or of sexual license.

Ford once described himself as "a sentimental Tory and a Roman Catholic," and it is in these two forms that convention functions in *The Good Soldier* (and in a number of his other novels as well). Society, as Dowell recognizes, depends on the arbitrary and unquestioning acceptance of "the whole collection of rules." Dowell is, at the beginning of his action, entirely conventional in this sense; conventions provide him with a way of existing in the world — they are the alternatives to the true reality which man cannot know, or which he cannot bear to know. From conventions he gets a spurious sense of permanence and stability and human intimacy, and the illusion of knowledge. When they collapse, he is left with nothing.

Leonora's conventions are her "English Catholic conscience, her rigid principles, her coldness, even her very patience," conventions which are, Dowell thinks, "all wrong in this special case" (it is characteristic of him that he refuses to generalize beyond the special case). Ashburnham's are those of a sentimental Tory — "what was demanded by convention and the traditions of his house." (A first draft of Ashburnham appears in *The Spirit of the People*, Ford's study of the English mind; there the scene between Ashburnham and Nancy at the railway station is offered as an example of the Englishman's characteristic reticence and fear of emotion.) It is by these conventions that the husband and wife act at crucial moments; but it is not conventions alone which bring about their tragedy. It is, rather, the interaction of Convention and Passion.

Passion is the necessary antagonist of Convention, the protest of the individual against the rules. It is anarchic and destructive; it reveals the secrets of the heart which convention exists to conceal and repress; it knows no rules except its own necessity. Passion is, of course, an ambiguous term. To the secular mind it is likely to suggest simply sexual desire. But it also means suffering, and specifically Christ's sacrificial suffering. I don't mean to suggest that Ashburnham is what it has become fashionable to call a "Christ-figure" — I dislike the critical method which consists in rewriting novels as Passion Plays — but simply that the passionate sufferings of Ashburnham (and even of Leonora) are acts of love, and as such have their positive aspects. Convention, as Dowell learns, provides no medium for the expression of such love. In conventional terms it is true, as Dowell says, that Edward and Nancy are the villains, and Leonora the heroine, but the expense of her conventional heroism is the defilement of what is best in her, and the destruction of what she loves, while the "villains" are, in their suffering, blessed; the epigraph of the novel is their epitaph: *Beati Immaculati*, blessed are the pure.

Between the conflicting demands of Convention and Passion, the characters are, as Nancy says, shuttlecocks. "Convention and traditions I suppose," Dowell reflects near the end of the book, "work blindly but surely for the preservation of the normal type; for the extinction of proud, resolute, and unusual individuals." Passion works for the reverse.

In the action of Dowell's knowing, he learns the reality of Passion, but he also acknowledges that Convention will triumph, because it must. "Society must go on, I suppose, and society can only exist if the normal, if the virtuous, the slightly deceitful flourish, and if the passionate, the headstrong, and the too-truthful are condemned to suicide and to madness." Yet in the end he identifies himself unconditionally with Passion: "I loved Edward Ashburnham," he says, "because he was just myself." This seems a bizarre assertion, that Dowell, the Philadelphia eunuch, should identify himself with Ashburnham, the English country squire and lover ("this is his weirdest absurdity," Schorer remarks of this passage, "the final, total blindness of infatuation, and self-infatuation"). But in the action of the novel the identification is understandable enough. The problem that the novel sets is the problem of knowledge, and specifically knowledge of the human heart: "Who in this world knows anything of any other heart — or of his own?' Dowell, in the end, *does* know another human heart — Ashburnham's, and knowing that heart, he knows his own. By entering selflessly into another man's suffering, he has identified himself with him, and identity is knowledge. He is, to be sure, ill-equipped for this knowledge; he lacks, as he says, Ashburnham's courage and virility and physique — everything, one would think, that goes to make an Ashburnham. But by an act of perfect sympathy he has known what Ashburnham was, and he can therefore place himself honestly in the category of "the passionate, of the headstrong, and the too-truthful."

With this confession, the affair is over. The action in Dowell's mind is complete, or as complete as it can be in a novel built on doubt. The repeated questions, which Ford uses as Shakespeare uses questions in the tragedies, almost as symbols of the difficulty of knowing, disappear from the last chapter; but they are replaced, not by an emergent certainty, but by resigned admissions of the limits of human knowledge: "I don't know. I know nothing. I am very tired" and "I can't make out which of them was right. I leave it to you." To know what you can't know is nevertheless a kind of knowledge, and a kind that Dowell did not have at the beginning of the affair. Of positive knowledge, he has this: he knows something of another human heart, and something also of the necessary and irreconcilable conflict which exists between Passion and Convention, and which he accepts as in the nature of things. Beyond that, it is all a darkness, as it was.

Conrad and *The Good Soldier*   Thomas C. Moser*

Despite his reputation for telling tall tales, Ford Madox Ford's contributions to the achievement of Joseph Conrad now prove to be pretty much what he said they were.[1] Not only did he provide the stories for all three collaborations, he elicited Conrad's two memoirs, supplied material for "Amy Foster" and *The Secret Agent*, backed up Conrad while he was

*Reprinted from *Joseph Conrad: A Commemoration*, edited by Norman Sherry (New York: Harper and Row, 1977), 174–82. Portions of this essay originally appeared in *Mosaic: A Journal for the Comparative Study of Literature and Ideas*, published by the University of Manitoba Press, 8, no. 1 (October 1974):217–27, to whom acknowledgement is herewith made.

writing *Nostromo*, and even wrote a few pages himself for the last. Especially, as Conrad's "large, blond, phlegmatic" friend, Ford gave Conrad the "moral support" he "passionately needed." As for exerting direct literary influence, Ford says modestly: "I don't really imagine that I really influenced Conrad at all."

But what, if anything, did Conrad contribute to Ford's masterpiece *The Good Soldier*, the book that Ford called, long after Conrad's death and shortly before his own, "the only novel of my own that I considered — and indeed consider — at all to count"? Ford did not write *The Good Soldier* until five years after the memorable decade (September 1898 to March 1909) of his real intimacy with Conrad. Ford's "place as general cook and bottle-washer in Conrad's literary establishment" had long been taken by their mutual friend Arthur Pierson Marwood, who was also "large, blond, outwardly placid, and deliberate."[2] Nevertheless, Conrad probably exerted two powerful influences upon *The Good Soldier* — the one literary and technical, the other biographical and deeply personal.

Graham Greene rightly finds the greatness of the novel in its "sense of Ford's involvement." The source of that involvement must be biographical: "A novelist is not a vegetable absorbing nourishment mechanically from soil and air: material is not easily or painlessly gained, and one cannot help wondering what agonies of frustration and error lay behind *The Saddest Story*."[3] Such agonies could have come only out of drastically altered relations with the people he was closest to: Elsie Martindale Hueffer, his wife of fifteen years whom he left in 1909 and who would not give him a divorce; Violet Hunt, who became his mistress in 1909; Conrad, his dearest and most distinguished friend, who had broken with Ford in March, 1909, but did respond in 1911 and 1912 to Ford's friendly overtures; and Marwood, the second-best friend of both Conrad and Ford, who also quarrelled with Ford in 1909 but who, along with his wife Caroline, appears very soon to have become temporarily reconciled with Ford and fond of Violet.

And yet, when, on his fortieth birthday, on 7 December 1913, Ford sat down to write *The Good Soldier* "to show what I could do," to put into that novel "*all* that I knew about writing,"[4] he must have felt that his personal life was, once again and more so than ever before, in ruins. By then, Violet Hunt tells us, she was feeling distinctly unsympathetic to Ford.[5] On 7 February 1913, in a highly publicised libel suit, Elsie had received £300 damages from a magazine that had applied the name Mrs Hueffer to Violet. Far more important, Marwood at this time ceased all communication with Ford, and Conrad, probably in sympathy for Marwood, apparently re-rejected Ford. At least, no letters from Conrad to Ford, datable between March 1913 and March 1915, have as yet appeared.[6] I believe, in short, that, by 1913, Ford must have realised at last that neither his artist-friend, who was like a father to him, nor his country gentleman-friend, who embodied the generous traditions of his beloved grandfather, Ford Madox Brown, that neither of these boon companions truly loved him anymore.

Yet, even granted that Ford in 1913 realised that those two English gentlemen could no longer bear him, why connect this with *The Good Soldier*? After all, Ford had been writing on its subject, marital complications, for over twenty years and had been suffering from them almost as long. There are, however, some interesting coincidences of dates and of characters between *The Good Soldier* and the Hueffers, the Marwoods and the Conrads. In the manuscript version of the novel, the crucial first meeting at Nauheim between the Ashburnhams and Dowells occurs in July 1906. Ford's first recorded mention of the Marwoods is February 1906. In May and June of that year, Ford and Conrad collaborated on *The Nature of a Crime*, that strange prefiguration of *The Good Soldier*. And, according to Jessie Conrad, Ford first brought Marwood to the Conrads in July 1906, just before Ford's departure for Germany.[7] In the book version of *The Good Soldier* Ford changed the date of the fatal meeting between the Ashburnhams and Dowells to 4 August 1904, another momentous occasion in Ford's psychic life. The winter of 1904 had marked the height of Ford's intimacy with Conrad, when he was helping with both *Nostromo* and *The Mirror of the Sea*. In the spring and summer of 1904, Ford suffered a severe mental breakdown. July found him weeping and staggering with agoraphobia under the hot sun of the Salisbury Plain. In response to Ford's cries for help, Conrad was unable to supply any financial, and very little moral, support. About 4 August 1904, under doctor's orders, Ford went off alone to seek psychiatric help in various German spas.[8]

The Good Soldier tells of an adulterous affair connecting two couples whose members are all, apparently, dear friends. The masculine Captain Edward Ashburnham, estranged from his wife Leonora, becomes the lover of Florence, wife of the epicene John Dowell, the only member of the quartet ignorant of the affair. Nine years of intimacy end with the suicides of Florence and Edward, the enlightenment of Dowell, and his estrangement from Leonora. Dowell writes down his tale of passion in order to get it out of his head. Both male characters, obviously and unsurprisingly, owe a great deal to physical and psychological aspects of Ford. Similarly, both female characters partake of various aspects of Ford's two women, Elsie and Violet. My own view, which differs from Arthur Mizener's, is that Florence principally reflects Elsie, and Leonora Violet. But Edward and Leonora, the model Tory couple, also owe something to the Marwoods. Elsie, moreover, told Ford in 1909 that Marwood had been making improper advances to her.

If, as I believe, Marwood was the chief model beyond Ford himself for Edward Ashburnham, where in *The Good Soldier* is Conrad to be found? In John Dowell, of course. Dowell's small stature and non-English origin place him among recurrent caricatures of Conrad in Ford's novels. But far more important, Ford gives us in Dowell an impressionistic narrator like Marlow. If the publication of Conrad's *Chance* at the end of 1913 pained Ford with its portrait of de Barral, it would also have provided technically the resurrection of the complex impressionism of *Lord Jim* with its time-shift, its personal narrator Marlow and its plethora of sub-narrators, including the naive Powell (ur-Dowell?).[9]

Dowell, as narrator, owes much to the four manifestations of Marlow. Dowell's life with Florence and the Ashburnhams proves ultimately as devastatingly enlightening to him as Marlow's trip to the Congo to him. Before Marlow embarked on his voyage of discovery, he was like "a silly little bird."[10] Dowell says that he himself was simply a fool. However, the contrast between the narrator's pre- and post-enlightenment phases is endemic to *The Good Soldier* as it is not to *Heart of Darkness*. In the recurrent juxtaposition of an older, wiser Dowell with a young, naive one, we can see a trace of the relationship between old and young Marlow in "Youth." Old Marlow recounts in amazement how his younger self foolishly leapt into a smoking hold, promptly fainted, and was fished out with a chain-hook. Dowell's tone is similar as he recalls how, on the night he eloped with Florence, he went up and down the ladder to her bedroom window "like a tranquil jumping-jack" (p. 84). Dowell's choice of a hero is Marlovian as well. Like Jim, Edward is a big, blond, handsome, likeable, inarticulate Englishman with considerable skill in the service-profession he espouses, and with a subtle unsoundness not at all apparent to strangers. But whereas Jim's plague spot relates, tragically, to his professional performance, Edward's does not. On the other hand, Edward's overwhelming need to comfort a mournful female recalls Marlow's last subject, Captain Anthony of *Chance*, and his Flora.

It surely goes without saying that Dowell especially resembles Marlow as a master (for the first time in Ford's career) of what Ford considered Conrad's greatest literary forte, the "architectonics" of the impressionistic novel. And so Dowell, in true Conradian style, gets in his strong first impression of Edward in the hotel dining-room, including the significant expression in the eyes, and then works backwards and forwards in time. "When one discusses an affair," Dowell says, "a long sad affair — one goes back, one goes forward" (p. 183). Both narrators handle the reader's feelings with such consummate skill that the main, titular character, who has acted in some respects like a villain, proves ultimately sympathetic, even heroic, if ambiguously, suicidally so. Dowell, again like Marlow, handles masterfully the meaningful, illustrative digression and manages beautifully the Conradian flexible chapter-unit. He uses apparently digressive, somewhat philosophical paragraphs to provide transitions between episodes of very different tonal qualities. Finally, Dowell recalls Marlow in his propensity to talk about how difficult it is to fulfil their common purpose to make the reader see and about how hard the impressionistic method really is. "I am, at any rate, trying to get you to see what sort of life it was I led with Florence," says Dowell early in the novel

(p. 14). He admits elsewhere: "I don't know how . . . to put this thing down" (p. 12). He uses Conrad's pathfinder metaphor from *Chance*: "I have, I am aware, told this story in a very rambling way so that it may be difficult for anyone to find his path through what may be a sort of maze. I cannot help it" (p. 183). Nevertheless, Dowell, like Marlow, insists upon the unquestionable, literal truth of his tale: "I console myself with thinking that this is a real story and that, after all, real stories are probably told best in the way a person telling a story would tell them. They will then seem most real" (p. 183).

One fundamental, technical difference between Dowell's tale and the tales told by Marlow forcibly reminds us how Fordian a narrator Dowell is. Although Dowell asks the reader to pretend that they are spending a fortnight together in a cottage by the sea and that Dowell is talking, in a low voice, to his sympathetic auditor, all this is emphatically pretense. Dowell is not talking; he is "really" writing down this sad story and over a period of two years. The closest Marlow comes to written narration is the packet containing the account of Jim's last days that he mails to his privileged listener. The difference is crucial because it allows Ford to give full rein to his solipsistic beliefs (Dowell is really writing only to himself) and to his devastating tendency to change his mind. Although Marlow's attitude always includes bewilderment, although *Heart of Darkness* and *Chance* are unique narratives inspired by special circumstances rather than frequently told yarns, and although Marlow's narratives are characteristically "inconclusive," one never has the sense that Marlow would change events or his attitude. But as Dowell writes, he comes to dislike Leonora, for whom he earlier would lay down his life. Again, as Dowell writes, he suddenly sees events very differently from his earlier recollection of them. His impression at one time is that during their married years Florence was never out of his sight. But later he decides that she was almost always out of his sight. The method is congenial to Ford and provides excuses for apparent errors and inconsistencies. On the other hand, it is a common experience suddenly to remember correctly something one has misremembered; it is not unknown to change one's attitude toward a friend and to harden one's heart even more against an enemy.

Marlow's auditors in *Heart of Darkness* exist as real presences who may, if they wish, talk back; Dowell's auditor is imaginary and therefore mute: "listener . . . you are so silent" (p. 14). Interestingly enough, whereas Marlow can recount long, complicated conversations, Dowell sticks to Ford's dictum that since one cannot, in reality, precisely remember long speeches, one should never quote more than a couple of lines.[11] Most significantly, Dowell gives us virtually nothing from his all-night-long conversation with Edward. Yet, since Dowell supposedly loves Edward more than anyone in the world, that night must have been a great event in his life.

Dowell differs from Marlow in one last, important, but rather indefinable way. Ford had said that it was all right for a novelist to use himself as a character if he was careful to make that character unsound, even villainous.[12] Clearly Ford has in mind a character very different from Marlow, who is not only Conrad (albeit anglicised) but also, despite his many claims to self-doubt, as perfect (in Conrad's terms) as anyone could hope to be. Dowell would seem to fit Ford's prescription of the author's self with many imperfections. In choosing Dowell to be his eyes and voice, Ford chose a man who would try to tell what he saw but who, like Ford, saw badly; who on rare occasions was involved in passionate scenes but was basically like the Ford of *The Soul of London* "not made for strong impressions";[13] who admired passionate creatures as Ford admired "the passion of Conrad"[14] and yet himself feared passion; who nevertheless was human and thus inevitably involved in suffering. To the extent that he can, Dowell suffers: "my mind going round and round in a weary, baffled space of pain" (p. 233). Blind as he has been and perhaps still is, he has seen suffering great enough to drive people he loves to madness and suicide. Dowell's conviction of the meaninglessness of existence is even more desperate than Marlow's. For the latter, Jim's dilemma has fascinating ethical and metaphysical implications for all men that make his story worth telling again and again. But characteristically of Ford, Dowell is unsure whether other people's lives are at all like the lives of those good people the Ashburnhams and the Dowells. Dowell's chief purpose in telling the tale is not to understand it but to get it out of his head.

If then we grant that, as Graham Greene suggested, Ford wrote *The Good Soldier* out of personal, agonised involvement, we might still speculate a little on what Ford's feelings were as he created his master-piece. How did he dare to do it, to write the first great work that follows Conrad's impressionistic manner, one in which Ford destroys or dismisses those formerly nearest and dearest to him? Ford's journalism of this period makes clear that he enjoys the role of ferocious critic. He acknowledges that it "is an exhilarating thing to do" to chuck his "cap into the faces of quite estimable people . . . we need the saeva indignatio . . . one wants to be reckless nowadays . . . One wants it desperately . . . I should respect myself more if I could . . . just for once, say what I really think of a few people. But I have not the courage."[15] Except that he did have the courage — in the guise of fiction — to admit his dislike for Violet, give Elsie prussic acid, cut Marwood's throat and consider spitting on his grave. He had the courage to defy Conrad, to write his own masterpiece of impressionistic fiction.

Ford had the courage because he had decided he was going to die soon. We can only speculate why that should be. Perhaps the *crise de la quarantaine* was upon him. He was also getting toward the age at which his father died. In a 1914 essay on impressionism, Ford says that he is "tired out" and "determined to drop creative writing for good and all."[16] In an article of 4 July 1914 he gives his *morituri salutamus*: "I who am, relatively speaking, about to die. . . ."[17] Thus, half-persuaded of his imminent demise, he who was so tender of skin could safely express his savage indignation.

And yet *The Good Soldier* is great not so much for its bitter tone as for the almost filial love that Dowell feels for Edward (analogous presumably to Ford's deepest feelings for Marwood). If Edward's flaws of stupidity, self-indulgence, and sentimentality lie exposed, they are simply aspects of the great, living human being Ford was determined to create once in his life. Even if we do not believe that Edward quite belongs, by virtue of his passion, among the "Beati Immaculati," he is appallingly human in his suffering.

Love of the father who had called him a "stupid donkey"[18] and guilt for having enjoyed his death perhaps won out after all and helped Ford make *The Good Soldier* the great novel that it is. We do not need merely to infer — from Ford's age, his death-thoughts, the misunderstandings with those two father-figures, Marwood and Conrad, and Marwood's mortal illness — that Ford would also have been thinking about his father at this time. We know it from the journalism. In September 1914, when he had just completed *The Good Soldier*, the image of his father and Swinburne talking together became for Ford the symbol of the good life lost: "some days ago . . . there suddenly jumped into my mind a dim recollection: . . . my father's high excited tones and Mr. Swinburne's mellow, exhortative, and beautiful organ . . . I like to think of my father and Algernon Swinburne discussing with heat the identity of Petronius Arbiter, or whoever he was. For that . . . is a picture of manners that I would very willingly see revived. . . ."[19]

Thus, at the very time Ford has apparently outraged Marwood and again dismayed Conrad, he is thinking of how as a child he just loved listening to his father talk. Ford's purpose in founding, with Marwood, *The English Review* was to promote discussion. In *Mr. Fleight* (1913), the Fordian Fleight's happiest moments are spent talking to the Marwoodian Mr Blood. But it was, after all, with Conrad — according to Violet Hunt — that "At Someries and The Pent they sat up all night helping each other to 'find the word'."[20] Or, as Ford put it, precisely fifty years ago: "For the writer [i.e., Ford himself] the pleasure of eternal technical discussion with Conrad was a sufficient motive for continuing our labours. . . . And it is to be remembered that, during all those years, the writer wrote every word that he wrote, with the idea of reading it aloud to Conrad."[21]

As a paean to both Conrad and Marwood, *The Good Soldier* succeeded only with the artist-friend. Although Marwood apparently never again communicated with Ford, Conrad wrote a warm letter (undated but presumably of March 1915, or shortly thereafter) in praise of *The Good Soldier*: "The women are extraordinary — in the laudatory sense — and the whole vision of the subject perfectly amazing. And talking of cadences, one hears all through them a tone of fretful melancholy,

extremely effective. Something new, this, in your work, my dear Ford—
c'est très, très curieux. Et c'est très bien, très juste."[22] Perhaps Conrad
realised, too, that Ford was throwing himself into the war effort by
writing propaganda, would soon enlist (making Conrad his literary
executor) and would suffer sorely while trying to be a good soldier.

Notes

1. Thanks, in particular, to the following: Bernard C. Meyer, *Joseph Conrad: A Psychoanalytic Biography* (Princeton: Princeton University Press, 1967); Arthur Mizener, *The Saddest Story: A Biography of Ford Madox Ford* (New York and Cleveland: World, 1971); Norman Sherry, *Conrad's Western World* (Cambridge: Cambridge University Press, 1971).

2. Ford Madox Ford, *Return to Yesterday* (London: Gollanz, 1931), pp. 191, 198; and *Mightier Than the Sword* (London: Allen and Unwin, 1938), pp. 278, 280.

3. Graham Greene, ed., *The Bodley Head Ford Madox Ford*, Vol. I (London: The Bodley Head, 1962), p. 12.

4. Ford Madox Ford, *The Good Soldier: A Tale of Passion* (New York, 1951), p. xviii. All further references are to this edition.

5. Violet Hunt, *I Have This to Say* (New York: Boni and Liveright, 1926), pp. 152, 200, *et passim*.

6. I am indebted to Professor Frederick R. Karl for confirming my own census of Conrad's letters to Ford.

7. Mizener, pp. 115, 118 ff., 544. Jessie Conrad, *Joseph Conrad and his Circle* (New York: Dutton, 1935), p. 116. Charles G. Hoffman, "Ford's Manuscript Revisions of *The Good Soldier*," *English Literature in Transition*, 9: 3 (1966), 151.

8. Thomas C. Moser, "From Olive Garnett's Diary: Impressions of Ford Madox Ford and His Friends, 1890–1906," *Texas Studies in Literature and Language* 16:4 (Fall 1974), 511–33.

9. Thomas C. Moser, "Conrad, Ford, and the Sources of *Chance*," *Conradiana*, 7:3 (Fall, 1975).

10. Joseph Conrad, *Youth and Two Other Stories* (London: Blackwood, 1902), p. 60.

11. Ford Madox Ford, *Joseph Conrad: A Personal Remembrance* (London: Duckworth, 1924), pp. 184 ff.

12. Ford Madox Ford, *The Critical Attitude* (London: Duckworth, 1911), p. 34.

13. Ford Madox Ford, *The Soul of London* (London: Alston Rivers, 1905), p. 58.

14. *Joseph Conrad*, p. 20.

15. *The Outlook*, 7 February 1914, p. 174; 2 May 1914, pp. 599f.; 9 May 1914, p. 636.

16. *Critical Writings of Ford Madox Ford*, ed. Frank MacShane (Lincoln: University of Nebraska Press, 1964), pp. 46 f.

17. *The Outlook*, 4 July 1914, p. 16.

18. Ford Madox Ford, *Ancient Lights* (London: Chapman and Hall, 1911), p. ix.

19. *The Outlook*, 26 September 1914, p. 399.

20. Hunt, p. 23.

21. *Joseph Conrad*, pp. 49, 203.

22. From Violet Hunt's transcription of an undated letter in the Cornell University Library. Quoted by permission of the Cornell University Library and the Trustees of the Joseph Conrad Estate.

Escaping the Impasse:
Criticism and the Mitosis
of *The Good Soldier*   Lawrence Thornton*

More than ten years have passed since Joseph Wiesenfarth's "Criticism and the Semiosis of *The Good Soldier*" (*MFS*, 9 [Spring 1963]) provided Ford's readers with an acute examination of the divisive critical responses to the novel, and the number of "new" interpretations which have appeared in the last decade offer little hope of any critical accord being reached before the millennium. Wiesenfarth accurately predicted this state of affairs in his essay. While he judiciously isolates what he feels to be the most promising areas of exploration, and presents his own interpretation that the novel "survives . . . as a tale of suffering" (p. 48), the overriding plea is for enlightened tolerance of others' views among critics faced with the apparently irresolvable ambiguity of *The Good Soldier*. He is, as Hugh Kenner says of Ford in relation to his characters, "in an impasse of sympathy for all sides."[1] But this impasse unnecessarily obscures *The Good Soldier*, and it can be escaped by examining a crucial nexus in the genealogy of the novel's critical history which Wiesenfarth overlooked.

Wiesenfarth chronologically reviews the criticism of the novel published between 1949 and 1961, but while he acknowledges that Mark Schorer originated the idea of Dowell's unreliability and christened *The Good Soldier* a novel of "comic irony" whose gull is Dowell, he does not see a pattern developing in the essays which, year by year, either align themselves with or against Schorer's "An Interpretation." These readings are challenging and often contradictory, but with the exceptions of Cox's and Meixner's they focus on the problem of Dowell's reliability, *as if* that were where a perceptive critic should inevitably begin his assessment of the novel. Yet it was not until after the publication of Schorer's essay in the 1951 Knopf edition of the novel that critics addressed themselves to this question; one searches in vain in pre-Schorer writings for comments about Dowell's veracity.

As I see it, the impasse Wiesenfarth encourages us to accept springs not from some inherent ambiguity in the novel's form or theme (an early review [1915] speaks of its psychological "truthfulness,"),[2] or from Ford's impish delight in obfuscation (we should remember that Ford maintained "one should address oneself to the cabmen round the corner"),[3] but rather from the editorial caprice which placed Schorer's essay at the front of the 1951 Knopf edition, the edition used by all the critics Wiesenfarth cites, as well as by those who have written about the novel since 1963. For *The*

*From *Modern Fiction Studies* 21, no. 2 (Summer 1975):237–41. © by Purdue Research Foundation. Reprinted with permission.

Good Soldier has been approached through the portal of Schorer's strangely biased essay rather than, as Ford intended, through the data on the title page and the "Dedicatory Letter." By responding to Schorer's version of the novel, critics have forced a mitosis of its theme and values, but with Schorer removed, and along with him what have become the semi-sacred critical touchstones of the unreliable narrator and "comic irony," the original text of *The Good Soldier* is restored. When the novel is read in the format intended by Ford, rather than that created by the Knopf editors to which critics since 1951 have felt obliged to respond, a much different reading suggests itself, one which supports Meixner's view of it as a tale of passion and suffering and which makes Wiesenfarth's ambivalent suggestion of a similar reading unnecessarily tentative. Although there is no need to review Schorer's argument at length, two details from his essay will establish the tense dialectic between his introduction to the novel and Ford's.

> [Describing his theory of "comic irony," Schorer asserts that] "*The Good Soldier* carries the subtitle "A Tale of Passion," and the book's controlling irony lies in the fact that passionate situations are related by a narrator who is himself incapable of passion, sexual and moral alike. His is the true *accidia*, and so, from his opening absurdity: "This is the saddest story I have ever heard," on to the end and at every point, we are forced to ask: "How can we believe him? His must be exactly the *wrong* view."[4]

This is the basic premise of his essay, and it has successfully deflected critical attention away from Edward Ashburnham to John Dowell. Yet as Ford makes abundantly clear on the title page and in the "Dedicatory Letter," Ashburnham is the protagonist around whom the tragic events of the novel spiral, cohere, and have their meaning.

Schorer is equally misleading when he has recourse to the "Dedicatory Letter," especially to Ford's allusion to *Fort comme la mort* which is, he says, "suggestive in the structural terms that Ford must have had in mind" (p. xii). Ignoring the *thematic* parallels Ford had in mind, Schorer quotes one sentence from Maupassant (a sentence describing, I might add, a character peripheral to the action) which prepares for what is perhaps the greatest distortion in his essay. The passage in question illustrates the radical dissimilarity between the critic's and the author's introductions to *The Good Soldier*, and it brings us full-circle to Schorer's original premise. "I wish . . . to call attention," Schorer says,

> to what may be the most accidental connection of theme. Of one of his characters Maupassant says: "He was an old intellectual who might have been, perhaps, a good soldier and who could never console himself for what he had not been."
>   The vicious consolations of failure form our narrator. "Men," said D. H. Lawrence, "men can suck the heady juice of exalted self-importance from the bitter weed of failure — failures are usually the most conceited of men." Thus at the end of the novel we have forgotten

the named good soldier, and we look instead at the nominated one, the
narrator himself. (p. xii)

As we will see, Ford most assuredly did not forget Edward Ashburnham,
but most of the critics writing about the novel have acquiesced to Schorer's
nomination of Dowell as its focal point, a character whose interpretation
of the novel's events "must be exactly the *wrong* view." If we read the novel
as Ford intended us to, with *his* directions, it becomes apparent that the
critical impasse in the face of which Wiesenfarth throws up his hands in
resignation was created by "An Interpretation," not by *The Good Soldier*.
    Ford's directions begin with the data on the title page:

THE GOOD SOLDIER
A Tale of Passion
"Beati Immaculati"

Marital, sensual, and spiritual signs mark the entrance to the world of the
novel, and these signs are much less ambiguous than Wiesenfarth suggests
when he says "one cannot even be certain of the meaning of its title page"
(p. 42). In the first place, it is clear that the good soldier of the title must
be understood in relation to the sub-title and epigraph. Weisenfarth is
right when he says that "passion," which at first glance probably denotes
lust, is tempered by the epigraph since it speaks of the happiness of the
blameless. And "passion" as lust is even more suspect when it is viewed in
the context of the epigraph which Wiesenfarth supplies:

Beati Immaculati
qui ambulant in lege Domini.
(Happy are they whose way is blameless
who walk in the law of the Lord.) (p. 43)

Given this context, there is no question that the "passion" of the sub-title,
glossed as it is by the epigraph, is double-edged, suggestive of both lust and
suffering. But Wiesenfarth is unnecessarily tentative in his conclusions
about what can be derived from this information. We should remember
that these signs constitute the portal through which Ford wanted us to
enter the novel, and the novel itself continuously glosses their meanings.
The most direct connection is with Dowell's coda which clarifies the title
page, arching back to illuminate all the events he has described: "Mind, I
am not preaching anything contrary to accepted morality. I am not
advocating free love in this or any other case. Society must go on, I
suppose, and society can only exist if the normal, if the virtuous, and the
slightly deceitful flourish, and if the passionate, the headstrong, and the
too-truthful are condemned to suicide and to madness" (p. 253). "Happy
are they whose way is blameless / who walk in the law of the Lord" —
happy, perhaps, and certainly socially acceptable, but incapable of
passionate love, the emotion which animates Edward and whose absence
allows the likes of Leonora and Rodney Bayham to survive and "flourish."

Contrary to Wiesenfarth's assertion of its ambiguity, the title page responds precisely to the world of the novel. Alluding to Rougement, whose purpose was to "describe the inescapable conflict in the West between passion and marriage,"[5] Cox rightly focuses on the tragedy of a man who embraces the romantic illusion in a society adverse to passion because it is antithetical to its concept of order. The unresolvable tensions between this society and Edward flare up not only in Dowell's coda, but also in the crucial allusion to Peire Vidal. Dowell's judgment (which is surely Ford's) is echoed in Cox's reference to Ford's "praise of passion at any cost" (p. 398), and the coda unmistakably evokes Pound's "Peire Vidal Old," whose persona is Edward's prototype, and in whose rhetoric we see the theme of *The Good Soldier* concentrated:

> O Age gone lax; O stunted followers,
> That mask at passions and desire desires,
> Behold me shrivelled, and your mock of mocks;
> And yet I mock you by the mighty fires
> That burnt me to this ash.[6]

Moreover, the "Dedicatory Letter" adds to what can be inferred from the title page, taking us even further from Schorer and Wiesenfarth. Just before he tells us that the novel was originally called *The Saddest Story*, Ford remarks that he "had in those days an ambition: that was to do for the English novel what in *Fort comme la mort* Maupassant had done for the French" (p. xx). Now *Fort comme la mort* deals with the relationship between a painter, Olivier Bertin, and his longtime mistress, Any de Guilleroy, who are troubled by the ravages of time and the growing fear of old age which will dim his artistic powers and her beauty. Any's young and beautiful daughter enters the scene, resembling so closely the portrait Bertin once painted of Any that he soon begins to confuse the two women and eventually falls in love with Annette. When he is aware of his feelings, he realizes that the only solution is death, and he eventually wanders into the path of an omnibus, killing himself. Maupassant's novel is not about Bertin's lust for either Any or Annette, but about the suffering he experiences after falling in love with a girl young enough to be his daughter, about the psychological turmoil engendered by such a socially unacceptable situation, and consequently about Bertin's "passion" which is as strong as death. The parallels to *The Good Soldier* are obvious, for Ford's novel is not primarily concerned with Edward's affairs. The focus of the novel is on the hopeless situation Edward finds himself in when he, like Bertin, falls in love with Nancy, his ward, a girl young enough to be his daughter. Despite his wife's bizarre attempts to promote it, the idea of an affair with Nancy is appalling, totally antithetical to his unwilled idealization of the relationship. And Edward, again like Bertin, kills himself when Nancy unwittingly destroys his illusion that she would love him forever. Thus the "Dedicatory Letter" illuminates the thematic nexus of the title page, provides a crucial allusion to Maupassant, and demonstrates that *The Good Soldier* is a novel preeminently about suffering, suffering for love in particular, and suffering as the lot of man in general. For the agony Edward experiences spreads out to encompass the lives of all the other characters including Dowell's who in the very act of writing the novel suffers (and for a second time at that) as he records the evidence of his ruined life.

The data on the title page and the information in the "Dedicatory Letter" indisputably point toward the tragic center of a novel where we find a "visceral intensity," as Meixner says, that we are "likely to associate with the Greeks."[7] When *The Good Soldier* is approached as Ford intended, the mitosis of its theme and values becomes as illusory as Schorer's hall of mirrors which seemed to fragment and distort its labyrinthine design. There is an impasse in that labyrinth only if Ford's instructions about its design are overlooked.

Notes

1. Hugh Kenner, "Conrad and Ford," in *Gnomon* (New York: McDowell, Obolensky, 1958), p. 168.

2. David Dow Harvey, *Ford Madox Ford: 1873–1939. A Bibliography of Works and Criticism* (Princeton University Press, 1962), p. 321.

3. *Critical Writings of Ford Madox Ford*, ed. Frank MacShane (Lincoln: University of Nebraska Press, 1964), p. 49.

4. Ford Madox Ford, *The Good Soldier* (New York: Vintage, 1951), p. vii; hereafter cited in the text.

5. James T. Cox, "Ford's 'Passion For Provence,' " ELH, 28 (December 1961), 383.

6. Ezra Pound, *Personae* (New York: New Directions, 1926), p. 32.

7. John A. Meixner, "The Saddest Story," *Kenyon Review*, 22 (Spring 1960), 235.

"An Extraordinarily Safe Castle": Aesthetics as Refuge in *The Good Soldier*

Miriam Bailin*

At the beginning of Part Four of Ford Madox Ford's *The Good Soldier*, John Dowell, the narrator, addresses his readers in the following manner: "I have, I am aware, told this story in a very rambling way so that it may be difficult for anyone to find his path through what may be a

*A condensation by the author of the essay published in *Modern Fiction Studies* 30 (Winter 1984):621–36. *Modern Fiction Studies.* © by Purdue Research Foundation, West Lafayette, Indiana 47907. Reprinted with permission.

sort of maze."[1] Dowell's words regarding the difficulty his narrative "may" present to the reader have been borne out by the nature of the critical activity *The Good Soldier* has generated. Critic after critic has set himself the task of finding a path through the maze of intricate reference and cross-reference, of "fact" and distortion, in an effort to make sense of the complex experience Dowell records and the complex character he reveals himself to be in the process—a character so contradictory in his responses that one critic can say he is "all feeling" and another that he has no feelings at all.[2]

Efforts to deal with this baffling narrative have frequently focused on attempts to distinguish between Dowell's maze-like rambling through the complexities of his experience and Ford's techniques which guide the reader through the maze despite Dowell's inadequacies as a witness. The purposeful artistry, in other words, is usually attributed to Ford alone and the psychologically motivated rambling to Dowell. Richard Cassell's comments on the form of the narrative are representative: "The device of memoirs written by a rambling narrator is a ruse. . . . it is a method to conceal art. . . . [Ford] sees the time-shift as an artificial structural device . . . to achieve a sense of the immediate present, to offer opportunities for the juxtaposition of actions, moods, temperaments, meanings, and metaphors, and to develop the *progression d'effet*."[3] As Cassell's mention of such Fordian techniques as immediacy of effect and *progression d'effet* indicates, the identification of the novel's various formal aspects with Ford's own aesthetic principles and aims has contributed to the critical tendency to ascribe the artistic methods of the narrative solely to Ford.

Although the division Cassell makes between Ford's art and Dowell's rambling is somewhat extreme, even those critics who do take note of Dowell as "the conscious imagist" (Meixner 165), the "Fordian viewer of scenes and maker of images,"[4] conceive of that artistic shaping primarily in terms of Ford's aesthetic or moral vision. As a result, they overlook the manner in which such aesthetic concerns constitute an intrinsic and revealing part of Dowell's psychology. Dowell, after all, is depicted as a man preoccupied with form, both aesthetic and social, and as a self-conscious storyteller vitally concerned with the aesthetic considerations involved in telling his story. Moreover, the subjective first-person narrative frame makes all formal concerns an inextricable part of his psychology. Aesthetics is thus implicitly portrayed in the novel as an essential attribute of such psychology rather than as an authorial means of clarifying the maze which that psychology produces. It is my intention to examine the ways in which Dowell himself employs aesthetic principles in order to control and evade the disruptive nature of the experience he recounts.[5] To view the form of the novel in all its aspects as a product of Dowell's psychological needs is not, however, necessarily to divorce it from Ford's aesthetic theory, but to suggest that Ford's theory was generated from the same personal needs and preoccupations that generated his fiction and his greatest fictional character, John Dowell—a suggestion which I will elaborate on at the end of the essay.

I

Dowell's "maze," like Daedalus's, is a shapely and ordered arrangement of confusing passageways leading in many directions at once. Rather than "a method to conceal art" it can be seen as an artistic concealment, or at least containment, of the Minotaur within—the imposition of controlled form upon the chaos of a world from which the protection of conventional structures of meaning have been withdrawn. Through Dowell's storytelling method Ford depicts not only the destructive conflict between private and public value, passion and convention, illusion and reality (as the conflict has been variously described), but also demonstrates man's need to seek out consoling forms to mediate such conflicts and to impose order and unity on that which is essentially intractable and chaotic. Moreover, the literary form of the novel can be viewed, in part, as Dowell's more private replacement for the social conventions he formerly relied upon for security and stability, but which to a large extent have failed him.

The connection in Dowell's mind between social forms of control and aesthetic forms is indicated by his choice of the intricate form of the minuet (itself both a form of art and a highly structured form of social and personal interaction) as an appropriate analogy to the carefully regulated intimacy of good people: "[Our] intimacy was like a minuet, simply because . . . in every possible circumstance we knew where to go, where to sit, which table we unanimously should choose; and we could rise and go, all four together, without a signal from any one of us, . . . always in the temperate sunshine, or, if it rained, in discreet shelters" (6). When the comforting "minuet" of Dowell's association with the Ashburnhams falls apart under the pressure of the private needs and desires it was meant to contain, he seeks the "discreet shelter" of his own aesthetic conventions. Dowell is able to distance himself from the disturbing implications of the story he feels impelled to record both by providing himself with a refuge in his self-designated role as detached storyteller and by variously containing and displacing in numerous aesthetic frameworks the emotional and moral quandaries with which he wrestles.

Dowell's imaginary setting for the telling of his "saddest story"—that of a cottage by the sea—is the most all-encompassing of his fictional refuges and is paradigmatic of the various ways in which subsequent aesthetic frameworks function in the telling of the story itself. Dowell introduces the cottage setting as an apparent solution to his dilemma concerning "how it is best to put this thing down" (12), thus initiating a series of speculations regarding his storytelling strategy which will continually divert him from the more serious personal and moral dilemmas presented by the experience he recounts. The choice he confronts himself with here is "whether it would be better to . . . tell the story from the beginning. . . . or . . . as it reached me from the lips of Leonora or from those of Edward himself" (12). His answer is rather puzzling if taken merely as an answer to the question of narrative sequence, for it poses yet a third alternative and one which has no apparent bearing on sequence at all: "So I shall just imagine myself for a fortnight or so at one side of the fireplace of a country cottage, with a sympathetic soul opposite me. And I shall go on talking, in a low voice while the sea sounds in the distance and overhead the great black flood of wind polishes the bright stars" (12).

If, however, we see this response as a solution to the philosophical dilemma posed in the lines immediately preceding his speculations on appropriate narrative form, it makes good psychological sense: "[W]hat is there to guide us," Dowell asks, "in the more subtle morality of all other personal contacts, associations, and activities? Or are we meant to act on impulse alone? It is all a darkness" (12). Confronted with the darkness and chaos of a world without conventional guides to regulate human contact in all its dangerous complexity, Dowell takes refuge in the inviting enclosure of a warm, secure cottage, populated by an imaginary sympathetic listener, while the sounds of potential disruption (the sea and the "black flood of wind") are heard only in the distance. Dowell thus immediately links his choice of narrative strategy ("how best to put this thing down") to this cozy setting, while relegating the devastating tangle of events that has left him solitary and grieving to the status of a fireside chat told to a friend.[6]

The choice of this particular refuge of the cottage as a central attribute of his storytelling strategy is not arbitrary. In his reminiscences about the Ashburnhams, Dowell continually associates the image of a home — or its more concrete counterpart, a house protected from the elements — with intimacy and security. For instance, he contrasts his feeling of "nakedness" in the "great open space" of the resort at Nauheim before he and Florence had met the Ashburnhams and "had no attachments," with the friendly reassurance of "one's own home" with its "particular chairs that seem to enfold one in an embrace" (21). Dowell refers to his and Florence's relationship with the Ashburnhams as just such a home, referring to their companionship on one occasion as "our foursquare house" (7) and on another as "an extraordinarily safe castle." "Where better," he asks, "could one take refuge?" (6).

There is some indication that the various elements of Dowell's imaginary setting have antecedents in his actual experience with Leonora. His storytelling situation is strikingly similar to the one in which he found himself when Leonora began her revelations to him: "It was Leonora's own little study that we were in. . . . I . . . was sitting in the deep chair. . . . I cannot tell you the extraordinary sense of leisure that we two seemed to have at that moment. . . . There was an extreme stillness with the remote and intermittent sound of the wind. . . . I knew then that Leonora was about to let me into her full confidence" (105–106). When Dowell later casts about for a way of telling his painful story it is not surprising that he tries to recapture this privileged moment of intimacy with Leonora, a woman he claims he once "desired . . . to possess" (252). In the fictional setting there is the same protected house, the same distant sound of the wind and the same intimate confidences to a sympathetic companion. But this time, in a reversal of roles, Dowell is the master of ceremonies while his unnamed imaginary listener is given attributes that Dowell elsewhere ascribes to Leonora: "She was tuned down to appearing efficient — and yet *sympathetic*. . . . When she listened to you she appeared also to be *listening to some sound that was going on in the distance*. But still, she listened to you and took in what you said, which . . . was, as a rule, something sad" (206 [emphasis mine]). Whether Dowell projects his ideal mode of presentation back on his past or actually borrows it from that past, the way in which these earlier moments with Leonora seem to haunt his imaginary setting reinforces the sense that that setting is an aesthetic substitute for the refuge the Ashburnhams once provided — in effect, an ideal re-creation of the best aspects of his past, now fully under his control.

Dowell not only uses the cottage as an enclosing form for his story but, by concerning himself with the formal considerations his chosen setting entails, he also retreats from pain and confusion into the rhetorical shelter it provides. His explanation at the beginning of Part Four for the difficult maze-like structure of his story is the most revealing example of this kind of retreat into his "cottage": "I cannot help it. I have stuck to my idea of being in a country cottage with a silent listener. . . . I console myself with thinking that this is a real story and that, after all, real stories are probably told best in the way a person telling a story would tell them. They will then seem most real" (183). Within the fictional construct of the novel, Dowell's justification for the verisimilitude of his own story is dizzying in its circularity. He *is*, after all, supposed to be a real person telling a real story in a real way, so that his need to justify the manner in which his account conforms to the way "a person telling a story would tell them" seems to call his actual existence into question. In essence, he is denying any agency as participant, observer or even teller of the tale; (he is only *like* a real person telling a real story).

Dowell deflects his attention (and ours) from the events that took place at Nauheim and Branshawe Teleragh and their consequences for him to a concern with the "realism" of his presentation — from a desire to know the truth to the desire to be true-to-life. Even the "life" he is being true to is not his actual situation, but rather the fiction of the storyteller in the cottage; he makes the real story "seem" real by first making it a fiction. In all his discussions of where, when and how to make his story "seem most real" he never mentions that he is actually in the bleak, deserted mansion of the Ashburnhams with the mad Nancy as his only companion—a fact we learn only at the very end of the novel. By attributing the confusing narrative structure to an aesthetic choice ("I have stuck to my idea of being in a country cottage . . .") rather than to his very real confusion, he can assert a kind of control which he in reality lacks, and he can insist on the realism of his consolatory illusions.

Dowell's manner of portraying the countryside seen from his train window on an excursion with the Ashburnhams provides another telling instance of the manner in which his impressionistic rendering (offered as an improvement on more conventional notions of mimesis) continually offers just another illusion. Safe within the interior of "a great big train" Dowell can look out the window at the natural world as if it were a picture behind glass. He informs us that the green of the countryside seen from the train window is merely an illusion ("the country isn't really green"), and goes on to describe what it "really" is: "The sun shines, the earth is blood red, and purple and red, and green and red. And the oxen . . . are bright varnished brown and black and blackish purple; and the peasants are dressed in the black and white of magpies. . . . [T]here are little mounds of hay that will be grey-green on the sunny side and purple in the shadows. . . . Still, the impression is that you are drawn through brilliant green meadows that run away on each side to the dark purple fir-woods"(41–42). Dowell's description of the countryside, offered as the truth behind the illusory appearance of conventional impression, is itself a fiction of sorts. With its minute attention to perspective, to diversity of color and to shades of light, the picture he paints is very like an Impressionist canvas. His earlier suggestion that the world seen through the train window is merely an illusion is thus reinforced rather than superseded—one picture merely supplanting another. The pictorial aspects of the scene are further emphasized by the subsequent appearance on the walls of the Prussian train station of "paintings of peasants and flowers and cows" (43) the same objects we have just observed through the train window and Dowell's aesthetic sensibility, this time securely and explicitly placed within a picture frame out of harm's way.

In general, Dowell's references to aesthetic perception and to the mechanics of his storytelling serve to cushion the impact of the material he presents by constantly reasserting the storytelling process as the primary focus of attention. When, for instance, he refers to Edward's confession of love to Nancy as "the most monstrously wicked thing that Edward Ashburnham ever did in his life" (113), Dowell immediately retreats from that "wicked thing" into his role as storyteller: "Before he spoke, there was nothing; afterwards, it was the integral fact of his life. Well, I must get back to my story" (116). (As if his story were other than such details—a curious division!)

Often Dowell's attempts to clarify the chronological sequence of his story provide similar diversions from startling and painful events. For instance, when he describes Leonora's agony at Nancy's remark that she would like to marry a man like Edward, he abruptly changes the subject to his own artistic problem in telling the story: "You are to remember that all this happened a month before Leonora went into the girl's room at night. I have been casting back again; but I cannot help it. It is so difficult to keep all these people going. I tell you about . . . Edward, who has fallen behind. And then the girl gets hopelessly left behind. I wish I could put it down in diary form"(222). In this passage, Edward, Leonora and Nancy become mere characters being moved about within Dowell's narrative frame rather than people both in pain and the cause of his own pain.

Self-conscious references to both his manner of telling his story and the fictional frame around that telling are only the most conspicuous examples of Dowell's use of aesthetic form to control and shape the raw material of experience and neutralize threatening emotions. Within the more general frame of the fireside tale, Dowell places individual scenes and perceptions within such other aesthetic frameworks as images of paintings, books, etchings and mythic tableaus—images which serve to distance and contain Dowell's painful or ambivalent feelings. Descriptions of negative events or perceptions are thus often made, at least in aesthetic terms, positive or benign. For instance, Dowell says of his feelings of dispossession: "[T]he whole world for me is like spots of colour in an immense canvas" (14). His ambivalent feelings of rejection and desire for Leonora are expressed in this visual image of her: "She seemed to stand out of her corsage as a white marble bust might out of a black Wedgewood vase" (32), and even his comparison of Nancy's madness to "a picture without meaning" (254) seems to make a negative presence (madness) merely an absence.

Just as Dowell uses aesthetic frames to avert the distressing impact of the material they enclose, so, too, does he use them to avoid moral judgment and the potentially painful assignment of guilt. When he attempts to come to terms with his ambivalent feelings about the Ashburnhams ("But what were they? The just? The unjust?" [70]), he characteristically offers a picture in the place of an answer and continually shifts his attention from the disturbing content of this "picture of judgment" and its moral implications to comment on its aesthetic aspects: "It is almost too terrible, the picture of that judgment, as it appears to me sometimes, at nights. It is probably the suggestion of some picture that I have seen somewhere. But upon an immense plain, suspended in mid-air, I seem to see three figures, two of them clasped in an intense embrace, and one intolerably solitary. It is in black and white, my picture of that judgment, an etching, perhaps: only I cannot tell an etching from a photographic reproduction"(70). Dowell does not pursue the important questions he initially poses concerning guilt and justice; his "judgment" of those who have hurt and betrayed him is merely a picture that "appears" to him "at nights," its "too terrible" force mitigated by his preoccupation with its formal attributes.

In all of the cases I have cited so far, Dowell presents the actual people and events of his story within aesthetic frames. Often, however, he resorts to even more indirect displacement by using secondary fictions and imaginary and historical characters to refer to the most distressing events of his story. While the parallel between the stories of such characters as Peire Vidal or Ludwig the Courageous and the experience of the Dowells and the Ashburnhams has been frequently noted by critics, it has been attributed only to Ford's artistry rather than to Dowell's need to find aesthetic forms to protect himself from the disruptive passions of those who have made him, as he puts it, "so happy and so miserable" (69). However, Dowell's own aesthetic designs and the palliative function they serve can be clearly seen, for instance, in his use of Peire Vidal's story. This tale of destructive passion, of a cold, manipulative female and her obliging chivalric husband, with its obvious parallels to Dowell's own experience is invoked by Dowell following his description of the setting he has chosen for his story, thus suggesting the connection between them: "From time to time we shall get up and go to the door and look out at the great moon and say: 'Why, it is nearly as bright as in Provence!' And then we shall come back to the fireside, with just the touch of a sigh because we are not in that Provence where even the saddest stories are gay. Consider the lamentable story of Peire Vidal"(12–13). Although Dowell again creates an illusory division between an imaginary world (Provence) and a "real" world (the cottage fireside), they are, in fact, two dream worlds. Having retreated into his fictional cottage by the sea to tell his story, he retreats even further by displacing that story upon the "lamentable history of Peire Vidal." Through the implicit parallel between the two stories, he manages at the level of presentation, at least, to have things both ways. He may bemoan the fact that he and his silent listener are not in Provence "where even the saddest stories are gay," but his own sad story is temporarily made gay by its transformation into a Provençal tale.

Dowell's attempt to contain the darkness and complexity of human experience within reassuring forms is not only evidenced by these individual units of composition but, in a less overt manner, by the rambling structure of the novel itself. Through the continually shifting motion of his storytelling, he encloses painful events in casual, anecdotal frameworks, delays the account of critical events and digresses from explosive scenes, producing in the process an intricate narrative maze leading away from the heart of darkness. Rather than a search for understanding, his tale is a constant retreat from the chaos of "personal contacts, associations, and activities."

Particularly troublesome events such as Maisie Maidan's death or the Kilsyte case are often dispersed throughout the narrative in numerous fragments which are themselves enclosed in various digressive contexts.

Such diffusions of plot allow Dowell not only to cushion the emotional force of these events but also to present and re-present the story in varying and at times contradictory ways so as to accommodate his own contradictory allegiances. On one occasion he says that Maisie dies "quite quietly — of heart trouble" (51), and, on another, that she is driven to her death by Florence and Edward. He sees Florence's alluring over-the-shoulder glance as intended for anyone else but himself (23), and later, as a tribute to his manhood (88). He characterizes Edward one time as "the fine soldier, the excellent landlord, the extraordinarily kind, careful, and industrious magistrate" (93), and yet elsewhere sees him as having nothing to him "inside and out" but his attention to his appearance and his banality of conversation (26). Edward's death is construed at first as an example of the cruelty of societal restraint over passion and then as a triumphant assertion by Edward of restraint over uncontrollable passion.

Dowell's contradictory perceptions do not reveal, as some critics contend,[7] a process of gradual illumination culminating in an overarching vision at the end. Rather, they reveal how Dowell under the pressure of an emotional and moral impasse produces a purely formal resolution to his conflict. The inconsistent versions of character and event scattered throughout the narrative allow him to have things both ways in his presentation in a manner not possible in his own life. He can have Edward both pure and sullied, both a fool and a god; he can love Leonora and hate her; he can admire social restraint and abhor it; he can blame and absolve each member of his coterie, and yet by separating these versions and placing them in contexts to which they are not immediately relevant he need never reach a conclusion based on an accumulation of insights, nor confront the implications of his various versions whole.

The meandering, digressive narrative actually allows Dowell to have two different endings to his story which correspond to his two versions of the world. In the first ending — the "truer" end in terms of chronological sequence — Dowell, now an attendant for the mad Nancy, is alone in his study at the Ashburnham mansion. Bitterly denouncing society, he identifies with Edward as a fellow victim of that society which he sees as flourishing at the expense of the "passionate, the headstrong and the too-truthful" (253). His condemnation of society is defiant and resolute, and he ends on a note of contempt for Leonora and her new life with the rabbit-like Rodney Bayham, proclaiming, "that is the end of my story" (255).

But this is not the final word. "It suddenly occurs to me," he continues, "that I have forgotten to say how Edward met his death" (255). This omission is rather surprising given the primacy of Edward's role in Dowell's story, and given that Edward's suicide is the one distressing event in which Dowell was directly involved. The postponement of his account of this crucial event cannot be justified simply by the difficulty he has earlier noted of "keeping all these people going," nor should it be attributed solely to Ford's desire to save the most important scene for the last.[8] It clearly fills two important psychological functions for Dowell. First, it provides him with the opportunity to blunt the impact of Edward's suicide (and his own complicity in it)[9] by depositing his account of it in a casual afterthought at the very end of his narrative; and, second, it allows him to end on a reassuring note which reverses his pose of defiance in his initial ending and reasserts his allegiance to social convention. For, this second, and final "ending" leaves him with Nancy still healthy and en route to India (where Dowell plans to go to wed her), with Edward behaving like the perfect gentleman, dying discreetly because he is too good for the world,[10] and Dowell himself on the best of terms with everyone, especially Leonora. In contrast to the first ending, this one is casual and inconclusive. The last we see of Dowell is not the lonely man in his study summing up his bitter conclusions about the human condition, but the proper, well-behaved man trying to please his friends without exceeding the bounds of approved social discourse. At Edward's request, he "trot[s] off" to Leonora with the telegram announcing Nancy's safe arrival in Brindisi. As the last words of the novel assure us, "She was quite pleased with it" (256). Dowell has crafted his tale so that the boundary of his fictional world is drawn at this reassuring moment of community with Leonora, the apparent model for his figurative auditor, rather than at the later rupture with her — a formal arrangement which might have pointed to a more likely and less desirable listener to his tale — the insane Nancy Rufford.

The major tensions and conflicts in the novel remain unresolved; the sense of completed development and emotional or moral recognition conveyed by the first ending is undercut by the anti-climax of the second. The resolution of Dowell's struggle with the contradictory claims of conscience and desire is finally merely one of formal organization. Ultimately there *is* no stable, all-embracing solution provided to the troubling questions he poses at the beginning regarding the relation between private and public value. Instead, Dowell has found a form which consoles him by maintaining a constant equilibrium between passion and convention, which gives the verbal appearance of the confusion and deceit of lived experience, but does so in a balanced, decorous and tightly controlled created world which he has woven in good company in his cottage by the sea.

Those readers, then, who seek a path through Dowell's maze to a consistent vision offered by the novel, even if that vision be only epistemological uncertainty,[11] will find the task not merely "difficult," as Dowell coyly suggests, but impossible. Attempts to make logical connections between discrete elements of the story and to trace cause-and-effect relations between those elements are impeded by the divagations of his fireside chat; and what connections one finally chooses to draw depend on which elements and versions of plot and character one chooses to connect.

Moreover, Dowell's indirect transmission of his story, his more general framing of all experience and emotion, and his continual digressions serve to displace, distance and ultimately disarm the force of the story. Like Dowell himself, we are usually prevented from direct engagement in the events he describes. Our energies are directed toward penetrating the intricate verbal surface of his account rather than toward participating imaginatively in the despair that engulfs the central characters. "There is nothing to guide us," Dowell insists before embarking on his exploration into the darkness. But there is one guide — the cunning Daedalian artifice of his own construction which provides the illusion of shapeliness and order as it steers us past the treacherous moral ambiguities of contemporary experience.

II

As I indicated at the beginning of this essay, the congruence between the aesthetic principles and techniques which Dowell employs to serve his psychological needs and those which Ford espoused for the modern novel suggests a more personal source for those principles than Ford acknowledged. Indeed, the artistic success of *The Good Soldier* can, at least in part, be attributed to the fact that Ford's technical principles were employed in that novel to accommodate the same personal dilemma which had given rise to them in the first place — an irreconcilable split in Ford's own moral and intellectual allegiances. As Carol Ohmann notes, Ford's early work was flawed by his inability to decide "between two moralities, one social and prosaic, the other purely personal and romantic . . . since he approved them both in turn" (19). Ohmann, however, attributes the success of *The Good Soldier* to a new stability in Ford's moral and emotional outlook rather than to his artistic techniques (111). I would argue, to the contrary, that just as Dowell does not move toward a greater clarity of vision in the novel, so Ford, rather than finding a stable code of values, found a stabilizing aesthetic instead — an aesthetic which in *The Good Soldier* took its rightful place as the tacit subject of his fiction. A brief look at Ford's critical pronouncements will, I think, suggest the manner in which they reflect his desire to remain loyal to two worlds in the same way his protagonists from his earliest novels to *The Good Soldier* try to be both consummate gentlemen and daring iconoclasts.

Dowell's storytelling fiction of a fireside chat with a sympathetic listener, so integral to his need to contain and control his conflicting emotions, is Ford's ideal situation for the novelist: "He must address himself to such men as be of good will; that is to say, he must typify for himself a human soul in sympathy with his own; a silent listener who will be attentive to him, and whose mind acts very much as his acts."[12] Furthermore, the "low voice" which prescribes for himself as storyteller conforms to Ford's prescription for his own narrative tone: "to evolve for myself a vernacular of an extreme quietness that would suggest someone of some refinement talking in a low voice near the ear of someone he likes a good deal."[13] In still another discussion of the audience to whom he addressed himself, Ford designates the same "good people" to whom Dowell writes, saying that he "tried to turn out the sort of book that . . . the English gentleman might read in his library."[14] Yet in his essay "On Impressionism" Ford discredited the "English gentleman" as an appropriate audience for his fiction: "His mind is so taken up by considerations of what is good form, of what is good feeling . . . that he will find it impossible to listen to any plea for art which is exceptional, vivid, or startling" (331). The reader he prefers is the man of peasant intelligence who is receptive to unaccepted ideas because he knows "that this is such a queer world that anything may be possible" (332). In short, the novelist — at least a novelist like Ford, who wishes to be both gentleman and peasant — needs someone like Dowell's "silent listener" who can be relied upon to observe good form, but who is willing to listen sympathetically to the unexpected and disruptive.

Ford's principle that no word, sentence, paragraph or element of plot stick out and call attention to itself also seems related to his desire to remain a gentleman despite his subject matter. Although he attributes this principle to a concern for verisimilitude, it is analogous to the upper-class British reserve which frowns on any gesture or remark which might stick out of the smooth surface of conventional intercourse. After all, his storytelling vernacular is meant to suggest someone *of refinement* talking in a low voice. Dowell's predominately casual and ironic tone, as well as his stated intention to speak as if in a low voice, reflects this desire for refinement as well as what dictates that refinement — the attempt to restrain or subdue unsettling impulses of passion.

Ford's insistence that a novel have "the same effect on the reader as life makes on mankind" (*Conrad* 180) — the central tenet of his impressionist aesthetic — is reflected in Dowell's insistence on verisimilitude in his presentation. For instance, Ford writes about the necessity of breaking up long speeches — whether the author's or his characters' — because they aren't lifelike or interesting: "But if you carefully broke up petunias, statuary, and flower-show motives and put them down in little shreds one contrasting with the other; you would arrive at something much more . . . life-like and interesting. . . . Into that live scene you could then drop the piece of news that you wanted to convey and so you would carry the chapter a good many stages forward" (*Conrad* 190). Dowell also breaks up his account into "little shreds one contrasting with the other," dropping the "news" he wants to convey unobtrusively into their midst. This diffusion of plot may be life-like, but, as I have shown, it also provides a means of conveying disturbing or unresolved material in a shock-proof manner.

Ford's personal use of his aesthetic principles to distance disturbing news and accommodate conflicting impulses is apparent in *Joseph Con-*

rad: A Personal Remembrance—a book which he claims to have written as if it were an impressionist novel (6). Just as Dowell contains his account of Edward's death in an addendum at the end of his story, Ford appends his description of his reaction to Conrad's death to the main body of his book. The appendix, written in French, is introduced in the following manner: "For those not dreading more emotion than the English language will bear, the writer appends what follows, which was written immediately after learning of the death of Conrad. It contains something that is not in the foregoing pages. The writer could not face its translation" (251). By separating this section from the rest of the text, Ford characteristically attempts to accommodate both the reader who "dread[s] more emotion than the English language will bear" and the reader who does not dread such emotion. Furthermore, he offers his spontaneous reaction to Conrad's death in French, the language of its original composition and a language which he implies is a superior vehicle for the transmission of strong feelings. The last sentence, however, undermines these implicit claims for the inclusion of this document on the basis of its realistic presentation and vivid impact. We learn that it has been printed in French because "the writer" (Ford prefers to avoid the too personal "I") could not "face" its translation into English, an act which presumably would require of him more emotion than *he* could bear. This tangle of self-cancelling motivations recalls Dowell's explanation of his own narrative principles, which, though ostensibly meant to make things more vivid and true-to-life (yet palatable to the refined listener), actually serve to comfort the "story-teller."

In his first eighteen novels, as Ohmann notes, Ford's inability to reconcile his inconsistent values resulted in "an evasion of internal tension, a facile solution to conflict" (31). In *The Good Soldier*, Ford at last found an artistic solution to his conflict. He displaced his own evasions, simplifications and conflicting desires onto a fictional self who displaced *his* onto yet another fictional self who employed a narrative strategy that allowed him to have things both ways. We can easily agree with Ford that the result is a superb demonstration of craftsmanship—but we can say still further that the realism of its psychological complexity is greater than its diffident author perhaps ever realized.

Notes

1. Ford Madox Ford, *The Good Soldier: A Tale of Passion* (New York: Vintage Books, 1955), 183. All future references, cited in the text, are to this edition; all ellipses are mine.

2. John A. Meixner, *Ford Madox Ford's Novels* (Minneapolis: University of Minnesota Press, 1962), 159; and, Mark Schorer, "An Interpretation," *The Good Soldier* (New York: Vintage Books, 1955), xv, respectively.

3. Richard A. Cassell, *Ford Madox Ford: A Study of His Novels* (Baltimore: The Johns Hopkins Press, 1961), 176.

4. Thomas C. Moser, *The Life in the Fiction of Ford Madox Ford* (Princeton: Princeton University Press, 1980), 165.

5. For an interesting general discussion of Dowell's evasive narrative strategy see John G. Hessler, "Dowell and *The Good Soldier:* The Narrator Re-Examined," *The Journal of Narrative Technique*, 9 (Winter 1979): 53–60. Hessler, however, does not link Dowell's moral and emotional evasions to his aesthetics.

6. In contrast, most critics see the cottage setting in terms of Ford's aesthetic purposes not Dowell's. For instance, Meixner observes that "in this paragraph Ford is both summing up in juxtaposed images the emotional dimensions of the novel and shaping the reader's responses and expectations" (166). Similarly, Arthur Mizener (*The Saddest Story: A Biography of Ford Madox Ford* [New York: The World Publishing Company, 1971], 267) sees the setting as a pretext for Dowell's casualness which is "Ford's means of bringing the significant particulars into dramatic relation."

7. See, for instance, Mizener, 265, 269; and, Elliott B. Gose, "The Strange Irregular Rhythm: An Analysis of *The Good Soldier*," *PMLA*, 62 (1957):495.

8. See, for instance, Mizener, 269; and, Carol Burke Ohmann, *Ford Madox Ford: From Apprentice to Craftsman* (Middletown, Conn.: Wesleyan University Press, 1964), 108.

9. Dowell does nothing to hinder Edward's obvious intentions: "I guess he could see in my eyes that I didn't intend to hinder him" (256).

10. "I didn't think he was wanted in the world, let his confounded tenants . . . his drunkards, reclaimed and unreclaimed, get on as they liked. Not all the hundreds and hundreds of them deserved that that poor devil should go on suffering for their sakes" (256).

11. See Samuel Hynes, "The Epistemology of *The Good Soldier*," *Sewanee Review*, 69 (1961): 225–35, for what is generally recognized as the standard treatment of this view.

12. Ford Madox Ford, "On Impressionism," *Poetry and Drama* 2:7 (September 1914): 328.

13. Ford Madox Ford, *The March of Literature: From Confucius' Day to Our Own* (New York: The Dial Press, 1938), 793.

14. Ford Madox Ford, *Joseph Conrad: A Personal Remembrance* (London: Duckworth & Co., 1924), 174.

Parade's End and Beyond

[Preface to the Tietjens Novels]   R. A. Scott-James*

In 1928 there was a sudden revival of interest in books about the Great War. It was then that Edmund Blunden's *Undertones of War*, and many other books of war reminiscences achieved success. At last the public was willing to recollect or study emotional experiences which for eight years it had been trying to forget. But Ford Madox Ford's *Some Do Not, No More Parades, A Man Could Stand Up* appeared in 1924, 1925 and 1926 — too soon. People were not yet willing to re-live the painful years of the Great War or ponder the social conditions at home which were associated with it. The Tietjens novels were praised by the reviewers and of course had a measure of success — greater, I believe, as is understandable in the circumstances, in America than in war-weary Britain. But it is perhaps significant of the period that the great public was much more willing to acclaim the *Forsyte Saga* of Galsworthy and study characters which peered back into the last century than fret itself with the fretful recent happenings with which Ford was concerned. And anyway, who was this Ford dealing in so tragical a manner with the painful experience of yesterday's all too gruesome world? Was he not that dexterous, fanciful, almost dilettante writer who had trifled so attractively and non-significantly before the war? What was he doing in this galley?

But that earlier Ford Madox Ford (or Hueffer, as he was till he elected to change his name) was not really so insignificant or even non-significant. He was not by any means distressed or even fully aware of the fact that during the first forty years of his life he was seldom taken seriously by any but the frivolous or the young. He liked to declare — doubtless with his usual exaggeration — that as a boy he had been looked upon as the fool of the family. "Fordie," as he had been called, had been indulgently patted on the head by his father, Dr. Hueffer, the musical critic, and by all the members of that circle — the Rossettis, Madox Brown, Swinburne, Watts Dunton, Holman Hunt and the rest. But before they had become

*From Ford Madox Ford, *Some Do Not* . . . , *No More Parades, A Man Could Stand Up —*, *Last Post* (London: Penguin Books, 1948). Copyright 1948 by Penguin Books Ltd. Reprinted by permission of Penguin Books Ltd. The preface is included in each volume.

accustomed to his growing up he was already writing books which appeared one after the other in quick succession, novels and biographical, critical, impressionistic studies, books which were received, not unfavourably, for they were so well written, but not quite seriously, since what he wrote was so unlike what serious people say. During the first fourteen years of the century, when English literature was being dominated by Shaw, Wells, Bennett, Galsworthy, and a number of zestful writers preoccupied with social problems or by lighter essayists like Chesterton whose lightness could not conceal the same essential purposefulness, Ford pursued his apparently aimless, fanciful course, reading novels and a little history in a desultory way, playing the piano, looking at pictures, visiting music-halls for an hour's recreation — feeling there, as he would say, "the great heart of the people" — talking about art much as the pre-Raphaelites had done. Pre-Raphaelitism was in his veins; perhaps it might be said that he was a sort of link between the votaries of pre-Raphaelitism in the nineteenth century and the neo-Georgians who fluttered into existence in the second and third decades of this century.

Highly serious critics like Edward Garnett were inclined to think of him as a dilettante — a fanciful, egotistic person who turned his back on "real life," moving irresponsibly from one unreality to another. And in a sense he did, in that his realities were often compositions of his active fancy, incompatible with hard fact, and not to be held down by any rules of severe common sense. None the less, the world in which he moved, smiling, egotistic, and seemingly irresponsible, was not wholly the invention of caprice. Within itself it was amazingly consistent; he clung tenaciously to certain governing ideas which were growing up in his mind. In the first place he wanted to be truthful to himself, to preserve "those ideas which are a part of ourselves, which are our very selves" — ideas that deserve to be "treated with some of the tenderness which is due to divine things." "It is not enough," he said in *The Critical Attitude*, that "the critic should say that we are nine parts gold to one part dross, for that one part will be to us dearest of all. And similarly for the novelist, it will be his function to present the world that he sees with tender regard for what it is, its gold and its dross, 'crystallising modern life in its several aspects.' " Hence the governing idea which he never abandoned, that the novelist should be intent "merely to register — to constater."

He was of course concerned, as so many conspicuous writers of his time were not, with the problem of style — but he would not have called it a problem — he disliked problems. He harped upon the expression *le mot juste*, as illustrated in Flaubert, though for him the search for it was no "martyrdom." Writing indeed was an art that had to be studied and even learnt — he audaciously affirmed that it was he who taught Conrad, with whom he twice collaborated, to write English — but once the faculty had been acquired it was as if for him style issued from inward grace and candour, through instinctive selection. He himself wrote fluently — perhaps too fluently — always giving as much heed to the sound and rhythm of sentences as to their meaning. A sentence that did not gratify his ear was to him intolerable.

In founding and editing the *English Review*, it has his avowed object to help to bring into being "a sober, sincere, conscientous and scientific body of writers" who would "crystallise modern life in its several aspects." This was very ambitious, very high-sounding, but perhaps not wholly convincing, coming from one who in those years just before World War I still had something of the air of a trifler in the realms of gold, dealing so lightly if agreeably with eternal verities, weaving his fanciful tapestries of history with so much exactitude and so little authority, moving in a charmed and charming world but not a world of recognisable realities. Indeed, at the age of forty-one, in 1914, when that war started, it seemed as if Ford might have gone on to the end, an exquisite, fascinating trifler, with no clear bent, no central core, certainly with no definable character capable of leaving any deep impress on literature; he might have gone on just being "Fordie," that and no more. But when certain things happened, one consequence of which for him was the present series of novels, the Tietjens novels, which have been compared to Galsworthy's *Forsyte Saga*, but surely outstrip that work by virtue of a finer sensibility and a more elastic sympathy with human nature.

The events that produced a crisis for him were of two kinds. The first were in his private life, which I shall not discuss, for this is not the time to rake up memories painful to persons still living. Enough that Ford became involved in an intricate emotional situation from which his vanity and obstinacy made it difficult for him to escape. At the same time he had been introduced into a wider social world than he had hitherto known through his association with Violet Hunt on one side and the politician Charles Masterman on another. The second event was the war. He was over military age, but got a commission in the Army. He spent a few weeks on not very active "active service" on the western front. But it gave him his picture of the war. A series of crises in his private life synchronising with a World War stirred Ford's emotional and perceptive life to the core. His writing acquired significance and poignancy. This combination of experiences produced the stimulus for his best books, *The Good Soldier*, and the four Tietjens novels, *Some Do Not, No More Parades, A Man Could Stand Up*, and *Last Post*.

Ford's avowed purpose in the Tietjens novels was to show "what the late war (1914–18) was like." "If, for reasons of gain or, as is still more likely, out of dislike for collective types other than your own, you choose to permit your rulers to embark on another war, this — or something very accentuated along similar lines — is what you will have to put up with!"

"You see here the end of the war of attrition through the eyes of a fairly stolid, fairly well-instructed man." From this it might seem that Ford, than whom none could have been less like a propagandist, had turned to the writing of propaganda. "I hope," he says, "that this series of books, for what it is worth, may make war seem undesirable." But the Prefaces in which these words occur are, after all, like most Prefaces, afterthoughts. All writing may become propaganda when it is poignant enough to stir the emotions, and thereby set up the train of thought which leads to opinions or convictions. It is only in this sense that these novels are propagandist. Ford's ostensible subject-matter is the war—the war as it is on the scene of action or the lines of communication, and the war as an atmosphere among the people at home, who remain their habitual pre-war selves, but modified by the unusual circumstances of war. His declared object is to make us look at this spectacle of war, and to show it without over-stating the horrors or the heroisms (thereby inducing in the reader indifference to both); and it occurred to him that he could not do better than view these struggles, mostly emotional struggles, through the eyes of a certain man he had once known, a Tory—"already dead, along with all English Tories." He is the Christopher Tietjens of these novels— "the last English Tory, omniscient, slightly contemptuous—and sentimental in his human contacts."

But the statement that the war is his subject must be qualified. The war was the governing factor in the life of that time, thirty years ago, just as the recent war with its sequel is the governing factor in the life of the present. War brings out the best and the worst in men and exaggerates the more primitive virtues and vices, but does not fundamentally alter human nature. It can afford the most amazing perspectives for the artist. Ford is concerned with the life, passionate and trivial, of certain people and groups of people, and the conflict arising from their loves, intrigues, vanity, ambition, obstinacy and weakness, honour and dishonour, a conflict which is heightened by the exceptional powers and disabilities conferred by the circumstances of war, and made more striking against the background of its more obvious tragedy.

It is for every reader to decide for himself whether he can quite believe in Tietjens as a real human being. "The English Tory" as such is perhaps a figment of Ford's imagination. This obstinately chivalrous English gentleman (with "the gentleman" somewhat over-emphasized) *sans peur et sans reproche*, masterful, arrogant, generous to the point of prodigality, reticent to the point of folly, honourable to the point of condoning dishonour, passionate yet steeled against passion, is a person hard to believe in, yet he does get across, striding powerfully through these pages, compelling some sympathy, some acceptance of his reality. We must, indeed, presuppose his reality, for all depends on him; and the fiction works. Whether such a person could ever have existed in real life we may question. But his existence is necessary for Ford's purpose. This Fordian ideal of an English gentleman is the peg on which this story had to be hung, and—fanciful or real—it acquires under his presentation reality at least within his system of thinking. Tietjens' personality is the foil against which the other characters are set in violent contrast.

The books present a series of conflicts. There is the conflict between him and his wife Sylvia, beautiful, arrogant, spoilt, and destitute of any sense of loyalty to country or husband, "who considered that the World War was just an excuse for male agapemones," of whose shamelessness Tietjens is in no doubt, though characteristically he refuses to divorce her, remaining in torture from love for another woman, Valentine, whom he neither accepts nor rejects. Sylvia is a brilliant piece of sardonic portraiture. In depicting Valentine, the clean, robust, courageous girl, in love with Tietjens as passionately as he with her, Ford reveals a capacity for probing genuine emotion such as one might never have suspected him capable of. There is no affectation here, no mere cleverness, but creative force of a high order in the long story of repressed passion between Tietjens and Valentine.

There is the conflict also between Tietjens and the whole order of established humbug which he discovers, first in the pre-war officialdom of the Government department he served before the war, and in many parts of the military machine which he is called upon to serve during the war. And there is the conflict between the private world of his domestic and social relations and his duty as an official or a soldier. Magnanimous to a fault, generous to the extreme of quixotry, we find him surrounded with careerists who borrow his money and exploit his talents and throw him over when they think he is down. Admirably drawn are the vain little coxcomb Macmaster, and the adroit Mrs. Duchemin (whom Macmaster marries) aspiring to salon fame and intellectual correspondences with budding celebrities. And there is Mark Tietjens, Christopher's elder brother, who is perhaps, like Christopher himself, a type rather than an individual — here the manner of portraiture is a little Galsworthian. But how Ford would have detested such a comparison!

The whole is a large-scale picture of English life in its public and its private aspects at moments when the world was approaching, enduring, or endeavouring to forget the war. The motive is the conflict between contrasted types of human beings living under the shadow of war or actually immersed in its ugly operations. The war scenes are done with a coolness, an insouciance, far more effective than any high-coloured rhetoric in conveying the cumulative horror of the thing. Ford may have had Tolstoy's *War and Peace* in his mind. These books are in no sense an imitation of that inimitable work, but Ford does, in his own way, seek to convey, as Tolstoy did, the pettiness and magnificence of individual human beings set against the terrific, ironic background of a fatuous war. I would not for a moment suggest that Ford can reach the splendour of Tolstoy. There are too many errors in tact, too many exhibitions of fancy or ingenuity, too many petulances incidentally revealed, for his work to stand up against so great a masterpiece. Nevertheless, I have little doubt that the Tietjens novels will come to rank far higher than the *Forsyte Saga*, and remain a significant expression of the time, a mature exhibition of passion, at a moment in literary history when so many of the more distinguished writers chose the insignificant and ran away from passion.

The Story of Ford Madox Ford
[Review of *Parade's End*]   Caroline Gordon*

In 1938 Ford Madox Ford made a talk before a class of girls who were studying "the novel" under my tutelage. It was in April. In North Carolina. April in North Carolina is like July in less-favored climates. Ford was then in his early sixties and already suffering from the heart disease that killed him; he seemed to feel the heat even more than we had feared that he would. My husband I debated as to whether it would be safe to let the old man make the talk he was bent on making. When we reached the classroom the next morning and I saw that his veined, rubicund face had gone ashen from the effort of climbing the stairs I wished that I had not accepted his offer to speak. He sat down at one end of a long table, his chair pushed well back in order to accommodate his great paunch, his legs spread wide to support his great weight.

Girls came in, by twos and threes and, as if feeling something strange and formidable in his presence, huddled in a group at the other end of the table. A copy of *The Saturday Evening Post* that somebody had been reading lay open before him. We were waiting for the last comer to seat herself. He cast his eyes down and began to read. For several minutes there was no sound in the room except his labored breathing. I remember thinking that he looked like a big white whale as he sat there, forcing the breaths through his wide-open mouth. Suddenly he looked up. The fish-like gaze brightened. He said, with a chuckle: "I see that our method has reached *The Post*."

The "method" to which he referred was the "Impressionist" technique which he used in collaboration with Joseph Conrad and later used to better advantage in his own novels. It is true that the author of the best-seller then running serially in *The Post* was using Ford's method — as much of it as he could handle. Many other writers have used it since then, some of them writers who have never even heard his name.

Ford's work — the body of it — may be compared to a huge stone cast into a pond; only the water which is displaced by its presence will have

*From *New York Times Book Review*, 17 September 1950, sec. 7, pp. 1, 22. Copyright 1950 by The New York Times Company. Reprinted by permission of The New York Times Company and Nancy Tate Wood.

intimate contact with the stone, but the tiniest ripple will in time carry its impact to the shore. Ford was the best craftsman of his day; we are only now beginning to realize how widespread and pervasive such a literary influence can be.

The wielder of this powerful influence was born in London in 1873 (he died in 1939), the grandson of the pre-Raphaelite painter Ford Madox Brown. His youth was thus spent among the Rossettis and their circle. At 17 he published his first book. His international background gave him ready access to the leading literary and artistic movements of his generation: his finest short novel, *The Good Soldier* (1915), he himself rewrote in French. And indeed, as John Rodker said of this book, it is the greatest French novel in English.

Breadth of view, immense knowledge of many literatures, and an unwavering loyalty to his great profession marked Ford as perhaps the last great man of letters in the nineteenth-century style. Whatever concerned the vitality of letters was within his province. He was one of the few great editors of this century. In reckoning his value one must not forget that as editor of the *English Review*, founded in 1908, he brought what we know now as "modernism" to England.

In the Knopf edition just published Ford's four war novels, commonly known as "the Tietjens series," appear at last for what they are — one great novel — under the title *Parade's End*. The novels which make up the tetralogy were written at the close of World War I and achieved a brief popularity. They were held to be a not too realistic account of one soldier's disillusioning experience in that war. They are being published on what is perhaps the eve of a third world war, with a preface by Robie Macauley, a young writer whose own work will doubtless be better known later on than it is today.

Mr. Macauley points out in his preface that *Parade's End* begins, as many great works of fiction have begun, with a journey: two young men sit in a perfectly appointed railway carriage; everything in the carriage is of the best material; the window straps are of the finest leather, the mirrors, immaculate, "as if they had reflected very little"; the air smells faintly of an excellent varnish. Christopher Tietjens, the hero, and his friend, Vincent Macmaster, are on their way to spend a week-end in the country. They are of "the class that administers the world." If they see anything wrong anywhere — a policeman misbehaving, an insufficiency of street lamps, a defect in public service — they feel it their duty to set the matter right. The train they are riding runs as smoothly (Tietjens thinks) "as British gilt-edged securities." However, it is running on the wrong track.

"Actually," Mr. Macauley says in his brilliant preface, "it is not running from London to Rye as they think, but from the past into the future, and ahead of them on their one-way journey is a chaotic country of ripped battlefields and disordered towns. Their fellow-passengers will grow hysterical and unpredictable; station masters will put up the wrong signals, troops will come aboard and get off again, the good furnishings of the train will get worn and broken, the schedules will go to pieces. And, experiencing all this, Christopher Tietjens will learn to expect that somewhere, beyond some bridge or tunnel, the tracks themselves will finally disappear into the dry sands of the wasteland."

It is easier now to read the Tietjens novels than when they were first written. It is becoming apparent that when he wrote them Ford was writing history, as any novelist is writing history when he records faithfully the happenings of his times. (It was Henry James who observed that the novelist's obligation to record faithfully is as binding, "as sacred" as that of a Thomas Macaulay or an Edward Gibbon.) Ford was one of the most brilliant and faithful recorders of his time. There is no one, not even James, who can bring a scene before us with more vividness.

In some of Ford's writing, however, there is too much going on. If the reader relaxes his attention he will soon not know where he is. Then, too, he must pay attention with his ear as well as his eye, for sound plays an important part in Ford's dramatic effects. The first part of the tetralogy ends with the words: "He had caught, outside the gate of his old office, a transport lorry that had given him a lift to Holborn." These cadences, which tells us that Tietjens' future life will be sober, if not mournful, fall on deaf ears if the reader has not read every word that precedes them.

Such demands were not made on English readers at the time when Ford began writing novels. They had not been made by Thackeray and were made only sporadically by Dickens; Arnold Bennett and Swinnerton and Galsworthy did not make them—and Joyce had only just been published.

It is easy to see why Ford's work was not popular in his own day, but it is hard to see why it has been neglected in our own, for he would seem, in these times, to have a special claim on our attention. He is a superb historical novelist, seeming as much at home in the medieval castle or in Tudor England as in Tietjens' twentieth-century railway carriage. At his touch some of history's driest, barest bones take on flesh. Yet he is comparatively unknown as a historical novelist in an age in which the historical novel enjoys the greatest vogue it has ever enjoyed.

It seems highly suitable that the preface to *Parade's End* should be written by a young, comparatively unknown writer, since Ford himself has as yet hardly been recognized as a writer. Or perhaps it is more exact to say that he has been recognized as a writer. Or perhaps it is more exact to say that he has been recognized only intermittently. Certainly he lapsed after his two modest successes—the publication of the Tietjens series and *The Fifth Queen* trilogy—into obscurity greater than he had known before.

It has been fashionable to regard this obscurity, deeper and darker than that surrounding any comparable talent of our time, as no more than he deserved: the proper reward for a misspent life. Ford during his lifetime was often the subject of gossip, his actions often seemed ill-advised; he made powerful enemies. In his late fifties his powers failed him; he was no longer able to write fiction and kept himself going by writing over and over a sort of fictionalized auto-biography.

Yet all this was part of one story, the same story he was all his life telling, for like most novelists he had only one story to tell. His novels are all either rehearsals for that story or variations of its pattern. The action is presented very vividly in the Tietjens series and it is possible that that is the version of the story by which Ford would prefer to be remembered.

Christopher Tietjens may be thought of as "the last Tory." Indeed Ford himself says that he so conceived him, a man who through no apparent fault of his own is at odds with his times. However, "he and she," as Chekhov sagely observed, "are the engine that makes fiction move." Tietjens is a fine fellow, but for all his virtues he is not at peace with himself; for one thing, he has made a bad marriage. Sylvia Tietjens, his wife, is a *belle dame sans merci*. Tall, beautiful, wealthy, she alternately hates and loves her husband and is hell-bent on his ruin. When she is not tormenting him she suffers from boredom. She is too fastidious to take a lover and, instead, practices on men "every variety of turning down."

As a novelist Ford is much preoccupied with those life-giving and death-dealing attributes of woman. Ford's heroes are all involved with some *belle dame sans merci* who looms to them a little larger than life.

The heroines who battle with these apparitions for the love of Ford's heroes are usually little, fair women, possessed of great filial piety, who have recently had reverses of fortune. In the earlier novels the white goddesses are triumphant. The hero and the woman who is attached to him are nearly always ruined.

Still, no matter how his fortune turns, Ford's hero stands always between two women whose natures are diametrically opposed, inclining a little toward the *belle dame sans merci*. Man naturally seeks his own ruination, the author seems to say, particularly if there is no exterior order to which his case can be referred. A priest usually broods over the conflict: in *Parade's End*, Father Consett; in *A Call*, a Greek Orthodox priest who sardonically points out to Robert Grimshawe what his own loss of faith has cost [him]. Man's plight, the novelist seems to say, is always the same: he must exercise his free will and choose between the good and the bad.

It does not seem to matter where or when Ford sets his stage; he is always able to make the action immediate and convincing. In *The Young Lovell* the young knight praying over his arms, "in the new French fashion," succumbs to the temptations of a sorceress, passes three months as a day in her company and thereafter finds his family, friends and fiancée unendurable. He finally follows her into barren pastures to spend his life in a long enchantment. In Ford's hands this variation of an ancient legend symbolizes the plight of the modern man; Tietjens' expensive railway carriage is heading for the same trackless wastes.

Ordered Life and the Abysses of
Chaos: *Parade's End*

George Core*

In the mists of early twentieth-century literary history the figure of
Ford Madox Ford will always bulk large, and not merely because the
ungainly proportions of the man himself always tend to be associated with
the strange shape of his career. Indeed, as Caroline Gordon persuasively
argued a few years ago, much of Ford's work has the inscrutable
massiveness of the elephant as well as its power, and none of the reports
about this particular instance of the animal reduce him to ordinary
stature. Ford remains easy to attack but impossible to wound at vital
points. One should always remember when the outline of Ford's portly
figure begins to lose its shape and when his best novels seem to take on the
coloration of James or Conrad that it was not for nothing that Ezra Pound
remarked in 1913: "F.M.H. happens to be a serious artist. . . . He and
Yeats are the two men in London."

On another occasion Pound said that he could leave Ford naked and
alone in an empty room and come back an hour later to find pandemo-
nium. Even if the remark were apocryphal the image would be right, as
Arthur Mizener's new biography confirms—and confirms not only in its
title, *The Saddest Story*. Only a few times in his long and productive
career was Ford able to overcome the distracting circumstances which
were characteristic of his life and bring all his vast experience, talent,
resourcefulness, and insight fully to bear on the making of a work of
fiction. Two of the three occasions were marked by the First World War.

In *The Good Soldier* and the first half of *Some Do Not*, Ford presents
Edwardian England on the eve of change: it is a society of immense
wealth, sharply defined social divisions, and absolute certainties about
itself and the world. Beneath the surface elegance and order runs the
powerful current of uneasiness, corruption, and disorder; and one is
reminded of the Tudor England that Ford pictures brilliantly in *The Fifth
Queen* or the England of two centuries hence as it is rendered by
Thackeray. *Parade's End* is a twentieth-century *Vanity Fair*. The first three
novels cover roughly a decade. (It should be understood throughout that,
with two exceptions, I am referring to the first three novels: *Some Do Not*,
No More Parades, and *A Man Could Stand Up*— hence to the trilogy. I see
The Last Post as a sequel to these novels, not an integral part of this
fiction.) By the time *A Man Could Stand Up* ends on Armistice Day in
1918, Ford has almost perfectly objectified what he felt upon returning to
England after the war: beneath "the merest film" of "Ordered Life itself
was stretched . . . the abysses of Chaos. One had come from the frail

*From *The Southern Review* 8 (1972):520–32. Reprinted by permission of the author.

shelters of the Line to a world that was more frail than any canvas hut. . . . The world of men was changed and our places were taken by strangers." The country which had existed from the Renaissance onward was now irremediably altered, and modernism had triumphed. The last vestiges of the feudal world were shattered, yet the tissue of order remained.

Ford depicted this cataclysmic change in the life of English society by doing precisely what he set out to accomplish—"to register my own time in terms of my own time," as he said. This in itself can be neglected as an achievement unworthy of particular notice, for novelists have been writing in this way since Defoe. But if we look more closely at the Tietjens trilogy and the circumstances surrounding their conception, gestation, and birth, the genuine importance of Ford's accomplishment can be weighed in the balances.

In writing *Parade's End* the author was faced with a fictive problem which involved far more than merely projecting a social history of England during the last years of the Edwardian regime. That would have been difficult and exacting enough, but the job was complicated enormously by the great war, which stands as a continental divide in English history. The modern world began for the British Empire in 1914, and Ford prophetically understood this.

Sensing the powerful currents of change and navigating the riptides of history is one thing; rendering the conflict as fable is quite another. As I view *Parade's End*, what Ford did was bring together two forms of fiction in order to achieve the right shape for the action. In so doing he combined the two greatest genres available to him: the historical novel of Sir Walter Scott and the novel of manners of Jane Austen. At the same time, Ford strenuously avoided what he disdainfully called the Literature of Escape— the popular romance. The essential substance in the white magic that he mixed on this occasion—the reagent—was what he and Conrad called impressionism.

Ford Madox Ford insisted time and again that a novel should begin with "an action or incident"—not an arbitrary subject or theme—and from what he has said about *Parade's End* and from the evidence of the novels themselves, it is plain that he thought in terms of action—the behavior of his various characters. As he remarked, "Every incident— anecdote—has of necessity subject, atmosphere and inevitabilities of character behind it." The coincidence of atmosphere—the larger action or "background"—and fable—or the action proper—as it concerns the leading figures is precisely the meeting ground of history and fiction, of common life and individual imagination, of singular experience and personal craft. The problem to resolve through the form of art—"the sound way to elaborate a novel"—lay in the past as Ford had lived through it as the last Pre-Raphaelite, the failed editor of the *English Review*, the overage shell-shocked captain, the rejected man of letters, the journeyman gardener who had left England for France.

The mystery is that Ford was able to triumph over numbing complications in his personal life — incredible marital difficulties, legal entanglements, scandalous publicity, financial reversals, wretched health, and neurasthenia — to write *Some Do Not*. One is tempted to unlimber a phrase after the manner of Lionel Trilling and suggest that Ford is the hero as man of letters. That would not take us very far and would indeed simply present another mask of the kind that H. G. Wells deplored in saying, "What he is really or if he is really, nobody knows now and he least of all; he has become a great system of assumed personas and dramatized selfs." It is more to the point to note that *Some Do Not* was written and published in that astonishingly fecund period in the early and mid-twenties that saw major work by Pirandello, Pound, Stevens, Mann, Forster, Yeats, Eliot, Joyce, and Hemingway, some of which Ford accepted for the *transatlantic review.*

Like his contemporaries Ford was responding to the vital forces unleashed by the great war, and he wrote a fiction which deals directly with the collapse of one culture and the simultaneous growth of another against the background of war. The wasteland that Christopher Tietjens confronts as he looks out over the no-man's-land between the English and German trenches has more in common with postwar England than one sees at first glance.

More than one critic has examined important facets of the technical brilliance in *Parade's End*. The character alignments are a significant feature, for instance: not only do we get a cross-section of English society, but the lives of the Scotsman Vincent Macmaster and his wife Edith Ethel counterpoint the lives of Christopher and Valentine Wannop. Many of the novels' most subtle and penetrating ironies inhere in the differences between the two couples — the one calculating, cold-blooded, dishonest, and successful in the world's eyes; the other ingenuous, generous, warmly human, and dogged by every possible reversal in an unfriendly and morally ugly society. The distinction in the couples is made clear at the outset when Edith Ethel Duchemin lectures the incredulous Valentine on the advantages of chastity; before the day is over Mrs. Duchemin and Macmaster have started their affair. The sight of their passion at the Reverend Duchemin's elegant table before Christopher's knowing glance is both comic and revealing of all that is to come.

Even though Tietjens knows his way around this society, he only moves through it — and with indifference. He is in it but not of it, knowing its shams too thoroughly and caring too little for its devices. Later he is alienated from it, largely because his wife Sylvia (whom Bernard Bergonzi has aptly called a sexual terrorist) sets out deliberately to punish him and to ruin his reputation — and because various others resent his great wealth, his vast intelligence, his rough manner, and his uninterest in what this world thinks important. As Graham Greene has put it, the story of Christopher Tietjens' life is "an appalling examination of how private malice goes on during public disaster."

The irony is that Tietjens is one of the great ruling class of Edwardian England—a man whose position should be unquestioned and secure. This brings us to one secret of Ford's fable: he took the usual plot of the novel of manners and reversed it. Rather than having an intruder, a Macmaster, attempt to enter a closed society, Ford quite properly decided to present the end of an era by having the new society—now open, fluid, and unsure of itself—victimize a member of the old establishment who had refused to change. (Ford knew exactly what Edith Wharton meant when she remarked that the only way to reveal a trivial society is to show what it destroys.) Tietjens, rather than adapting himself to the new ways, simply yearned for a place where a man could stand up—a retreat like George Herbert's Bemerton parsonage—the place "that produced the stock of . . . Anglican sainthood." It is a hopelessly simple yet impossible request to make of a complex, decadent, and inhuman world. In the end he must apparently lose nearly everything—his father, his ancestral home, his son, his fortune, his reputation, his peace of mind, and his health—to gain it.

This, then, is the stuff of Ford's plot, and he makes great use of what Henry James called "the irresistible determinant and the incalculable advantage of [the novelist's] interest in the story *as such* . . . the prime and precious thing." James went on to say that "what makes for it, with whatever headlong energy, may be said to pale before the energy with which it simply makes for itself." The story growing out of Ford's friendship with Arthur Marwood and his own experience produced its own energy and motion, and out of that was also generated the larger action of the novels.

The enveloping action of *Parade's End* deals with a crumbling world which in its death throes produces a modern society run by the bureaucrats who stayed home while the backbone of English manhood was broken by four years of trench warfare. It is a world run by aggressive women like Sylvia Tietjens and Lady Macmaster and effeminate men like Perowne, Sylvia's bumbling lover; Brownlie, the duplicitous young banker who dishonors Tietjens' checks; Levin, the uxorious officer on Campion's staff; Ruggles, Mark Tietjens' meddling roommate; Sir John Robertson, the antiques dealer whose prices depend upon innuendo and rumor; and so on. The veterans of the war, as Pound wrote, had "walked eye-deep in hell / believing old men's lies, then unbelieving / came home, home to a lie, / home to many deceits, / home to old lies and new infamy; / usury age-old and age-thick / and liars in public places." And many of those who did not come home were "of the best" who gave up life "for an old bitch gone in the teeth, / For a botched civilization."

The botched civilization is the world that "preyed most on the mind of the majority of soldiers in the field." As Ford himself knew, "wounds, rain, fear, and other horrors are terrible but relatively simple matters." What the fighting man found almost impossible to bear was the news of an unfaithful wife, the dun from an unscrupulous merchant, the insane requirements of civilian and military bureaucracy, the disquieting unease of hearing nothing from home. Such an imbroglio is conveyed particularly well in Book II of *A Man Could Stand Up* when Tietjens' battalion commander goes to pieces — not under the strain of four years duty in the lines or the threat of an impending offensive or the fear that he has terminal cancer or the weight of his alcoholism — but because of the absurdity of an official inquiry into the battalion's accounts for August, 1914. Tietjens takes his place, but shortly thereafter he is relieved of his command by his godfather, Lord General Campion, because his uniform is soiled and because Campion believes the rumors about his godson. It makes no difference that the battalion has just come under an artillery barrage and that Tietjens has nearly been killed while rescuing some of his men, and here one feels most keenly the fearful pathos of Greene's superb insight about the trilogy: "The private life cannot be escaped and death does not come when it is most required."

The Tietjens trilogy ends, appropriately, in Christopher's empty London flat. He and Valentine are beginning life anew after the impromptu celebration is over — and so are their maimed friends who have survived the war. In the meantime Sylvia Tietjens and Lady Macmaster continue to run amuck.

One sees in the opening and closing books of *A Man Could Stand Up* that historical event and common life have merged — that Ford has dramatized and explored the coincidence of personal destinies within what George Lukács calls "the determining context of a historical crisis." Ford has accomplished this considerable feat without writing a fiction which follows the usual pattern of the historical novel: indeed the only historical event in *Parade's End* is Armistice Day. Furthermore, no historical figure appears on center stage or in the wings. The novels therefore gain in unity and singleness of effect, and little or nothing is lost. The historical context is firm from beginning to end, even without the introduction of historical figures and incidents; and Ford avoids the problems inherent in introducing an actual person — the British commander-in-chief Douglas Haig, for example — or in developing a particular military campaign or domestic crisis.

One part of Ford's strategy was to deal with the impact that events made rather than the events themselves. Another complimentary aspect of his approach ensued from his shrewd judgment that nine-tenths of war was agonizing over what had been and waiting nervously for what might be. He knew that combat played a relatively insignificant role in a war of attrition — and that there is no place for the hero in modern warfare. Much of this comes through clearly in a conversation he had with Wyndham Lewis, when Lewis was worrying about the soft civilian jobs held by members of the Bloomsbury group. Ford said, "When this War's over, nobody is going to worry, six months afterwards, what you did or didn't do in the course of it. . . . Within a year disbanded 'heroes' will be selling matches in the gutter. No one likes the ex-soldier—if you've lost a leg, more fool you."

Parade's End dramatizes the impact of a historical crisis upon individuals—concretely realized persons who are representative of every level of English society; and the inner life which the author thereby reveals is always consonant with and reflective of the outer world. As Ford delicately probes the minds and psyches of his characters he illumines the history of their times. We get neither history with a subplot—fiction overwhelmed by recalcitrant fact or abstract speculation—nor do we get romantic chronicle—history popularized into the literature of escape. *Parade's End* is a work of fiction in which Ford seized upon the possibilities inherent in two great forms and modified them both for his own purposes. But more than this is involved.

The shape which emerges is peculiarly Ford's own: the architectonics derive from his conviction that a novel should consist of "one embroilment, one set of embarrassments, one psychological progression" which provides its motive force and unity. That embroilment belongs especially to Christopher Tietjens, it goes without saying; yet it is also a matter of World War I, the collision of conflicting forces at home and abroad. The social and psychological forces chiefly interest Ford—not the logical and historical: he was far more concerned with how it felt to be living at this particular time and with what individual and collective life involved than he was about why certain events occurred. He knew also that it was impossible to present a complete picture of English life from 1908 to 1918: therefore he shows us the various spheres of action at random but representative moments: country estate and town house, smoking car and cramped cottage, elegant watering place and shabby hotel, open field and enclosed trench, rear lines and battleground.

As Ford said of himself, he was a master of the "time switch." The shifts back and forth in chronology were Ford's answer to what James called the eternal time-question which "always insists on the effect of the great lapse and passage, of the 'dark backward and abysm.' " The time shift is of crucial importance to *Parade's End*, where time is almost invariably presented in the present tense: this gives the action its immediacy and lifelike quality.

The disjunction of normal chronology and the restricted post of observation are of course cardinal aspects of the impressionistic novel in which objective scenes are counterpointed against the subjective workings of the mind. The *progression d'effet*—the steady turning of the main engine—provides the pressure which controls the action, pushing it forward and gradually intensifying it.

These dimensions of fiction as Conrad and Ford practiced the craft remind us that Ford was by no means writing a hybrid form which one can properly call a historical novel of manners. "Fiction is history," Conrad said, "human history, or it is nothing. But it is also more than that; it stands on firmer ground, being based on the reality of forms and the observation of social phenomena." We should remember at the same time that *Parade's End* is not a series of war novels, even though they embody characteristic themes of the First World War novel: the virtual disappearance of the hero, the longing for a simpler pastoral world, and the alienation of the soldier from his countrymen.

The comprehensiveness and diversity of *Parade's End* are but one measure with its greatness. Another way of gauging its power is to compare it with contemporary and similar novels such as *The Forsyte Saga*, *A Farewell to Arms*, and *Three Soldiers* or to subsequent novels such as Evelyn Waugh's *Sword of Honour* and Richard Hughes's *The Fox in the Attic*. None of these fictions have the scope, density, and credibility of the Tietjens trilogy.

This, of course, is a partial reading of a great (but by no means flawless) work of fiction. Ford's achievement in *Parade's End* cannot be completely charted, and it is not quite enough to show how he remade certain artistic conventions, radically modifying them as his purposes demanded, and at once remaining faithful to the irresistible determinant of circumstance. Precisely here lies the limitation of criticism — or one kind of criticism — the naming and defining of modes. (Hence I want to examine the trilogy from another perspective.) I suspect that the innermost secret of these novels will remain immured in what Allen Tate has called the masonic tradition of the craft of fiction — the efforts of Wayne Booth and others nothwithstanding. What we know is that the novel from Flaubert, Turgenev, and James to Conrad and Ford depends upon the scenic art, the dramatizations of the intersections of social life and individual conscience. What we do not know as exactly as we would like is the mysterious chemistry of a great scene like the lavish, hilarious, and pathetic meal at Breakfast Duchemin's estate. Even so it is perfectly clear that on this occasion — and I speak particularly of *Some Do Not* — Ford Madox Ford was as fortunate and sure in his art as he deserved to be at many other points in his career but wasn't.

As I have insisted, it is not enough to measure the technical accomplishment of *Parade's End*, considerable and even occasionally breathtaking though it may be. The author's achievement in this sense is of course only a function of the whole, a means of enabling his larger vision to operate to best advantage. In the Tietjens trilogy Ford did not let technique overwhelm action, a fatal weakness. Technique alone is never enough to produce a great work of art, and that is what Ford meant in saying that impressionism exists only to "attain the sort of odd vibration that scenes in real life really have." As Conrad pointed out, "Technical perfection, unless there is some real glow to illumine and warm it from within, must necessarily be cold." Technique, then, should be limited to the executive means by which the author brings his fable to life, or as R. P. Blackmur remarked, "its final purpose [is] to bring into being—to bring into performance, for the writer and for the reader—an instance of the feeling of what life is about . . . the tensions, the stresses, the deep relations and the terrible disrelations that inhabit them as they are made to come together in a particular struggle between manners and behavior, between the ideal insight and the actual momentum in which the form of life is found."

The ideal insight in *The Good Soldier* and in the Tietjens trilogy, as well as in many characteristic fictions of Ford's older contemporaries James and Conrad, revolves around the difference in private and public behavior; and what is especially impressive about the Tietjens trilogy is that Ford deals at once with both inner and outer reality, with the conflict between social man and his dark self on the one hand and man and society on the other. We are here faced with politics in the broadest and most profound sense, what Trilling has called "a quick responsiveness to the details of the outer world, an explicit awareness of history, of the grosser movements of society and civilization."

Revolution is not a theme of *Parade's End*, but the society which Ford pictures after August, 1914, is obviously closer to anarchy than at any time since Napoleon. To confirm this point and show its impact on Ford, one need only consider the difference between the action of *The Good Soldier* and *Some Do Not*. Political considerations accordingly play a greater role in the Tietjens novels than might otherwise be supposed, for Edwardian England and British imperialism are now in obvious decline. We are not concerned here with an alien ideology in conflict with an ordered society (as in *The Secret Agent*, a novel which Ford suggested to Conrad) but with the end of one way of life—feudalism at home and abroad—and the beginning of the modern world. "The telling thing," Robie Macauley has said, "was not that the world had changed physically to any great extent, but that the lines of communication had broken down. There was no longer a recognized continuity between past and present or present and future." The experience of disruption is the fulcrum upon which the action of *Parade's End* turns. Ford instinctively understood with James that "experience . . . is our apprehension and our measure of what happens to us as social creatures . . . The picture of the exposed and entangled state is what is required."

The crucial action of these fictions is manifested in the way that human beings are pushed by society and the way that they in turn try to enforce their will upon others or resist such pressure. This is the recurrent and inescapable pattern the experience takes. Thus in the largest sense politics spring from the relation of character and society: this is at the heart of Ford's geometry of relations, and it is even more central to James.

The modern novelist's problem is to maintain the continuity between the individual and his world, while simultaneously delineating the character's inner life. The individual is of his world, yet apart from it, straining to be himself but affected continuously by others. The pattern of one life therefore reflects the wider pattern of civilization: the life of the individual is measured against the life of society; character is measured against society in a moral sense. The degree of variance between the individual and the collective experience—between man alone and society as a whole—ultimately involves whether the shape of the action will eventuate in reconciliation or renunciation, in triumph or defeat, in comedy or tragedy. For the reader character and society must complement and reinforce one another, must add up to what James called the authenticity of concrete existence, as that life has been shaped by art and refined by value. When the elements react properly, one gets a novel like *Some Do Not*; when the solution does not yield such a precipitate, a fiction such as *Under Western Eyes* ensues.

In that novel the action is "exclusively concerned with ideas," as Conrad admitted. It lacks a significant public dimension, as Walter Sullivan has shown, and it therefore degenerates into random individual behavior which is too strongly affected by ideology. In contrast, a political novel like *The Princess Casamassima* presents a believable and richly detailed world, but the characters within that world do not move us to participation and belief in their lives. In *Parade's End* Ford simultaneously gives us both the world of public event and the world of private conflict; one complements and modifies the other: the larger action is instanced in individual behavior, and the characters act in terms of the moving world; they are part of a civilization, not simply a local society, for various levels of life cross and merge, touch and move away.

In *Parade's End* the connection between society and the individual is provided by the family, especially in the House of Tietjens but also in the domestic arrangements of the Wannops, Satterthwaites, Macmasters, and Fittleworths. The breakdown of society is mirrored in the breakdown of the family, instanced not only in Christopher's life but also in the lives of his friends and enemies. It is important that there are many widows and bachelors, that divorce is commonplace, that most marriages are childless, that marriage in general is a social convenience and nothing more. Domestic politics affect public considerations: the best example of this occurs when Edith Ethel Macmaster encourages her husband to fake statistics for the English government in order to undercut the French position in the war. He does and the trick earns him a knighthood. There are many other instances, and in them we see the emergence of a new ruling class which is motivated far more by personal considerations than by an impersonal standard of obligation.

Christopher Tietjens finally prevails, but he does so through withdrawal from the society which he should serve and administer: the last

Tory retreats into the timeless green world of England. Thus *The Last Post* presents a pastoral coda where "the land was pleasant and green and comely. It would breed true."

In *Parade's End* the author has dramatized a way of life as it turned rotten: he has struck its chronicle in the twilight of its going. In *The Princess Casamassima*, James's English political novel of the public world, and in *The Golden Bowl*, his international novel of the private life (or domestic politics), the author foretells what will occur in the Tietjens story; the same is true of *The Secret Agent* as a prophecy. In each instance the author pushes us to the frontiers of tragedy and beyond, and this is particularly true of Ford's "tetralogy" as the redemptive movement of the sequel carries us beyond the historical crisis to a transitional period which suggests that England will lose its empire and be overshadowed by the United States: the portent of *The Golden Bowl* and *The Good Soldier*.

Parade's End leaves the reader with the moving image of a society in transformation, suffering the concomitant strain to the body politic which is nothing less than civilization itself. The subject is not new: its newness involves only the form it will take, the configuration the particular artist would choose in order to enclose and reveal this pattern of experience. What is of greater importance is the comprehensiveness of the fable — perhaps the most exacting and ambitious that a writer can choose. It is an action which can only be controlled by an immensely powerful engine, and for the last century that engine has been the novel.

Fifty years ago Ford Madox Ford wrote that "modern life is so extraordinary, so tenuous, with still such definite and concrete spots in it, that I am forever on the look-out for some poet who shall render it with all its values." *Parade's End* is an instance in which this man of letters met his own high standards. In this fiction he was able to look directly into the heart of the matter — what he himself said was "the world as it culminated in the war" — and get it down for good.

Images of Collapse and Reconstruction: Ford's Vision of Society in *Parade's End*

Richard A. Cassell*

Vision is the right word. Images of experience are transformed into shapely illusions of reality: the actual into the possible. That which is seen; an activity of the imagination; seen in a way beyond ordinary sight;

*A shortened, revised version of "Images of Collapse and Reconstruction: Ford's Vision of Society," *English Literature in Transition: 1880–1920* 19, no. 4 (1976):265–82. Permission granted by the journal.

dream; revelation to a prophet: an image without substance, an object of the mind alone: fictions. "The business of Impressionism," Ford wrote "is to produce an illusion of reality." On the one hand, "the Impressionist author is sedulous to avoid letting his personality appear in the course of his book. On the other hand, his whole book, his whole poem, is merely an expression of his personality."[1] This tension is evident in almost everything he wrote.

Ford was a visionary, an "halluciné," as Pound called him, who went outside his social milieu and class for his major protagonists and who made the places where he lived or dreamed of being into symbolic environments that expressed both the realities he had to face and understand and the ideals he sought to hold on to. Ford lived all his life within artistic-intellectual circles, and even when he periodically retreated from their centers in London, Paris or New York to the countrysides of Sussex or Provence or the American midwest, his women and his friends were artists and writers. He knew a few among the landed gentry, the politicians, the anarchists, the farmers, but he was not of them, as we say. Rather, at various times in both his life and fiction, they would serve as imaginative projections of himself, borrowed personas. He most admired artists and martyred saints and those, whoever they were, who served society with a comparable integrity, and who, whatever they gave up, never surrendered their integrity to the people or forces determined to destroy them.

The people and places Ford knew and the events they involved him in might well be called images of experience that Ford in his life and more successfully in his major novels integrated, along with imagined images, into fictions, into illusions of reality. I want to investigate the world he envisioned at the time he was writing his postwar fictional masterpiece *Parade's End*, 1924–28, and to consider less the people and events than the images of place the tetralogy projects and only as far as they illumine Ford's vision of society. It is a vision that can be caught best, if it can be caught, by indirection and by approaching it warily, fragment by fragment.

In his pre-war masterwork *The Good Soldier*, Ford's lens is microscopic. Contemporary political or historical references are completely lacking, except for the coincidental dating of key events that keep happening over a period of years on August 4th, which foreshadows that August 4th of 1914 when the Germans entered Belgium near Gemminich. Brought into focus is a representative couple of the landed gentry as they move leisurely between watering place and country estate; they avoid London and Paris as much as they avoid concern with current political affairs. Other classes are peripheral: Edward Ashburnham's tenant farmers he helps, and those women from the lesser ranks he chooses for attention. Since Ashburnham is revealed as a representative, not of the current crop, but of the last vestige of the once great feudal landlord and gentleman, the novel is less an "unbiased picture of the world we live in" than it is a lament. Nevertheless, the events preceding the Great War, if not mentioned, are there by implication: because Ashburnham is lost, so is the best of England, and the way is open for the betrayals by the newly entrenched bureaucracy which precipitates and somehow wins the war and then ruins the peace which follows. As far as he is an historian of his own time, Ford in *The Good Soldier* leaves a provocative chronicle prophetic of our century's literature of exhaustion.

If *The Good Soldier*, confined as it is to a small circle, defines a private yet representative destruction of the old order, *Parade's End* describes its public collapse and further asks how to comprehend and face it. Novelist, not really historian, Ford judiciously avoids reference to most of the political and military events one could check in a history book; and all those that are referred to are filtered through the consciousness then opened to us. The impression of an event is always more real to Ford than the facts surrounding it, but because he tells this story in the hopes it will move society to give up wars, a corrective intention his previously stated artistic principles deny, he had to, as Samuel Hynes phrases it, "create in *Parade's End* a novel in which impressions and facts were the same," and in which "there was no disparity between imagination and history."[2] Ford succeeds because he makes the time scheme clear enough so that dates of scenes can be determined at least as to year, or season, if not always, as in the case of Armistice Day, to month and day. His success is also indebted to his handling of place, of where his characters are in relation to the public and private whirl of events. The techniques of recreating setting used in earlier novels are here, but more complexly and with others added, commensurate with Ford's epic intentions. Several fine critics have already guided us through the outer and inner rooms and corridors and countrysides of Ford's world in *Parade's End*, and what follows is indebted to them.[3] In my own selective tour I will fuse their insights into a kind of summary Baedeker.

The novel was inspired by neither a place nor an event, though Ford once said the idea came to him, in September, 1916, at a battlefield "in a region called the Salient."[4] Remembering his old friend Arthur Marwood, he wondered how the war would have looked to him, a Tory of the old stamp, "a man of infinite benevolence, comprehensions and knowledges." By a curious yet characteristic alchemy, Ford, as we know, idealized himself through Marwood into the creation of Christopher Tietjens to whom he gave Ford's own "lasting tribulation . . . of a moral order and something inscrutable": a bitch, attached like "a permanent shackle and ball on his leg." Ford couldn't dramatize his affair with Violet Hunt, of course. But once he heard, or imagined, the story of a poor devil named Waring pressured into a marriage with a woman picked up on a train, and never certain that her son was his, he discovered the "tribulations for my central character." He was to be a man who "was to go through the public affairs of distracted Europe with that private cannonball all the time dragging at his ankle!"[5]

Christopher Tietjens, observer and participant, endowed with both insight and the capacity for suffering, serves as the gauge by which Ford measures and finally comes to terms with the losses entailed in the slow transfer of power and influence from the landed gentry to the commercial middle-class completed during the Great War. Every lens focuses on the eighteenth-century Tory protagonist being forced into the cold wastes of the twentieth century, where he has to find new shelter. Ford's scope is panoramic, the method dramatic. Even as he slips into relative obscurity and anonymity, Tietjens is in the center. With all that he has given up, he never surrenders. Although emotionally and intellectually exhausted, he can realign his sights and discover modest shorings against the general ruins. From patrician to journeyman; from Groby to cottage by way of command and barrack huts and trenches and hills of mud. The mythic journey, if you please, but—in the way of an impressionist—real and immediate enough to Tietjens and to the reader.

Ezra Pound once complained that since the impressionist is bound to the visual, "the logical end of impressionist art is the cinematograph. The state of mind of the impressionist tends to become cinematographical. Or, to put it another way, the cinematograph does away with the need of a lot of impressionist art."[6] But Ford's impressionism as one experiences it in his best work is no longer merely visual or "a surface art." It is emotionally substantive; the private view can be transformed into symbolic vision. Of course, the world is diminished to the self. The limited consciousness is explored and exploited as larger assurances dissolve. That is the track of Ford's story in *Parade's End*. From the body politic to private survival: Tietjens is suspended in a succession of numbing events which assault his ideals, challenge, deny his view of things, and pare him down to essentials and simplicities. *Parade's End*, as well as *The Good Soldier*, follows that inclination of fiction since early James "to transform the art of narrative into an act of cognitive discovery, which sets modern fiction apart from a large number of eighteenth century and even nineteenth century novels."[7]

The early chapters of *Some Do Not . . .* with skillful economy introduce us to the complex inner and outer trials of Christopher Tietjens of Groby. Only twenty-six but third in command in the Imperial Bureau of Statistics, he is caught between a present he cannot face emotionally, trained as he is to suppress emotions, and a past he will not out of principle relinquish. An anachronism, he doggedly maintains his eighteenth-century ethical and political idealism even as he is forced to come to terms with both the morally slackened twentieth century and his long submerged passions. The varied settings of the early chapters reflect and enforce these tensions. One instructive scene occurs between Tietjens and

Valentine as they take their prophetic and symbolic walk from Duchemin's estate to her cottage, where she lives with her mother.[8]

Already Tietjens has been seen in some of the conventional haunts of the ruling class: a perfectly appointed railway carriage, a golf course, an expensive inn made over from old cottages, the elegant home of a wealthy country cleric. All of the splendid exteriors disguise signs of decadence inside, from the luxuriant scarlet and yellow upholstery with a minute dragon pattern in the railway car to the eighteenth-century rooms of Duchemin's home, bedecked with Chippendale pieces and numerous silver urns and candelabra, invaded by paintings of Turner and Simeon Solomon, and pervaded by the spirit of Ruskin. For Tietjens the Pre-Raphaelites signify a moral weakening through an emotional overindulgence that threatens the rational moral order of society. Their sloppy show of love emotions and their heavenly sanction of illicit sexual unions assault Tietjens' code of "monogamy and chastity. And for no talking about it" (p. 18). A similar vulgarity has invaded the once protected walls of the golf course clubhouse, and Duchemin himself proves to be a sexual psychopath who shouts vulgarities in Latin as the ambitious Macmaster and Mrs. Duchemin launch their Rossetti-inspired adultery.

Even before the country walk, we have seen analagous assaults upon Tietjens' assurance that he was entitled to "the best that first-class public offices and first-class people could afford" (p. 5). Earlier in a hotel room, furnished with "disinterred and waxed relics of the past," as he rationally tries to plan the conditions of Sylvia's announced return to their marriage after a four month adulterous escapade, his emotions explode into panic as he tries to calm himself by liquor, solitaire, and statistical calculations. He is paying the price for allowing himself in a rare moment of passion to have been seduced by Sylvia in a first-class railway carriage and then drummed into a loveless and sexless marriage because of her claim the child she carried was his. He will never divorce her, because his code of honor will not allow him to: do what you want (or have to) and take what you get for it. The inference is clear that with all that he will get he will not forever be able to take.

As Tietjens and Valentine walk together, his mind shifts between the promise of pastoral peace with an attractive young girl in the Rye Countryside and the surfacing of erotic emotions suppressed by his marital commitment to Sylvia. The irresolvable tension threatens his sanity and principled reserve. "This, Tietjens thought, is England! A man and a maid walk through Kentish grass fields. . . . The man honorable, clean, upright; the maid virtuous, clean, vigorous; he of good birth; she of birth quite as good. . . ." He muses in pastoral cadences ("Each knew the names of birds that piped and grasses that bowed") and in fond exclamations ("Attractive young woman's back. English midday summer. Best climate in the world!"). Suddenly he pauses to strike down some weeds with his hazel stick; it is a sexual strike, surfacing from the unconscious. " 'Now I'm a bloody murderer,' Tietjens said. 'Not gory! Green stained with vital fluid of innocent plant . . . And by God! Not a woman in the country who won't let you rape her after an hour's acquaintance!' He slew two more mulleins and a sow-thistle! A shadow, but not from the sun, a gloom, lay across the sixty acres of purple grass bloom and marguerites, white: like petticoats of lace over the grass!" and then suddenly: "All the governing class! All rotten! . . . Then thank God for the upright young man and the virtuous maiden in the summer fields. . . ." The shadow is Sylvia. He realizes he is being as hysterical as "that large-eyed whore" Mrs. Duchemin and that "Sylvia's as bad as Duchemin!" He knows Valentine will become a screen for Sylvia; no wonder he later says aloud: "I hate roads when there are fieldpaths." This part of the scene ends absurdly when Valentine, thinking an approaching dogcart carries police, runs across a field to a kissing gate; Tietjens runs after her; they end by being "jammed in together: face to face, panting! An occasion on which sweethearts kiss in Kent. . . ." Not Tietjens: his imagination can create a pastoral romance out of scenery, fair maid and all, but his emotions are still too imprisoned for human romance.

In the cart, Mrs. Wannop is in danger from her rearing horse, maddened by a tight harness and a choking bit. Tietjens skillfully calms the horse and repairs the harness. "I suppose you think that a mighty fine performance," Valentine says after her mother rides off. "Setting poor weak women in their places. Soothing the horse like a man with a charm. I suppose you soothe women like that too. I pity your wife. . . . The English country male! And making a devoted vassal at sight of the handyman. The feudal system all complete. . . ." She hits the mark well and goes on in her clear friendly way to complain of his maddening reserve and, less kindly, of his heartless replies to a show of emotion in others. She comes too near the matter of Sylvia's denunciations.

Sylvia herself keeps invading Tietjens' consciousness, battering the visions of peace and affection he had found in the countryside and finds at the Wannop's cottage: "He liked this house; he liked this atmosphere; he liked the frugality, the choice of furniture, the way the light fell from window to window; the weariness after hard work; the affection of mother and daughter; the affection, indeed, that they both had for himself, and he was determined, if he could help it, not to damage the reputation of the daughter of the house." Yet, paradoxically, he "cared more for his wife's reputation than for any other factor in a complicated world." Sensing his dilemma, Mrs. Wannop confesses she has lived "in a bath of scandal" all her life, and then leans over his high-backed chair and strokes the hair of his right temple: " 'My dear boy,' she said. 'Life's a bitter thing. I'm an old novelist and know it. There you are working yourself to death to save the nation with a wilderness of cats and monkeys howling and squalling your personal reputation away. . . . My dear boy; it doesn't really matter. You'll live it down. The only thing that matters is to do good work . . . Or perhaps you won't; that's for God in his mercy to settle. But it won't matter; believe me, as thy day so shall thy strength be.' " Tietjens weeps, starved for tenderness: "at bottom his was a perfectly direct, simple and sentimental soul." He already senses beneath Valentine's somewhat athletic brusqueness the same solace this saintly surrogate mother offers. But a startling Fordian juxtaposition assures him he will go through hell first. Valentine brings him the telephone message of Sylvia's cable from Lobscheid: ten words, beginning with "Righto." "A cavernous eternity of weary hopelessness" opens up before him. "Perhaps God then, after all, visits thus heavily sexual offences." Panic also grips him in the image of his and Sylvia's breakfast room, "the *decor* of the room seeming to burn into his mind": a collection of mechanical appliances, hothouse flowers, the Sotheby guaranteed prints on the wall ("pinkish women in sham Gains-borough hats"), Sylvia's mother rattling the *Times*, Sylvia herself pacing up and down, exclaiming: " 'I'm bored! Bored!': Sometimes even breaking the breakfast-plates," forever talking. And then Sylvia in the railway carriage the night of their passion: "An extravagantly beautiful girl! Where was the physical attraction of her gone to now?" As a gentleman he won't admit she had seduced him but doubts her child is his. He fears he has had a stroke. He struggles to get back to Mrs. Wannop's talk. He has a vision: "he felt a sudden strong pleasure: sunlight on pyramidal red roof in the distance: themselves descending in a long diagonal, a green hill. God, yes, he wanted open air." The way seems to be set for *The Last Post*; at least the image is planted. Mrs. Wannop takes him under her protection and assures him that she will back, if not approve of, whatever Valentine does against the cats and monkeys, even her living with a married man or having illegitimate children. That said, she returns to work on her novel, and the scene ends.

Although a scene is better read than summarized, the one surveyed here suggests the ways Ford makes of a scene a microscopic image of his whole imagined world and of the course of his protagonist through it. Settings, both the immediate and the remembered, are fuses for associational bonfires that will slowly burn away everything not essential for Tietjens' survival. As the novel progresses, the reader's position in relation to him changes: more and more Ford relinquishes narrative omniscience to enter directly the private consciousness,[9] primarily that of Tietjens during the war and of his brother Mark afterwards. Tietjens is the only one of the main characters in the camps and trenches; Sylvia, near his camp in Rouen for a while, believes that warriors are nothing but schoolboys at play. Robert Liddell describes the method exactly in his chapter on backgrounds in fiction: he calls it kaleidoscopic, the stream of consciousness, where the character lives concurrently in several worlds, both physical and of the mind. Tietjens, at one point, calls his vision stereoscopic, though that may be closer to what Liddell calls "the second background," "the countries of the mind" where characters' "hearts are present in memory, fear, hope or desire . . . ," by which he means fantasy, but that is Tietjens' mental mode, too.[10]

The painful contraries that beset Tietjens, intense enough before the war, become almost catastrophic during it. Everything expands: the burnt-in mental image of the breakfast room will blow up into the grotesque sights of soldiers killed and maimed; gossip will billow into conspiracies and betrayals, not only by Sylvia, their chief messenger, but also by the War Office and all of society. In short, everything that Tietjen perceives, suffers, represents in the early scenes of the novel enlarges into a composite image of the entire holocaust; indeed, at times it seems as though the whole war is being fought against Tietjens alone. It is truer to say it is being fought within him. He is finally to make a separate peace, on his own terms, drawing upon the restorative images of Valentine and rural fields and cottages, which slowly take precedence, and which he builds into a dream before he finds its realities.

Because Tietjens descends from the social heights, unlike conventional protagonists who struggle toward them, he has to relinquish or have taken away what he can neither accept nor be allowed. He has to be measured not by his relation to an essentially natural and right society where wrongs can be corrected but by his stand against a corrupt society that threatens his survival, a society characterized by its "divorce of principle from life" among those who govern, and by a docile resignation among the governed.[11] Tietjens can survive because in Ford's view some integration is still possible; there is "in the world a place to return" (*England*, p. 341). The world and self are not both lost, though in *The Good Soldier* he had suggested they were. In *Parade's End* Tietjens abdicates the social for the private consciousness and responsibility. Since we see Tietjens' fortunate fall mostly through the kaleidoscopic and stereoscopic lenses of his mind, it is through him we discover the novel's vision of society, a vision, as we might expect, hazy in its boundaries and demarcations.

Tietjens has his reputation snatched from him, but mostly he relinquishes what he could have kept with some stain upon his honor. Early in the war he resigns from the Imperial Department because he will not fake statistics that will falsely compromise the French. During his first rest leave, he resigns from his club, when a banker enemy of his refuses to honor a small overdraft of his. Later he renounces the Groby money, and in effect Groby, since he will neither divorce Sylvia nor commit adultery with Valentine. Long into the war, and after all the assaults upon him, he remains a Tietjens of Groby: "no man could give him anything, no man could take anything from him" (p. 556). He finds he is still "the sort of man who automatically lent money": in this case to his alcoholic C.O., dying of cancer: "After all, it didn't matter what kind of a man this was, it was a question of what sort of man Tietjens was becoming" (p. 615).

That is the crux: still of Groby but changing through suffering. Although the horrors of war are burnt into his consciousness, "home-worries" plague him most. "You were there, but great shafts of thought from the outside, distant and unattainable world infinitely for the greater part occupied your mind."[12] Tietjens' worries center on Sylvia and the War Office: unpredictable and irrational instruments of mental pain which frustrate and betray the established order of both public and private affairs. From the Boodlers in Whitehall, countermanded orders again countermanded; from Sylvia a love-hate desperately trying to break through his impenetrable stolidity and bring him to her bed.

Everything conspires to drive Tietjens underground and to join hands with the Other Ranks. As his trials expand, place contracts; more and more he suffers the psychological pressures of confined space. After his return to duty, Tietjens moves between two huts, emblematic, on a diminished but more clearly etched scale, of the old division within him between the public and the private man. In the command hut he takes satisfaction in doing the prolonged and complex work of arranging the drafts and doing it better than anyone else. There he learns that, like himself, the Other Ranks suffer most from home-worries, primarily sexual. Theirs he can manage when called upon and gain their respect. In this way he becomes one of them. His own worries he cannot manage so well. These he carries to "the Rembrandt-beshadowed hut" where he sleeps, his furniture a canvas cot, a canvas table and his flea-bag: stripped, caught up in the nightmare contest between Sylvia and Valentine, past and present converging into a nebulous future, trying to think matters through, coming to see that Sylvia had really thrown him into Valentine's arms. After O-Nine Morgan, to whom he had refused home leave in order to save his life, dies in his own blood in the orderly room; and after Sylvia appears, wreaking havoc in that other confined enclosure in which Tietjens finds himself, the hotel room in Rouen, any order left collapses into chaos, with only fitful dreams of Valentine to sustain him.

He is soon borne underground, literally and figuratively. His progress is a metaphor of his mental tribulations, his journey through hell. Sent to the front lines, second in command, confined now to dugouts, a "reeling cellar," the trenches, and the mud he fears most, and with nightmares of underground picks at work and a voice saying, *Bringt dem Hauptmann eine Kerze*," he approaches madness and is much in need of light. Amid the deafening orchestra of the bombs he hears one dawn a bugler playing an air by Purcell to Herrick's words, and thinks of Bemerton and George Herbert: the seventeenth century, "the only satisfactory age in England!" Now "what chance had quiet fields, Anglican sainthood, accuracy of thought. . . . Still, the land remains. . . ." (p. 566). He envisions standing up on a hill near Bemerton, "a lean contemplative parson, looking at the land sloping down to Salisbury spire" (p. 567). Unlike Ashburnham and Dowell, he is to relinquish the dream: he comes to Mrs. Wannop's realization that reputation does not matter, and he will live in adultery with Valentine near "a downland road, with some old thorn-trees" in Kent and hold out the dream to their children.

But he has to come to another equally important realization. When he is caught near an exploding German shell, the concussion elevates and then buries him in the mud and slime he loathes. To the plea of Aranjuez, the young soldier near him, "save me Captain!" he answers, "I've got to save myself first" (p. 637). Saving others—the Suffragettes, Mrs. Wannop, Macmaster, MacKechnie, and many more, even Sylvia—had always seemed with Tietjens to be more an official than a personal act, reflecting one of *les droites des Seigneurs* he cherished. Now he must be pulled out of the mud and needs help to pull Aranjuez out. When Tietjens carries the still dazed youth over his shoulder like a rolled blanket, the boy is hit by a sniper's bullet and loses an eye: Tietjens' responsibility. He is no longer in assured command; he realizes that when responsibility involves the lives of others, it is ambiguous at best, at its worst more than he can emotionally bear. He is found vulnerable and rendered cautious.

Not only renunciations will save him. He must also find his way in a world that has shoved him aside. Society and mankind being what it is, he himself must will the conditions under which he can live. Mark once figures that Christopher "wanted to be out of the world. . . . He wanted to be out of a disgustingly inefficient and venial world, just as he, Mark, also wanted to be out of a world that he found almost more fusionless and dishonest than Christopher found it" (p. 740). But Mark is wrong; it is he, more truly than his brother, who is the last Tory and who wills himself out. Christopher will remain, like the land. From the very first, in the railway carriage with Macmaster, he has realized that the lower classes (by which he usually means the middle) would rule the land and win the war, a perfectly natural process, he adds. He is willing to help a green-grocer's son like Macmaster to rise to the ranks of the ruling class and to live in elegant apartments managing literary teas, and can accept as natural the deceits, the devious maneuvers by which he arrives there, but Tietjens himself will not touch pitch. He expects the boodling that will crazily countermand orders and the moral grubbiness that will make the game more important than the player. The Tietjens kind of Tory had always after all aloofly tolerated the materialists, those masters of the expedient who serve and save only themselves; but when the returning Tommies are cheated out of their jobs and their girls by the civilians, and when the British fail to pursue the Germans to Berlin; when, one might say, St. George corners the dragon and then frees it; when boodling becomes betrayal, the Tietjenses of Groby must retreat either to death or go underground.

During Christopher's early appraisal of Valentine at the Duchemin breakfast, the narrator tells us that "Tietjens held very strongly the theory that what finally separated the classes was that the upper could lift its feet from the ground whilst common people couldn't" (p. 87). He is to discover that they can: O'Nine Morgan, Sgt. Cowley, Gunning, and all the other heirs of Meary Walker, the Fordian prototype of the peasant cottager. Hard-working, wise, "broadminded, temperate, benevolent, cheerful and cynical, she could confront every hap and mishap of life, whether her own, her neighbour's, or the state's, with a proper fortitude or a sane sympathy." In danger of becoming extinct, in the face of "the Anglo-Saxon-Teutonic-industrial-commercialism that is Modernity," Meary's kind persists and will "keep all on gooing" (*England*, pp. 184–93). When Valentine, at the end, muses that "they had to keep all on going" (p. 822), the connection is clear; they have simplified their lives and their loyalties and have discovered the spirit of Meary Walker within them, "the bedrock," "the raw material," "the mud from which our finer clays are baked." It is a spirit not yet lost, and for Ford who held a cyclical view of history, it might again prevail. The field laborer "is the stuff from which we have all developed, and to him, no doubt, we shall all return sooner or later" (*England*, pp. 219–20).

In such an imagined world, no legislation can be passed, no one can be put in jail for the ills of society under which Tietjens and the others suffer. Ford defines society less by its class structure than by its character, less by the masses than the individual. The vision is a moral, not a political or class-centered one. The ruling class may arise from the factories and shops rather than from the land, class structures may shift, political parties come and go, but as Tietjens once remarks, "the thing is to be able to stick to the integrity of your character, whatever earthquake sets the house tumbling over your head" (p. 454). Human nature being what it is, the house is always in danger. Even before Mrs. Wannop assures him that society is composed of cats and monkeys, Tietjens has arrived at the same metaphor as he ponders why it is that humanity "next to always agreeable in its units, was, as a mass, a phenomenon so hideous" (p. 79). The world is composed of a number of artists and saints, Ford was fond of saying, and the rest of mankind is the stuff to fill graveyards. Tietjens, no artist, but at the end something of a humbled saint, takes his stand among those who "keep all on going."

On Armistice Day, returning to his house in London, stripped of its furniture by Sylvia, now in her desperate, vulgar, pitiful last stand, Tietjens places his canvas cot, canvas table, and flea-bag in the empty drawing room, tries unsuccessfully to get a loan on the one cabinet Sylvia has left him, and returns to be with Valentine and a few maimed survivors from the other ranks he has befriended to celebrate the victory. Tietjens and Valentine dance over the debris of the past.

Later, living in their rural Sussex cottage with Mark Tietjens and his wife, Marie Leónie, they seem to have achieved "the hard, frugal life" of Christopher's long-standing dream. But they are slow in finding the peace he had expected, glimpsed long before at Mrs. Wannop's cottage and in his front-line visions of Bemerton. Life proves to be no pastoral romance; Tietjens, in Mark's words, is merely "an old-furniture dealer who made a stink in virtuous nostrils" (p. 732). Beneath their determination is a mild undercurrent of regret in the alternative they have chosen. He and Valentine "had surrendered Groby in order to live together and she had endured sprays of obloquy that seemed never to cease to splash over the garden hedges" (p. 818). One summer's afternoon, Sylvia, with her and Christopher's son, Michael Mark, and other ghosts of times past peer over the hedges to spy, carp, and gaze in wonder before retreating for good to leave Christopher and Valentine and the child she carries to make their own way.

Relinquishing Groby proves a less painful, less sentimental surrender for Tietjens than the cutting down, by Sylvia's order, of Groby Great Tree. The mansion which is scantily described and which the reader never gets to see, is strictly the object of the novel's "second background," and stands as a remote, almost inert symbol of the Protestant feudal ruling class, now turned over by lease to a brash American lady (of the kind who stalks destructively through the standing grass needed for fodder) and in time is to go to Michael Mark, a Catholic. But Groby Great Tree is the spirit, the soul of the mansion, associated with legend, superstition, magic ritual, and curses. Its cutting down is the final release for the Tietjens clan from all the ghosts and romance of the past, including the curse put upon the house when it was first turned over to Protestants in the time of old Dutch William. Since then the tree "never seemed to like anybody," Mark once muses, though Christopher, "a romantic ass" cherished it (pp. 733;760). It is the loss of the romance and some of the reality of the past that Christopher regrets so much. He brings back a souvenir of the tree to show Mark on his deathbed. But the reality of the present has taken over; wearily he has to go to recover some prints he had forgotten. "How are we going to feed and clothe a child if you do such things?" Valentine scolds him (p. 835).

Tietjens does not renounce his integrity. He holds on to values his faith assures him are some place beneath the collapse and lives in the hope that the regimen of personal honor will again be elevated to the consciousness and protection of society. He, along with Valentine and their child, will be keepers of the flame against those who would snuff it out, backing those, like T. S. Eliot, who refuse to surrender to the wasteland of this century. Thus we see Tietjens at the end, after his troubled symbolic descent, returned from his sentimental pilgrimage to Groby, the talisman in his hand (to hang on the wall or keep in a trunk of mementos?), seeking valuable and genuine artifacts of the past to be saved for the future. Our final image is of a man subdued and wordless, a survivor of the flood, stripped to essentials, forgetful yet knowledgeable of what counts, having discovered that love is possible and that he can carry on without swank.

Exhausted but not defeated, he rides off on his bicycle into new beginnings, as Ford liked to phrase it, beginnings promised and given before,
but which Ford would feel the generations after him have not found or
even expect to be there.

Notes

1. Ford Madox Ford, "On Impressionism," Poetry and Drama, I (June–Dec. 1914), 323.

2. Samuel Hynes, "Ford Madox Ford: 'Three Dedicatory Letters to Parade's End' With Commentary and Notes," *Modern Fiction Studies*, XVI (1970–71), 518.

3. I want particularly to acknowledge James M. Heldman, "The Last Victorian Novel: Technique and Theme in *Parade's End*," *Twentieth Century Literature*, XVIII (1972), 271–83; T. J. Henighan, "Tietjens Transformed: A Reading of *Parade's End*," *English Literature in Transition: 1880–1920* XV (1972), 144–57, and, most of all, Ambrose Gordon, Jr., *The Invisible Tent: The War Novels of Ford Madox Ford* (Austin: University of Texas Press, 1964).

4. Ford Madox Ford, "Dedication: To William Bird," *No More Parades* (New York: Grosset & Dunlap, 1925), p. vii.

5. Ford Madox Ford, *It Was the Nightingale* (New York: Lippincott, 1933), pp. 208–10.

6. Ezra Pound, *Gaudier-Brzeska* (New York: New Directions, 1960), p. 89.

7. Irving Howe, *A World More Attractive* (New York: Horizon, 1963), p. 80.

8. Ford Madox Ford, *Parade's End* (New York: Knopf, 1950), pp. 104–24. (All references are to this edition.)

9. Heldman, pp. 271–83.

10. Robert Liddell, *On the Novel* (Chicago: University of Chicago Press, 1969), pp. 113–15.

11. Ford Madox Ford, *England and the English* (New York: McClure, Phillips, 1907), p. 290. (Hereafter referred to as *England*.)

12. Ford Madox Ford, *Joseph Conrad: A Personal Remembrance* (London: Duckworth, 1924), p. 192.

[Christopher, Sylvia, and Valentine]

Sondra Stang*

Ford's impressionism, the literary theory comprising the whole set of
artistic assumptions that enabled him to write his novels, provided the
"rules" for working into coherence the raw material the world presents.

*From *Ford Madox Ford* (New York: Frederick Ungar, 1977). © 1977 by Frederick Ungar Publishing Co., Inc., pp. 103–04; 108–23. Reprinted by permission of the publishers.

But rather than deal with the raw facts themselves — that is, the phenomena of the external world — he tried to get at the very nature of experience, to study the impact of the external world upon human consciousness. In other words, he was interested not in "realism" but in psychological reality.

And in rendering the experience of each of his characters — Tietjens, Sylvia, their son Mark, Valentine, Christopher's brother Mark, Mark's wife, Marie Léonie — Ford was as much interested in the individual way each mind experienced as in what it experienced. The characteristic sound of its thoughts, the psychological rhythms of perception and speech, the special syntax of each separate consciousness — through these the reader can grasp each character's unique psychological experience as well as the facts to which he responds. The reader is forced to stand, with each of the characters, "at different angles"[1] to the perceived world and to experience twice every act of perception: once with the character, and once for himself, reassembling all that he has learned from the implications of the text. In getting the facts, the reader simultaneously experiences the whole range of the characters' responses to them.

Perhaps the greatest critical problem the book offers is the character of Sylvia Tietjens. How are we to understand her and her relationship to Christopher? What, by inference, are we to make of Christopher, who married her? She has often been taken to be the embodiment of evil, an allegorical figure, and one of the great *femmes fatales* in literature. How can we square such an image with Ford's novelistic method, which rests upon the idea that the sympathetic imagination can enlarge the reader's capacity for identification with other people and understanding of them?

Ford's idea of the art of the novel derived largely from Flaubert's principle "ne pas conclure." Ford would often quote that phrase, intended for the practicing novelist, and it meant do not sum up a character; do not draw the reader's conclusions for him; allow him to see and understand for himself. Like Flaubert, Ford seldom gives us a complete physical description of a character. Instead, the character — even the way he looks — emerges from different contexts, always freshly to be perceived, and never totally grasped. In this respect Ford's men and women are like human beings outside the novel, at every meeting needing to be reinterpreted and never finally to be wholly understood. More than any character in Ford's novels — that is to say, more than any of the hundreds of characters he created, Sylvia is the most problematic and difficult to understand.

She had first presented herself to Ford's imagination as a pagan goddess. As he tells us in *It Was the Nightingale*, he once saw a woman in the railway station at Amiens:

> She was in a golden sheath-gown and her golden hair was done in bandeaux, extraordinarily brilliant in the dimness. Like a goddess come in from the forest of Amiens!

I exclaimed:
"Sylvia!" So I didn't have to cast about for a name.

Sylvan, of the woods: the original shining figure became, before Ford was done with her, a character of tantalizing complexity. "Who is Silvia? What is she?" Shakespeare's song may have had as much to do with Ford's naming her as did the fresh and arrestingly pagan quality of the actual woman he once saw in Amiens.

Early in *Some Do Not . . .* , Sylvia is compared to the mythological Astarte, Phoenician goddess of love and fertility, and Lamia, in Greek stories the witch who sucked human blood. Though the mythic dimension is certainly implied, and at times implied very strongly, Sylvia *is* neither of these. What is significant is her many-facetedness, and it was present in Ford's original inspiration as a quality of light—coruscating, brilliant, flashing different images at different times, now a goddess, at other times a woman, never reducible to a single fixed aspect.

Virgin and courtesan, devil as well as "a picture of Our Lady by Fra Angelico," she is presented in paradoxes, with each quality calling up its opposite. Perverse, unpredictable, her character is "a matter of contrariety." "To be seductive and to be chaste" is the condition she aspires to. To do wickedness and not be wicked: it is a theological distinction she makes, and perhaps it is the ultimate paradox of her nature. Ford repeatedly uses the verb *coil* in connection with Sylvia to suggest a snake, yet the imagery of writhing is, as often as not, connected with her suffering. And she speaks of the "almost painful emotion of joyful hatred." "Coldly passionate," she goes to the front to torment and allure Christopher in the hope of a *rapprochement.* She loves him for his mind, she says, but she hates his ideas. "There was no end to the contradiction in men's characters"—or women's. That she loves him as she does is, of course, "the impossible complication." The character of Sylvia needs four books to unfold itself, and Ford is at great pains to present her point of view with scrupulous fairness.

The Tietjens books have been described by Graham Greene as "almost the only adult novels dealing with the sexual life that have been written in English." In the story of Sylvia and Tietjens, the relation between the sexes is seen as a condition of warfare. Christopher's problem *is* "the whole problem of the relation of the sexes." Sylvia's "sex viciousness," her "sex ferocity," her "sex cruelty" are plain. But that repeated note cannot obscure the fact that the struggle between them is neither simple nor one-sided and that they are two antagonists of considerable subtlety, whose antagonism is made all the more subtle by the similarities between them. Their story is a study in obstinacies—two strong wills engaged in a war. On the one side Sylvia acts out of a strongly instinctual nature; on the other side Christopher distrusts his instincts and acts from a set of principles which, as he comes to recognize, can no longer serve. In order to use them, he is forced to reexamine them.

Curiously, the novel insists on how similar Christopher and Sylvia are. They are both *hallucinés* (Pound's word for Ford), given to actual hallucination. They are both venerators of the ideal of chastity as a state of physical and moral purity. And their sensitivity to one another's psychological processes is expressed by Christopher's compulsion (his "obsession") to shield Sylvia against gossip and slander, and on her side, by her pity and revulsion at how far she has succeeded in destroying him. There are moments when they meet and fight with the "friendly weariness of old enemies." Even their child—the young Mark—speculates about the basis of their enmity.

> Questions of . . . sex-attraction, in spite of all the efforts of scientists, remained fairly mysterious. The best way to look at it . . . the safest way, was that sex attraction occurred as a rule between temperamental and physical opposites because Nature desired to correct extremes. No one in fact could be more different than his father and mother—the one [Sylvia] so graceful, athletic and . . . oh, charming. And the other [Christopher] so . . . oh, let us say perfectly honourable but lawless. Because, of course, you can break certain laws and remain the soul of honour.

It is Sylvia who is generally regarded as lawless, but as she sees Christopher, it is he who is immoral. His principles are so baffling—for example, his systematic refusal to stand up for himself—that they make no sense, and they are so outmoded that she cannot even identify them. He "unsettles" society. As Christopher explains to General Campion: ". . . I've no politics that did not disappear in the eighteenth century. . . . I'm a Tory of such an extinct type that she might take me for anything. The last megatherium. She's absolutely to be excused." Christopher understands her difficulties.

Their relationship began as a "courtship of spiders," with the female enticing the male. Having married Sylvia "on the hop when he was only a kid," as his brother Mark puts it, Christopher forgives her her "sin." (She believed herself to be pregnant after an affair with a man named Drake.) As Sylvia perceives her marriage to Christopher, she is perpetually the woman taken in adultery. Though she grants that Christopher is more Christian than any man she knows, she finds it unbearable that with her he should play the part of Christ. "But our Lord was never married. He never touched on topics of sex."

Christopher is, in his remarkable selflessness and detachment from the world, correctly regarded as a saint, and his wish for saintliness is one of the repeated themes of the book. But Sylvia's view is to be considered. Christopher cherishes forgiveness (and, as Mark realizes in *Last Post*, Christopher cherishes unforgiveness as well), but Sylvia wants neither his forgiveness nor his saintliness. "How could any woman live beside you . . .

and be forever forgiven?" If he had denounced her or cursed her, he "might have done something to bring us together." But his aloofness and self-containment—she complains that he closes himself in "invisible bonds"—make him seem merely cold and feelingless, though he is neither.

Everything in his training as an Englishman and a Yorkshireman (a point Ford makes much of) has worked against the ready and spontaneous show of feeling. To make a display of one's deepest emotions is against the rules. His "calculatedly wooden" expression, his "terrifying expressionlessness," make him as much an enigma to Sylvia as she is to him. Intellectual, abstract, he has a monolithic quality she cannot deal with, except to attack it. She perceives him as a rock, a frozen marble statue. His extraordinary self-control, which puts him beyond her reach as he accepts the consequences of her wildest efforts to humiliate and slander him, is, as she understands it, a form of aggression against her, a way of refusing to acknowledge that she can touch him. It is a tacit statement that she is excluded from his life.

Christopher's brother Mark, who is Sylvia's most implacable enemy, understands this: that she is unable to attract her man is the mainspring of her behavior. It is a case of thwarted love become destructive. A woman unused to frustration or failure with men, she is "sappily in love" with him; that she is "forgiven" but not loved by him is the basic fact of their relationship. Jealous even of Christopher's battalion because he cares about his men so deeply, she says to one of them: "I'm glad the captain . . . did not leave you in the cold camp . . . For punishment, you know."

There is something anarchic about Sylvia; her jealousy and destructive passion resist containment. It is not evil as an absolute that she represents, even at her worst, so much as chaos, irrationality, impulse gone berserk. She is an unhappy, even masochistic woman who must have weak things to torture. She sees Christopher "with a mixture of pity and hatred" as a "tired, silent beast" whom she takes pleasure in lashing, as she once thrashed a white bulldog. On the other hand, "Tietjens' words cut her as if she had been lashed with a dog-whip." Ford is suggesting a mysterious identification here.

All the plumb lines are so entangled, as Ford liked to say about human relations and motives, that human behavior seems incapable of simplicity. Though the marriage is improbable from the start, and Sylvia's adultery makes it even more so, Christopher refuses, out of his sense of honor as a gentleman, to divorce her—a refusal that keeps them connected, and at the same time, alienated. The perversities of her nature make it impossible for her to leave him alone, and the game she plays is to torment him, to provoke him into intimacy. Tietjens understands this side of her and calls it "pulling the strings of the shower-bath." Her game is impulsive rather than systematic. She wants to see where and how and whether Christopher is exposed, and she stops only when he seems to have nothing more to lose, having lost money, property, position, and reputation. Her sense of decency makes an attack on Valentine and her baby unthinkable. Besides, by the time of *Last Post*, it seems to her that "God has changed sides."

Christopher's strength inheres in the fundamental principle of his being, his certainty about his own autonomy, his own outlines. Sylvia's sense of herself is a good deal weaker. She wants to possess him, but possession, as she comes to see, is meaningless without self-possession. And rather than fight back, Christopher merely waits for her ("anguish is better than dishonour" is his battalion's motto) to expend herself, as she finally does.

Christopher's metaphor of the shower bath is, in its understatement, intended to deflate Sylvia's effectiveness. But not even his clearness of mind and temperamental affinity with eighteenth-century rationalism can dissipate the sense of evil that hovers around Sylvia. We first see her in Lobscheid, the "last place in Europe" to be Christianized. There, Father Consett, her "saintly" confessor, hears "the claws of evil things scratching on the shutters" and tries to attribute Sylvia's "evil thoughts" to the "evil place" they are in. But the suggestion remains, no matter how much we understand Sylvia's psychology, that Christopher is under her spell and that she herself may be under a spell. The possibility of magic in Sylvia's capacity for destructiveness inheres in the book, emerging often enough to demand interpretation.

Magic has been defined by the late Hannah Arendt as an "intensification of the world to such a pitch of extraordinariness that reality would necessarily fail to come up to its expectations."[2] Sylvia lives in such an intensified world, but not consistently. Standing away from it long enough to try to understand it, she asks: "How was it possible that the most honourable man she knew should be so overwhelmed by foul and baseless rumours? It made you suspect that honour had, in itself, a quality of the evil eye. . . ."

No matter how farfetched her charge or inaccurate her aim, her success in hurting Christopher is uncanny and not to be wholly explained in terms of cause and effect. "I have always been superstitious myself and so remain—impenitently," Ford wrote in 1932. "The most rationalist of human beings does not pass his life without saying: 'I am in luck today!' " In *No Enemy* he had spoken of the "type of feeling" that men engaged in agriculture often have and that makes them "so often passionately disagreeable and apparently unreasonable"—the sense of "wrestling with a personal devil," of an "intelligent, malignant . . . being with a will for evil directed against you in person." "I think that, whilst it lasts," he wrote, "it is the worst feeling in the world."

Ford's belief in a kind of animism—really more significant than his nominal Catholicism for an understanding of his novels—that is, his sense of a universe full of unknown and living forces creating "an atmosphere of loaded dice"—is surely at work in his conception of the Catholic Sylvia.

Insofar as she suggests Astarte or Lamia, Sylvia is, in spite of her Catholicism, a creature from the world of romance. Throughout his long career, the pendulum of Ford's imagination swung back and forth between two kinds of fictional reality—the subjective and the objective: which is to say that he wrote two kinds of fiction—those he called romances and those he referred to as novels, and he was usually careful to designate by a subtitle which was which. Roughly half of his works of fiction bear the subtitle *A Romance* (*Romance*, which he wrote with Conrad, surely needed no subtitle) or some equivalent like *An Extravagant Story* or *A Just Possible Story* or *A Sheer Comedy*. And the historical novels are often, though not consistently, designated as romances. What *Parade's End* represents is a merging of the two genres—the combination of psychological reality and fantasy in the same framework, a conjunction that offers an interesting critical problem.

Tietjens has, as in a fairy tale, incurred the malignity of a dangerous woman. In putting himself beyond her influence, he moves from the world of romance, where cause and effect are incommensurate, to a small corner of the real world. In Ford's early fairy tales and romances, metamorphoses occur and miracles heal and bring back to life. The natural law of cause and effect is suspended, and we are in the realm of magic and divine intervention, in "that sacred and beautiful thing Romance," Ford called it. In *Parade's End*, Tietjens must face the tangled consequences of every small action—his own or Sylvia's—and live them down, as Ford put it when he discussed the genesis of the novel in *It Was the Nightingale*. If Tietjens is to have a new life, he must make it for himself. Ford is clear about keeping Tietjens in this imperfect world: the resolution of the book is coincident with Christopher's growing sense of reality. And *Parade's End*, unlike *The Good Soldier*, is about learning how to live rather than how to die.

As Ford wrote in another context, the purpose of philosophy was "to teach a man how to bear himself during, and what to expect from, life. All else is stamp-collecting."[3]

Christopher can make a new life ("a man could stand up") because of Valentine.

> But, positively, she and Sylvia were the only two human beings he had met for years whom he could respect: the one for sheer efficiency in killing; the other for having the constructive desire and knowing how to set about it. Kill or cure! The two functions of man. If you wanted something killed you'd go to Sylvia Tietjens in the sure faith that she would kill it; emotion: hope: ideal: kill it quick and sure. If you wanted something kept alive you'd go to Valentine: she'd find something to do for it. . . . The two types of mind: remorseless enemy: sure screen: dagger . . . sheath!

He can respect both women for their opposite perfections. Sylvia kills; Valentine cures. And he asks: "Perhaps the future of the world then was to women?"

Valentine is a militant suffragette. When we first see her, she is on a golf course where she has been demonstrating for the vote. She is exercising one of the suffragette movement's chracteristic tactics — to invade the traditionally male preserve. Ford himself had helped the suffragettes by writing for Mrs. Emmeline Pankhurst, leader of the Women's Social and Political Union, a pamphlet entitled *This Monstrous Regiment of Women* (1913), published by the Women's Freedom League, and he had a strong sense of the women's movement as the beginning of a new consciousness.

Valentine, whose name suggests love, health, and strength, is a fitting heroine for a novel that is as turned toward the future as *The Good Soldier* was turned toward the past. "She would have to be a militant if my book ever came to anything," Ford wrote later. But Valentine is also the daughter of Professor Wannop, the classical scholar, and from him she has received a sound classical education. Her intellectual roots are in the past, and she longs to read Euripides by the Mediterranean. Christopher admires not only her Latin, which is superior to his, but the fact that her head "is screwed on right." Having worked as a "slavey" to support herself and her mother, Mrs. Wannop, the aging and neglected novelist whose work Christopher so much admires, Valentine has a larger firsthand experience of the English class system than Christopher, and a grasp of reality he admires: "I daresay you're a heroine all right. *Not* because you persevere in actions the consequences of which you fear. But I daresay you can touch pitch and not be defiled."

Although Valentine is as unlike Sylvia as to be her mythical opposite (healer vs. destroyer), Ford has not created a simple antithesis. Instead, he deals with a "civilized ambiguity":[4] in many ways they are similar — and unlike Christopher. For example, neither woman can bear the thought of war: both are pacifists, and though Christopher does not share their views, he understands them: "Not three hours ago my wife used to me almost the exact words you have just used. Almost the exact words. She talked of her inability to sleep at night for thinking of immense spaces full of pain that was worse at night. . . . And she, too, said that she could not respect me. . . ."

Both are blonde, both are athletes (unlike the slow and heavy Tietjens). Sylvia is strikingly tall and calls Valentine, who is small, a miniature of herself. Both women are presented along with their mothers, so that we see them as daughters. Both express the same irritation with Christopher in the same language. Valentine feels "something devouring" and "overwhelming" in him that "pushed you and your own problems out of the road." She notes his "calculatedly wooden expression and his omniscience" and his "blasted complacent perfections." Like Sylvia, she feels he has insulted her by not making love to her. When they first meet, Valentine says: " 'I pity your wife . . . The English country male! . . . The feudal system all complete. . . .' Tietjens winced. The young woman had come a little too near the knuckle of his wife's frequent denunciations of himself."

Ironically, although Sylvia was conceived as a pagan, it is Valentine whose outlook is more authentically pagan. She is free of the burden of sin and the sense of dualism (body and soul leading separate lives) that Sylvia's Catholic upbringing has given her. In Valentine, body and mind work together. She can be as critical as Sylvia of Christopher's faults. But free of Sylvia's conflicts and morbid engrossment in her own capacity to sin, she has no wish to destroy. Harmony, discipline, "bread-and-butter sense": with these qualities she offers Christopher a "little, tranquil, golden spot" in an unstrung world.

In *The Education of Henry Adams*, Adams had asked: "What could become of such a child of the seventeenth and eighteenth centuries, when he should wake up to find himself required to play the game of the twentieth?" As if in answer, Christopher says: ". . . It is not a good thing to belong to the seventeenth or eighteenth centuries in the twentieth. Or really, because it is not good to have taken one's public-school's ethical system seriously. I am really, sir, the English public schoolboy. That's an eighteenth-century product. . . . Other men get over their schooling. I never have. I remained adolescent. These things are obsessions with me."

Christopher suffers from the defects of his qualities, and the scrupulousness with which he has adopted this code of behavior makes him slow to know his own feelings, which are often in conflict with his principles. Sitting on his mind as if it were a horse, "a coffin-headed, leather-jawed charger," he is at the same time aware of and aloof from the claims and needs of his "under mind," with all its repressed impulses. "He occupied himself with his mind. What was it going to do?" He is a man "in need of a vacation from himself," as he realizes. Under the double stress of the war and Sylvia's harassment, his mind becomes more and more detached until he sees his own dissociation as a danger signal, a portent of the madness he fears.

His decision to live with Valentine is a way of freeing himself and healing himself so that he can adapt to a new set of conditions. "Today's today," he tells himself. "The world was changing and there was no particular reason why he should not change with it." His brother Mark refuses to change; his muteness is a refusal to speak in a world he has come to loathe and despair of, and he wills his own death. In his book on Henry James, Ford had spoken of "the journey towards an entire despair or towards a possible happiness." It is toward the possible happiness that *Parade's End* moves: ". . . He would no longer stand unbearable things. . . . And what he wanted he was prepared to take. . . . What he had been before, God alone knew. A Younger Son? A Perpetual Second-in-Command? Who knew? But to-day the world changed. Feudalism was finished; its last vestiges were gone. It held no place for him. He was going — he was damn well going! — to make a place in it for . . . A man could now stand up on a hill, so he and she could surely get into some hole together!"

Christopher has inherited, through the deaths of his older brothers, the vast ("between forty and sixty rooms") Yorkshire estate of Groby that his family had acquired at the time of William of Orange. He renounces Groby because his disaffection with his own class makes it impossible for him honestly to accept its privileges, not the least of them being the immense income the estate yields. But more importantly, by giving it up, Christopher divests himself of the whole unwieldy feudal structure he has inherited. In exchange, he can, for the first time, recognize the legitimacy of personal happiness; "noblesse oblige" comes to include the obligation to oneself.

Christopher has learned that his sanity and his life depend on knowing what to preserve from the past and what to discard. He would like to keep "the old goodnesses" — without their old trappings and parade. And he reinterprets — by the spirit rather than the letter — the laws that have kept him second-in-command of his own life. Salvaging himself from the wreckage, he trims and consolidates his world, selling what is left of his beautiful old furniture, withdrawing from public life to a private life of "infinite conversations," a life of frugality, self-sufficiency, and comparative serenity. He will live his own life, rather than a predetermined model of it — and it will have order and meaning.

"In contentment live obscurely the inner life," Ford wrote later in *Provence*. In *Last Post*, we see Christopher mislaying some precious old prints and Valentine ashamed of the condition of her underthings and Sylvia and her entourage invading the landscape: Ford cannot offer an ideal solution for Christopher and Valentine, and that is the point. He makes it clear in his dedicatory letter to *Last Post*: "And so he will go jogging along with ups and downs and plenty of worries and some satisfactions, the Tory Englishman, running his head perhaps against fewer walls, perhaps against more. . . ." His descendants will carry on the country "without swank."

Christopher has to rethink his connection with the life he has been born to, and for that way of life Ford created one of the memorable symbols in modern literature, that of Groby Great Tree. The tallest cedar in Yorkshire, the fantastic tree was planted to commemorate the birth of Christopher's great-grandfather who "had died in a whoreshop." The tree was said never to forgive the Tietjens family for transplanting it from Sardinia, and it was connected with the family's bad luck, darkening the windows of the house and tearing chunks out of its foundations: ". . . Groby Great Tree overshadowed the house. You could not look out of the school-room windows at all for its great, ragged trunk and all the children's wing was darkened by its branches. Black . . . funeral plumes. The Hapsburgs were said to hate their palaces — that was no doubt why so many of them . . . had come muckers. At any rate they had chucked the royalty business."

Though the tree "did not like the house," Mark knows how much Christopher loved the tree. He would "pull the house down if he thought it incommoded the tree. . . . The thought that the tree was under the guardianship of unsympathetic people would be enough to drive Christopher almost dotty."

The spell is broken through Sylvia's agency, as a final act of revenge on Christopher for the peace he and Valentine share. Sylvia allows the tenant who was renting the ancestral house "furnished" to have the tree cut down — "to suit the sanitary ideas of the day." It is cut down before Christopher can intervene. The act cannot be undone, and Sylvia, recognizing this, assigns the part to an American. But the curse is removed, as she realizes: "God was lifting the ban." And ironically, Sylvia is the agent by whom the curse of the past is removed.

The ancestors against whom she sins had taken Groby from its rightful owners when the first Tietjens had come over from Holland with William III. The tree, with its great roots and yet its baleful influence, is an ambiguous symbol of the past. In any case, the tree will not darken the house for the generations to come.

Just before Mark dies, Valentine asks him "How are we to live? How are we ever to live?" Her question too is ambiguous, and at last breaking his silence, he answers indirectly, in the old Yorkshire dialect.

He whispered:

> " 'Twas the mid o' the night and the barnies grat
> And the mither beneath the mauld heard that."

. . . "An old song. My nurse sang it. . . . Never thou let thy barnie weep for thy sharp tongue to thy goodman. . . . A good man! . . . Groby Great Tree is down. . . ."

Thinking of the future — Valentine's unborn child — Mark reverts to the oldest words he knows. They express the wisdom of the past, the wisdom of the folk. Having heard them as a child from his nurse, Mark uses them to express the continuity of the generations. To Valentine's question "How are we to live?" he answers — in harmony with Christopher, for the sake of the child. The message is for the future, and since he and Marie Léonie have no children, it is clear to Valentine why she should not tell Lady Tietjens of his last words.

> She would have liked to have his last words. . . .
> But she did not need them as much as I.

Notes

1. The phrase is Christopher's in *Some Do Not . . .* , Part II, chp. 4. *Parade's End* (New York: Alfred A. Knopf, 1950).

2. Hannah Arendt, *Rahel Varnhagen* (New York: Harcourt Brace, Jovanovich, 1974), p. 60.

3. *When Blood is Their Argument* (New York and London: Hodder and Stoughton, 1915), p. 267.

4. The phrase is by Paul Fussell, *The Great War and Modern Memory* (New York and London: Oxford University Press, 1975), p. 80.

Ford Madox Ford: Art Criticism and *Parade's End*   Christopher Brightman*

Frank Kermode once observed that while Ford Madox Ford's *The Good Soldier* is marginally canonical, *Parade's End* lingers among the great unread books of English letters.[1] Clearly, many readers have felt that the trilogy's self-indulgent prose together with the unseemly aspirations of its hero, Christopher Tietjens, to Anglican sainthood, militate against its entry into the canon. Their judgment may be correct. I would claim, however, that the trilogy possesses considerable virtues, and that these lie in the construction of the narrative itself. The examination of Ford's critical ideas and narrative technique that follows is especially indebted to Richard A. Cassell's study of the novels, in particular to his chapter on Ford's view of Pre-Raphaelite painting. Cassell observes that "the criteria by which Ford discovered the Pre-Raphaelites' weaknesses and their virtues laid the foundations of his later criticism of fiction and for his own fictional theory and practice."[2] Here, then, is my starting-point.

Readers of Ford's literary criticism will have noticed that he employs visual metaphor to express his perception of the relation between reader and text. He always describes himself as an Impressionist, though he has little to say about Impressionist painting. He uses the term instead to describe the rendering, by means of certain technical devices, of the impressions he has received. In an article written in 1914, the year before the publication of his first mature novel, *The Good Soldier*, Ford offers an impression of Impressionism. He says: "I suppose that Impressionism exists to render those queer effects of real life that are like so many views seen through bright glass—through glass so bright that whilst you perceive through it a landscape or a backyard, you are aware that, on its surface, it reflects a face of a person behind you."[3] The observer sees the view through

*From *Theoria* 59 (October 1982):63–74. Reprinted by permission of the University of Natal Press.

the window, the reflection of himself and of the person behind him. Ford cannot resist the drama in his scene: in a continuation of the same piece, he insists that "a picture should come out of its frame and seize the spectator."[4] There are, it would seem, two dramas: the drama of the mind and memory (the face behind you can be a remembered face and you, the reader, can become the protagonist) and the drama of the relationship between the text (whether bright glass, a painting or narrative prose) and the spectator / reader. The first of these dramas, that of mind and memory, is enacted in Ford's fiction by means of the time-shift; the second, that of text and reader, by means of what he calls the "progression of the effect," and what we might call the structure of the text. Before leaving the bright glass analogy, I should add the point that it provides us with a clue to Ford's perception of the modernist text. In pre-modernist fiction, we may infer, the text is transparent, giving us an uninterrupted view of the landscape of the *histoire* with some authorial guidance about where we are to look and how we are to look. The modernist text, on the other hand, confronts us with the "thingness" of the text, a reflexive construct that frustrates our expectations and can, indeed, threaten us its readers who no longer have the comfort of a genial narrator's guiding hand. This is, of course, the view of a man writing in 1914; we post-moderns might find the issue less clear-cut.

The foundations of Ford's modernism have already been identified by Cassell in Ford's reading of Pre-Raphaelite painting. Ford's involvement with the Pre-Raphaelites was unavoidable: his maternal grandfather was Ford Madox Brown, painter of *Work* and *The Last of England*; he was a cousin of the Rossetti's and, if his accounts of his childhood are to be believed at all, he enjoyed (and suffered) the attentions of relatives and friends determined that he too should be "trained for a genius."[5] Ford's feeling for Pre-Raphaelite painting is expressed in the conclusion to his book on the Brotherhood: "They never convey to us, as do the Impressionists, or as did the earlier English landscape painters, the sense of fleeting light and shadow. Looking at Millais' nearly perfect *Blind Girl* or at Mr. Hunt's nearly perfect *Hireling Shepherd*, one is impelled to think, 'How lasting all this is!' One is, as it were, in the mood in which each minute seems an eternity. Nature is grasped and held with an iron hand."[6] It is the way the "iron hand" works in controlling particular techniques of spectator-response that Ford observes most acutely, and which forms the focus of his dramatic and narrative concerns.

Drama is not difficult to find in Pre-Raphaelite painting, and D.G. Rossetti's portrait of Lucrezia Borgia, which possesses very obvious dramatic qualities, leads Ford to this observation: "In the *Lucrezia*, in the mirror near the left shoulder of the sumptuous woman is shown Lucrezia's husband, Duke Alfonso of Biscaglia, whom she has just poisoned and 'who is being walked up and down the room by Pope Alexander IV, in order to settle the poison in his system.' This device of narrating in a mirror the happenings in the part of the room occupied by the spectator — of thus completing the anecdote — was a trick much beloved by both Rossetti and Madox Brown. The latter had already adopted it in his *Take your son, Sir*. In the *Lucrezia*, its use, dramatically speaking, is singularly effective and indeed admirable."[7] Paul L. Wiley, in *Novelist of Three Worlds*, notes an echo of the *Lucrezia* mirror in a passage in *Parade's End*, in which Sylvia, wife of Christopher Tietjens, is seated at her dressing-table; her lover enters the room, and the whole is observed through the dressing-table mirror.[8] Wiley may well be correct, but Ford's interest in the mirror in the *Lucrezia* has broader implications for his fiction, in particular for the rapport between reader and text. The *Lucrezia* "anecdote" needs a spectator to observe and complete it, and, by encroaching on the space occupied by the spectator, it obliterates him in order to complete itself. The spectator, at first involved in the anecdote, becomes, in fictional terms, a victim of the action. I have to describe this effect as a process because language is sequential: a mirror in a painting can achieve such an effect instantaneously — paintings have no endings.

Rossetti's painting offers the spectator a threat: Lucrezia's expression suggests that she might well treat us as she has treated the unfortunate Duke. Madox Brown's *Take your son, Sir*, in which a newborn baby is offered out of the painting to the spectator, presents a threat too — at least to the male spectator — for we see in the mirror facing us near the woman's shoulder a bewhiskered seducer, hands spread in a gesture of despair. We note that Rossetti offers us merely a threat, whereas Madox Brown's painting is accusatory. Ford is not enthusiastic about the white wing of moral purpose he perceives in Pre-Raphaelite painting but attends instead to the device itself. The mirror that does not show us ourselves but projects the fiction upon us achieves, in spatial terms, what, in the dimension of fictional time, can be achieved by the ending of a Maupassant short story. "The short story of genius," says Ford, "demands from the reader — nay, it exacts — an amount of strained, of breathless attention that is nothing short of a cruelty; and the final *coup de pistolet* — the last word — is the killing of a living thing, the breaking of a back, since it finishes the vital rapport between writer and reader."[9] This achieves the same effect as Rossetti's mirror in that it breaks the reader's connection with the story and, at the same time, reflects back upon the story with a sudden explosion of understanding. Maupaussant's *The Field of Olives*, in which the last sentence reveals the possibility that the murder has been committed by the intended victim, is an example of the use of the *coup de pistolet*, and is a story which Ford often recommended for study.

Both the mirror and the *coup de pistolet* are devices clearly useful in the creation of engrossing narrative, narrative of the kind Ford had admired from his youth. His early reading was, he recalls, "advanced," but he read adventure romances and Gothic novels with equal enthusiasm: *Melmoth the Wanderer*, *The Mysteries of Udolpho*, *Frankenstein*, *Lorna*

Doone, and *Westward Ho!*[10] His early enthusiasm remained with him; assertions of the following kind appear frequently: "art is nothing more nor less than the faculty, conscious or unconscious, of engrossing the attention of passers-by,"[11] and "the real great novelist . . . has the sense to see that the reader must be caught by his humanisms and retained by his tale."[12] The application of principles such as these to the reading of paintings is nowhere clearer than in Ford's biography of Ford Madox Brown, published in 1896. Ford notes that Madox Brown chooses to illustrate moments of drama and sentiment, in, for example, *Parisina's Sleep*, of which Madox Brown himself says, in his *Catalogue of the Piccadilly Exhibition* of 1865:

> Parisina in her sleep mutters a name which first gives weight and direction to the suspicions already planted in the mind of her husband, the Prince Azo:
>
>> "He plucked his poinard in its sheath,
>> But sheathed it ere the point was bare;
>> Howe'er unworthy now to breathe,
>> He could not slay a thing so fair. . . ."[13]

Madox Brown's illustration for *The Corsair*, his *Death of Sir Tristram* and *Christ Washing Peter's Feet* provide further examples of dramatic subject-matter. The last of these, the *Christ*, has an additional element mentioned by Ford later in relation to *Take your son, Sir*: the direct appeal to the observer. Madox Brown says, of the nimbus of Christ: "This, however, everyone who has considered the subject must understand, appeals *out* of the picture to the *beholder* — not to the other characters in the picture."[14] As an alternative to a dramatic moment, Madox Brown may choose a special and momentary effect of light, as he does, for example, in *Chaucer at the Court of Edward III*. Of the painting *Work*, Ford claims that it "was not to be, and should not be regarded as, a work of generalisation or allegory, but as an actual moment, caught and recorded."[15] Within this recorded moment a number of complex relations are shown. Of *Cromwell on His Farm*, Ford says, "the exposition of the subject, the maze of references and cross-references in the picture, is every whit as astounding as in *Work* itself."[16]

The internal references that Ford notices raise a further point of comparison between Ford's treatment of narrative and painting. In 1914, Ford reviewed an anthology of Imagist poetry for *The Outlook*. In common with many of his reviews, his subject-matter extends beyond the work under review and here he finds himself led to discuss Futurist painting in terms of its narrative qualities, claiming that it achieves much the same effect as Flaubert and Maupassant aimed at in their writing: "They [Flaubert and Maupassant] gave you not so much the reconstitution of a crystallised scene in which all the figures were arrested — not so much that, as fragments of impressions gathered during a moment of time, during a period of emotion, or during a period of travel."[17] In paraphrase, the rest of Ford's review goes on to say that a Futurist canvas tells a story without chronological sequence: there are many images in it and they appear simultaneously. The painting does not alter our fundamental perception of the nature of an object as a Cubist painting might, but is instead an example of "materialist-realist" art, that is to say, it alters our perception of the relation between objects rather than our perception of the objects themselves. He continues, "Futurists are only trying to render on canvas what Impressionists *tel que moi* have been trying to render for many years. (You may remember Emma's love scene at the cattle show in *Madame Bovary*.)"[18] He raises, incidentally, the criticism that Futurists are literary painters, but avoids the issue, significantly, by abruptly concluding that all experiment is self-justificatory and not to be labelled. Although Ford professes to admire the Cubist analysis of matter, he regards himself, by 1914, as entrenched in the "materialist" school. The comparison he draws between the seduction of Emma by Rodolphe and the multiple images of a Futurist painting suggests that he sees narrative as being like a number of lines on a flat canvas — the lines can interweave in a complex fashion, but they all do so on the same plane of recorded observation.

Turning now to Ford's practice of fiction, I shall attempt a new reading of the structure of *Parade's End* in the light of Ford's narrative-conscious reading of painting. *Parade's End* first appeared as a tetralogy, consisting of *Some Do Not . . .* (1924), *No More Parades* (1925), *A Man Could Stand Up* (1926) and *Last Post* (1928). Ford later dropped *Last Post*, saying that he had never liked the novel and had always intended to end with *A Man Could Stand Up*. That the three books were intended to form one whole there is no doubt. Ford wrote in a letter to Percival Hinton in 1931: "I think the GOOD SOLDIER is my best book technically unless you read the Tietjens books as one novel in which case the whole design appears."[19]

The trilogy opens with Christopher Tietjens and Vincent Macmaster, both public officials in the Imperial Department of Statistics, travelling on the 11.40 from London to Rye to play golf. Everything in their compartment is brand-new, like the novel and themselves; even the mirrors under the luggage-racks look as if they have reflected very little. Macmaster, small, precise, Scottish, from a humble background, is correcting the proof-sheets of his first book (on the Pre-Raphaelites) with a specially purchased gold pencil. He is disconcerted to find that no corrections need to be made. Tietjens, large, untidy, son of a Yorkshire landowner, is immersed in his own thoughts which carry us back to a point four months before when his wife Sylvia ran off to Brittany with a man called Perowne. On the morning of the train-journey a letter has arrived from Sylvia in which she asks to be taken back. Markers are introduced into the flow of Tietjens's thoughts — *at breakfast, in the cab* — in order to locate them in the fictional chronology of the novel and to prepare the reader for the time-shifts or chronological loops that follow. The first of these loops opens with Tietjens sitting in his hotel bedroom playing patience, He starts violently when Macmaster enters. Their conversation is fragmented and largely incomprehensible since it evidently refers to events that have not yet been narrated, but which have already occurred during their afternoon's golf. Macmaster then recalls these events but during the course of his recall events are narrated that he does not know about: in this way recall slips into narration. The loop ends after thirty-seven pages with Tietjens suffering the same shock that it opened with:

> Back in his room under the rafters, Tietjens fell . . . at once a prey to real agitation. For a long time he pounded from wall to wall and, since he could not shake off the train of thought, he got out at last his patience cards, and devoted himself seriously to thinking out the condition of his life with Sylvia. He wanted to stop scandal if he could; he wanted them to live within his income, he wanted to subtract that child from the influences of its mother. Those were all definite but difficult things . . . Then one half of his mind lost itself in the rearrangement of schedules, and on his brilliant table his hands set queens and kings and checked their recurrences.
>
> In that way the sudden entrance of MacMaster gave him a really terrible physical shock. He nearly vomited: his brain reeled and the room fell about. He drank a great quantity of whisky in front of Macmaster's goggling eyes; but even at that he couldn't talk, and he dropped into his bed faintly aware of his friend's efforts to loosen his clothes. He had, he knew, carried the suppression of thought in his conscious mind so far that his unconscious self had taken command and had, for the time, paralysed his body and his mind.[20]

Usually, the content of loops is recalled by the principal protagonist in the events of the loop, but here Tietjens has been consciously avoiding recall of the events of the day — an attack on a Cabinet Minister by two suffragettes and their escape, facilitated by Tietjens — so these events are introduced instead by a passage of Macmaster's recall. As the loop progresses, however, omniscient narration takes over, with Tietjens at the centre of the action and Macmaster on the periphery. Macmaster, then, is not permitted the whole of the loop he has begun and is relegated to the status of a secondary character by the construction of the loop itself, confirming the reader's initial impression of him as small, precious and weak. The rest of the loops in *Some Do Not . . .* , except for the last, are given to Tietjens. It is, incidentally, quite appropriate to treat Tietjens in this way since he has the capacity to perform tasks and think about a number of other matters at the same time. He is also not a man to discuss his personal affairs. Towards the end of the novel a long loop is given to Valentine Wannop, Tietjens's prospective lover, establishing her importance to him and to the remainder of the trilogy (III, 284–342). Episodes between loops are presented in straightforward narrative: either because Tietjens is not present, or because he plays only a small part in them. In the latter case, small loops covering only four minutes or so of fictional time are given to those playing major rôles in the action. At a breakfast given by the Reverend Duchemin, for example, Macmaster is allotted a small loop as the hero of the hour for subduing Duchemin, who suffers in public a fit of scatological lunacy (III, 122).

The reader's response to chronological looping is a more complex one than such an elementary device would appear to warrant. Clearly, looping is dramatic: the reader is invited to enter the loop if he wishes to discover the cause of Tietjen's state of mind. Looping is, equally clearly, not a grossly dramatic device: the reader knows the outcome of the events contained in the loop before they begin. The loops enact, then, a drama of mind and memory and invite the reader's participation in the often taxing experience of unravelling their complicated chronology. The loops recall, too, the bright glass analogy discussed earlier. Throughout the reading of the loop, the outcome remains in the reader's memory as though imprinted on the text, or reflected in the window. Tietjens shares this experience, though for him the events of the moment correspond to the landscape on which his thoughts are superimposed. The reader's sympathetic interest in Tietjens and his sufferings leads him through a beguiling sequence of loops in which he shares Tietjens's most intimate reflections. Interspersed with the loops are episodes of conventional narrative treating Sylvia, who first appears in the company of her mother and her mother's priest at Lobscheid, "an unknown and little frequented air resort" deep in the pinewoods of the Taunus Wald. The setting is redolent with evil: " 'Sometimes,' the priest said, 'at night I think I hear the claws of evil things scratching on the shutters. This was the last place in Europe to be Christianised. Perhaps it wasn't ever even Christianised and they're here yet.' " (III, 43). Sylvia, looking "like a picture of Our Lady by Fra Angelico," sits well amidst these surroundings as she horrifies the priest with her plans to haunt and persecute the wretched Tietjens. Sylvia's episodes contrast sharply with Tietjens's loops, not only in construction (Sylvia has no recall-sequences) but also in texture. The heavily adjectival and metonymic language of the Sylvia scenes contrasts with the spare prose of Tietjens's recall. Tietjens is not a man accustomed to think comparatively and his rare similes burst upon him accompanied each by an exclamation mark. It is the beginnings and the endings of loops that capture Tietjens for us in fleeting moments, fragments of time held and extended at length for the reader's inspection of the interweaving lines on the canvas.

At the end of each loop, whether long or short, the reader is snapped back, like an elastic band stretched and released, to that moment in the text as much as sixty pages before, where he left Tietjens or Valentine musing. Ford's remarks about the ending of a Maupassant short story come to mind: if the loop is the anecdote, the ending of the loop severs the reader's connection with that narrative, completing the story and bringing him, not to the very end but back, in circular fashion, to the point the reader began with. Ford's comment on the mirror in the painting of Lucrezia Borgia bears repetition here too: "This device," he says, "of narrating in a mirror the happenings in the part of the room occupied by the spectator — of thus completing the anecdote — was a trick much beloved by both Rossetti and Madox Brown."[21] At the end of a loop, then, the reader, intimately concerned with the narrating consciousness of Tietjens or Valentine, is brought back to the beginning: he is no further forward but has been carried for a considerable length of reading-time through a loop that is, in terms of the fiction, timeless. He is carried by his own effort and enjoyment, flattered perhaps by the intimacies confided to him, precisely nowhere. He has merely caught up with the moment he began reading the loop. What Rossetti achieves in the mirror — the completion of the anecdote by means of the anecdote's encroachment upon the spectator's space — is achieved in the loop by virtue of its own sequentiality: the reader gives time but gains none.

By the end of *Some Do Not . . .* , the reader has grown accustomed to the association of loops with characters who are presented sympathetically and to the association of conventional narrative with the evil Sylvia. All this begins to change in the second volume as the "progression of the effect" becomes clearer. There is, however, one more aspect of the series of loops in the first volume to consider. Part One of *Some Do Not . . .* takes place two years before the outbreak of the First World War and is set in England, except for the one episode with Sylvia at Lobscheid. Part Two of *Some Do Not . . .* is again set in England three years into the war, with Christopher Tietjens coming to the end of his invalid leave and in the process of being ruined by one of Sylvia's admirers and the machinations of English polite society. The circularity of the loops may well represent the hopeless struggles of Christopher and Valentine to escape the social net cast around them (their thoughts make no progress). The loops may also, more generally, reflect the stasis of pre-war English society. The last sentences of the first volume, in the past perfect tense, "He had caught, outside the gates of his old office, a transport lorry that had given him a lift to Holborn. . . ." (III, 356) prepares the reader for the plunge into the dreadful continuous present of a transport depôt in Flanders during an air raid in *No More Parades*.

The second volume opens with language that is metaphorical and onomatopoeic: "An immense tea-tray, august, its voice filling the blank circle of the horizon, thundered to the ground. Numerous pieces of sheet-iron said, 'Pack. Pack. Pack.' In a minute the clay floor of the hut shook, the drums of ears were pressed inwards, solid noise showered about the universe, enormous echoes pushed these men — to the right, to the left, or down towards the tables, and crackling like that of flames among vast underwood became the settled condition of the night" (IV, 9.). Tietjens, now a seriously overworked transport officer, has little time for reflection. No chronological loop follows the first shock that he receives, and the loop that follows the first event of importance in his personal life is of an unusual kind. Instead of being made up of shifting reflection and recall, the loop records Tietjens's thoughts about his marriage as he writes them down on paper in the style of a military report. He records all the main events of his relationship with Sylvia, summarising in chronological order the complex narrative of the previous volume (IV, 68–87).

The change in technique in this loop signals a change in the movement of the whole trilogy. The first part of the second volume, devoted mainly to military matters, contains a number of bizarre parallels with the world of peace in Part One of *Some Do Not. . . .* A runner is killed and dies bloodily in Tietjens's arms, recalling for him an injury done to a horse he drove in *Some Do Not. . . .* As he waited for the knacker's van at the end of the first part of the first volume, so he waits for an ambulance stretcher on bicycle wheels at the end of the first section of *No More Parades.* The injury to the horse was caused by a car driven by General Campion, the same General now commanding the Front. Tietjens is billeted with a lunatic brother officer who, it transpires, is Macmaster's nephew; Tietjens's treatment of him recalls Macmaster's handling of the lunatic clergyman Duchemin. The changes that have overwhelmed Tietjens's world extend even to Sylvia. In Part Two of *No More Parades* a loop is given over to Sylvia's reflections on the subject of a reconciliation with Tietjens, whereas in *Some Do Not . . .* her thoughts were never revealed. She is transformed from an evil icon to a conscious, though still perverse, human being. Her efforts in the direction of a reconciliation lead to Tietjens's arrest for striking her lover, now Major Perowne.

At this point in the final part of *No More Parades* the construction of loops is decisively changed. The narration of the circumstances in which Tietjens strikes Perowne is held back in the usual way, the loop opening with Tietjens already under arrest (IV, 193). One of the General's staff officers elicits the details of the assault from Tietjens and an explanation is offered to the General himself. The loop, however, never closes: the circularity of reflection in *Some Do Not . . .* is slowly opened out in the course of *No More Parades* to the point where the open-ended loop leads the reader forward in fictional time rather than leaving him in the stasis of the closed loop. The rubber band, it seems, can now be stretched indefinitely; the reader no longer enters loops with the expectation of being drawn back when they end. The reader's relation with Tietjens is no longer defined by the loop; both are freed. In the scene immediately following the unclosed loop, a small closed loop is allotted to the General, who, we can infer, is still held bound to the structure of the first half of the trilogy and to the social codes of pre-war England (IV, 217–224). The offer

of freedom from loops and codes, however, has as we shall see in the next
volume, a fatal consequence for the relation of the reader to the text.
    The third volume of *Parade's End*, with a tentative modal in its
title—*A Man Could Stand Up*—brings us to the end of the war, the
beginning of Tietjen's life with Valentine, and, of course, the severance of
the reader from the text. Ford, throughout the earlier part of the trilogy,
has presented us with the intimate reflections of people intensely private,
both by nature and station; Tietjens affirms that he would rather be dead
than an open book (IV, 70). Paradoxically, with the gradual liberation of
Christopher and Valentine, the reader, equally gradually, becomes less
and less privileged to share loops with them. The only loop in *A Man
Could Stand Up* appears at the beginning and traps Valentine between a
telephone call and an interview with the Head of the girls' school at which
she teaches at the very moment the maroons are sounding to announce the
cessation of hostilities. She escapes her loop with a speculation:

> "No more respect . . . For the Equator! For the Metric system. For Sir
> Walter Scott! Or George Washington! Or Abraham Lincoln! Or the
> Seventh Commandment!!!!!!"
>   And she had a blushing vision of fair, shy, square-elbowed Miss
> Wanostrocht—the Head!—succumbing to some specious-tongued be-
> guiler! . . . That was where the shoe really pinched! You had to keep
> them—the Girls, the Populace, everybody!—in hand now, for once you
> let go there was no knowing where They, like waters parted from the
> seas, mightn't carry You. Goodness knew! You might arrive anywhere—
> at county families taking to trade; gentlefolk selling for profit! All the
> unthinkable sorts of things! (IV, 272.)

After this a fast and fantastic narrative takes charge, peppered with
exclamations, capital letters and snatches of music, until the final scene
with Valentine and Christopher dancing together on Armistice Night
1918, described by Graham Greene in his Introduction to the trilogy as "a
day out of time—an explosion without a future." (III, 6.)
    The reader, accustomed to the beguiling but frustrating techniques of
the earlier part of *Parade's End*, accustomed too to the text's insistence
that he be drawn into its complexities, delayed, frustrated, leaping
forward only to return to the beginning again, is now confronted with
narrative that moves forward with dangerous speed. The prose of *A Man
Could Stand Up* is explosive and no longer beguiling. The privacy of
Christopher and Valentine is asserted; the anecdote no longer needs the
listener; the mirror reflects its own story, not ourselves. The lovers, amidst
the confusion and excitement, the carnival of the trilogy's end, are no
longer accessible to Sylvia, to society's codes or to us. We, the readers, are
no longer required; our time is no longer measured alongside fictional
time. The severance of reader and text is made complete: Valentine and
Christopher have each other but have excluded us; with the connivance of
the text they have achieved true privacy, not merely that of loops. Loops

no longer appear, the intimacy they offered is ended; we read ourselves out of the text and are left alone at our point of severance from it. The drama of reader and text is over; we diverge from the text and find at last that special, lonely freedom of the text's ending.

Notes

1. "Posterity," *London Review of Books*, 3, No. 6 (1981), 3 and 5.
2. *Ford Madox Ford: A Study of His Novels*, (Baltimore: Johns Hopkins Univ. Press, 1961), p. 12.
3. "On Impressionism," *Poetry and Drama*, No. 2 (June 1914), p. 174.
4. "On Impressionism. Second Article," *Poetry and Drama*, No. 2 (Dec. 1914), p. 328.
5. *Thus to Revisit*, (London: Chapman and Hall, 1921), p. 211.
6. *The Pre-Raphaelite Brotherhood: A Critical Monograph*, (London: Duckworth, 1907), pp. 164–5.
7. *Rossetti: A Critical Essay on His Art.* (London: Duckworth, 1902), p. 107.
8. *Novelist of Three Worlds*, (New York: Syracuse Univ. Press, 1962), p. 54.
9. "Literary Portraits, 34: Miss May Sinclair and *The Judgment of Eve*," *The Outlook*, 2 May 1914, p. 599.
10. See Arthur Mizener, *The Saddest Story: A Biography of Ford Madox Ford*, (London: The Bodley Head, 1971), p. 11; F.M. Ford, *The English Novel From the Earliest Days to the Death of Joseph Conrad*, (London: Constable, 1930), pp. 108–10.
11. "Literary Portraits, 9: Mr. Thomas Hardy and *A Changed Man*," *The Outlook*, 8 Nov. 1913, p. 642.
12. "Joseph Conrad," *John O'London's Weekly*, 10 Dec. 1921, p. 323.
13. Quoted by F.M. Ford in *Ford Madox Brown: A Record of His Life and Work*, (London: Longman, 1896), pp. 29–30.
14. Quoted by F.M. Ford in *Ford Madox Brown*, p. 81.
15. F.M. Ford, *Ford Madox Brown*, p. 165.
16. F.M. Ford, *Ford Madox Brown*, p. 415.
17. "Les Jeunes and *Des Imagistes*. Second Notice," *The Outlook*, 16 May 1914, p. 682.
18. "On Impressionism," *Poetry and Drama*, No. 2 (June 1914), p. 175.
19. Richard M. Ludwig, ed., *Letters of Ford Madox Ford*, (Princeton: Princeton Univ. Press, 1965), p. 204.
20. *The Bodley Head Ford Madox Ford*, ed. Graham Greene, (London: The Bodley Head, 1963), III, 103–4. All subsequent references are to this edition.
21. F.M. Ford, *Rossetti*, p. 107.

The Epistemology of Ford's Impressionism

Paul B. Armstrong*

Ford Madox Ford claims that his theory of impressionism "founds itself upon analysis of the human mind."[1] Ford radicalizes the conventions of realism by insisting that the novel must not just represent the world but must, if it wants to give an accurate account of the conditions of life, render how the world is known. In his view, traditional narration is not true to how the world originally presents itself to the perceiver. "[T]he general effect of a novel must be the general effect that life makes on mankind," he argues; "A novel must therefore not be a narration, a report."[2] In a famous statement of the epistemology of impressionism, Ford explains that he and Conrad "saw that Life did not narrate, but made impressions on our brains. We in turn, if we wished to produce on you an effect of life, must not narrate but render impressions" (*Joseph Conrad*, pp. 194–95).[3] By opposing "impressions" and "narration," Ford distinguishes between two levels of meaning-creation: the perceiver's first unreflective engagement with the world and the later acts of synthesis and criticism which create order and clarity out of what was first shimmering, unstable, and obscure. By insisting that the novelist give "the impression, not the corrected chronicle" ("On Impressionism," p. 41), Ford argues that unreflective meaning-creation is more authentic and basic than self-conscious judgment because reflection comes after and depends on primordial perception. An epistemologically fundamental realism must consequently, in Ford's view, try to capture the hazy, confusing surge and flow of the perceiver's pre-critical experience of the world, before self-consciousness imposes clarity, stability, and coherence.

Ford does not ignore reflection completely, however. The vicissitudes of memory occupy an important place in the theory and practice of his impressionism because only through retrospection can we recapture our first perceptions of a scene. Ford justifies his representational techniques by citing the workings of both memory and perception:

> If to-day, at lunch at your club, you heard an irascible member making a long speech about the fish, what you remember will not be his exact words. . . . So that, if you had to render that scene or those speeches for purposes of fiction, you would not give a word for word re-invention of sustained sentences. . . . No, you would give an impression of the whole thing, of the snorts, of the characteristic exclamation, of your friend's disquisition on morals, a few phrases of which you would intersperse into the monologue of the gentleman dissatisfied with his sole. And you would give a sense that your feet were burning, and that the lady you wanted to

*This essay was written for this volume and is published here for the first time by permission of the author.

meet had very clear and candid eyes. . . . In that way you would attain to
the sort of odd vibration that scenes in real life really have; you would give
your reader the impression that he was witnessing something real, that he
was passing through an experience. ("On Impressionism," pp. 41–42;
ellipses mine)

Ford's argument here invokes two different epistemological principles. It
would not be realistic, he claims, to give a complete, clear, and orderly
account of the scene because memory does not recall events precisely and
in an organized manner. But it would also not be realistic to do so, he
suggests, because the scene originally presented itself to the perceiver not
as a coherent narration but as a shifting ebb and flow of loosely associated
thoughts and sensations.

One connection between these two lines of argument is that both
memory and perception have similar structures. Although the goal of
retrospective reflection may be clear, coherent understanding, the way it
gets there is marked by the same lack of order, the same liability to sudden
shifts in attention, which characterizes unreflective experience. A further
and perhaps more surprising connection is that by depicting the digressions and dissociations of memory an artist may actually give the reader a
sense of the jumble and confusion of the immediate event itself. Ford
suggests that rendering the ramblings of retrospection can reinforce the
novelist's effort to recreate in the reader's experience of the text an
analogue of pre-critical perception because both modes of meaning-
creation are similarly shifty and incoherent.

The Good Soldier is an extended exploration of the relation between
memory and perception. The structure of the novel recapitulates Ford's
distinction between "impressions" and "narration" inasmuch as the act of
telling the story is the narrator's attempt to clarify and organize his earlier,
unreflective experience. Dowell apologizes at one point: "I have, I am
aware, told this story in a very rambling way so that it may be difficult for
anyone to find his path through what may be a sort of maze. I cannot help
it. . . . [W]hen one discusses an affair — a long, sad affair — one goes back,
one goes forward."[4] Dowell's tendency to ramble is attributable to both
levels of meaning-creation which concern Ford. Dowell's narration is
frequently marked by confusion and incoherence not only because his
original experience was often obscure but also because the act of reflecting
on his past is not a straightforward, step-by-step progress toward a goal.

"Well, those are my impressions," Dowell reports, for example, after
rendering his confused perceptions of the night Florence died; "What had
actually happened had been this. I pieced it together afterwards" (p. 109).
And he goes on to sort out what he had not fully understood at the time.
Dowell's original impressions are both dazzling and baffling. Instead of
people's faces, he sees "floating globes" bobbing back and forth before him
(p. 107). Instead of connected speeches, he hears scattered phrases whose

sound matters more than their sense (" *'Ja, ja, ja!'* each word dropping out like so many soft pellets of suet," or *"Zum Befehl, Durchlaucht"* sounding "like five revolver-shots" [p. 108]). Dowell is open here to sensations and associations which a more controlled, critical consciousness would censor out, but he is also blind to what is actually happening because the shifting gestalts through which he perceives the scene do not stabilize and harmonize into a consistent pattern. One reason why Dowell could be duped for so long—here believing that his wife died of a heart attack, not suicide—is that he habitually fails to subject his original experience to the retrospective critical scrutiny necessary to organize, clarify, and correct it. Especially striking examples are his dazed refusal to think critically about Leonora's outburst at the Protest and his odd indifference to Florence's peculiarly long delay in coming down the ladder the night of their elopement. These episodes are not isolated events, however, but part of a pattern of almost willful resistance to examining and criticizing his experience, no doubt to protect himself against what he might discover there. When Dowell finally, belatedly does begin to reflect, he finds that his world "is all a darkness" (p. 12) in large part because the ambiguity and obscurity of his unreflective impressions had never before been seriously challenged.

After Leonora opens his eyes with her surprising revelations about Florence's suicide and her affair with Edward, Dowell does not suddenly have before him a transparent, orderly vision of his past. When he picks up his pen and writes the words "This is the saddest story I have ever heard" (p. 3), he actually does not yet know the story he is about to relate. He hears it for the first time as he tells it because the act of narration is for him a process of reflection and discovery. His goal is a lucid, coherent account of events which he now finds he understood only partially or not at all. On his way toward this goal, however, he repeatedly changes his mind or shifts from one topic to another only to return to it later because reflection is itself a temporal process which cannot deliver a correct chronicle of the past complete and ready-made from the start.

The more Dowell reflects, the more he finds he has to reexamine and reinterpret. Correcting one mistake calls up a series of other related errors which demand revision. Every new revelation he achieves forces him to reevaluate many other matters which are interdependent parts in the complex whole he is trying to piece together. Whenever Dowell's sense of the whole changes, he must reassess its parts—most notably, perhaps, when he finds that "It wasn't a minuet that we stepped; it was a prison—a prison full of screaming hysterics" (p. 7), a gestalt-shift which compels him to reinterpret every aspect of his world. Conversely, a new understanding of any individual element can necessitate a rearrangement of the larger scheme to which it belongs—as when Dowell discovers that the bottle in his dead wife's hand contained not heart medicine but poison, a small detail with enormous implications. In all of these ways, Dowell's rambling mode of narration dramatizes the difficulty and tenuousness of any attempt to mold "impressions" into a coherent "narration."

The notorious dilemma of deciding whether Dowell is a reliable narrator is due at least in part to the impossibility of determining whether his reflections finally achieve a successful synthesis. On the one hand, it is possible to argue that Dowell achieves ever more mastery over his story the longer he tells it. His frantic thrashing about in the early pages as he desperately searches for a way of making sense of his distressing discoveries differs greatly, for example, from his controlled, deeply moving account near the end of the torment which Leonora, Nancy, and Edward put each other through during their last days together. This difference can be taken as a sign that Dowell understands them and himself better than he did before he began his reflections.[5] On the other hand, it is also possible to contend that his new syntheses are deceptive and incomplete. When Dowell confesses, for example, "that I loved Edward Ashburnham — and that I love him because he was just myself" (p. 253), this can be seen not as a profound act of sympathetic identification but as a sign of an incompletely understood desire for the sexual pleasures which Edward indulged in but which the repressed, celibate narrator simultaneously longs for and fears.[6] If so, then the darkness of Dowell's unreflected experience even to the end resists full illumination by the light of self-consciousness.

What both sides of this argument share is agreement that Dowell's task is to clarify and criticize his too little reflected-upon thoughts, feelings, and desires; they disagree about whether he successfully meets this challenge. If the dispute about Dowell cannot be conclusively resolved, one reason is that the unreflected always exceeds reflection from the moment self-consciousness takes aim at it — and that we cannot consequently ever be sure that it has been fully elucidated. Because reflection always comes after experience, it can never completely catch up with it. The ambiguity of *The Good Soldier* calls attention to the inescapable provisionality and incompleteness of the syntheses through which reflection reinterprets our original experience. Although the coherence of a self-conscious narration might seem to make it more trustworthy than the impressions it organizes, even this level of meaning-creation is not as stable and certain as the interpreter might like to believe.

Parade's End differs from *The Good Soldier* by offering a more direct approach to pre-critical experience. Perhaps paradoxically, the tetralogy's third-person mode of narration allows Ford to render a character's sensations, thoughts, and feelings with more immediacy than a fully dramatized first-person narrator permits. Where Dowell can only present his experience as remembered and reconstructed, the narrator of *Parade's End* has access whenever he wants it to Tietjens' often baffled interiority in the moment of perception itself. This omniscience may be epistemologically unrealistic in the strict terms Ford argues for elsewhere, but leaping over the boundaries which prevent us from experiencing another person's immediate perceptions of the world can give the reader such a powerful illusion of participation in an event that the theoretical absurdity of the narrative method goes unnoticed.

Where Dowell devotes most of his narrative to reflecting on his past and only occasionally tries to recreate his original impressions, *Parade's End* offers a series of strikingly vivid renderings of perceptual experience caught in the moment of happening. A typical example is Ford's treatment of this scene from *Some Do Not . . .* :

> Not ten yards ahead Tietjens saw a tea-tray, the underneath of a black-lacquered tea-tray, gliding towards them, mathematically straight, just rising from the mist. He shouted, mad, the blood in his head. His shout was drowned by the scream of the horse; he had swung it to the left. The cart turned up, the horse emerged from the mist, head and shoulders, pawing. A stone sea-horse from the fountain of Versailles! Exactly that! Hanging in air for an eternity; the girl looking at it, leaning slightly forward.[7]

The reader of this passage can only make sense of what has occurred by retrospectively piecing together fragmentary, ambiguous evidence. In order to recognize that General Campion's automobile has crashed into the horse-cart in which Tietjens and Valentine are riding, the reader must correct Tietjens' mistaken perceptions (a "tea-tray" for the body of a car) and discover a consistent pattern in disconnected events (the collision as the reason why the cart tilts, the horse rises strangely and screams, Tietjens shouts, and Valentine stares). This process of discovery recreates for the reader Tietjens' own experience of only later understanding the full significance of an event which he first lived through with a good deal of bafflement and obscurity. The implication is that we live forward but understand backward because only after having an experience can we elucidate it fully.

The challenge of reading this passage and the many like it in *Parade's End* is, however, not to let the need to figure out what is actually going on drive out one's sense of the instability and incoherence of the immediate moment. Ford makes contradictory demands on his readers — asking us to immerse ourselves in Tietjens' angry, bewildered, but curiously calm perceptions of the event and at the same time to engage in critical analysis of what must be giving rise to them. These two phases of consciousness cannot coexist. The discovery that Tietjens' unclear jumble of perceptions and associations is caused by a crash can only come after the reader steps back and looks behind them for the consistency which their seeming incoherence lacks. But after establishing a coherent explanation, the reader must not forget the impressions which his interpretive scheme has organized and clarified — even though that scheme now presents itself as their replacement because it is what they meant all along. If the reader lets the scheme suppress the confused, fragmentary thoughts and feelings which triggered it, he will gain clarity only by losing the richness and fullness of Tietjens' bewildered consciousness. To read Ford's renderings of pre-critical perceptions is to oscillate back and forth between sharing an unreflective experience and reflecting on its implications. The contradictory demands which Ford makes on his readers recapitulate in our construal of the text the interaction between the two levels of meaning-creation which fascinate him.

Unreflective experience might seem to be a formless flux, but this is not quite accurate.[8] Although Tietjens' experience of the crash is confused and incompletely coherent, it is not totally unstructured; if it were, it would be meaningless, and not a particular way of construing the event. Tietjens perceives the crash through gestalts which help him to make sense of events at the same time as they register his bafflement because they are not the categories which a fully lucid consciousness would employ—a "tea-tray" for an automobile, or the horse's oddly elevated posture compared to a statue of a fish. These are mistaken assignments of types, but the perceiver discovers their error only subsequent to their use, and then he should realize as well that they are not totally wrong because they capture aspects of the object which a clear, critical description might leave out (how better render a horse suspended upright than by invoking a stone sea-horse?).

The relation between the elements of Tietjens' experience might still seem formless, however, even if they themselves are structured. But their relation is indeed organized, if only in rudimentary ways. The connection between a tea-tray, an angry shout, and a statue might not seem evident at first glance, and the narration does not explain it. But they must be connected or else the reader could not discover without further clues how to fit them together as parts of a coherent whole. They are not a purely random listing of unrelated elements like, say, the items in a Dada-esque word-salad. They are instead connected by such factors as contiguity, simultaneity, and succession—low-level modes of organization which await replacement by more powerful explanatory syntheses based on principles like cause and effect. The relation of primordial perception to self-conscious understanding is not formlessness to form or meaninglessness to meaning. It is, rather, a movement from one set of structures to another which we only later, on reflection, recognize as more adequate—a movement from rudimentary gestalts, linked by proximity and association, to more fully articulated perceptual schemes organized by clearer, more sophisticated rules of coherence.[9]

One of the best summaries of Ford's epistemological realism is Thomas Moser's claim that "the impressionistic method serves not to render the external world but to dramatize a mind in a state of dislocation."[10] For Ford, however, bafflement is not an unusual occurrence. It is instead a common characteristic of everyday perception which ordinarily goes unnoticed precisely because we do not subject it to reflection. In

Ford's view, "the whole of life is really like that; we are almost always in one place with our minds somewhere quite other" ("On Impressionism," p. 41). Ford assigns special importance to experiences of distraction or absent-mindedness in order to contest the view that deliberate acts of judgment or predication are the hallmark of consciousness. By elevating "impressions" over "narration," Ford questions the assumption that consciousness is customarily — or even frequently — in fully lucid control over itself and its world.

Ford asks us to think of the mind not as a transparent medium with unlimited powers over its acts and objects but as an inherently divided realm where reflection constantly pursues but can never completely assimilate the ambiguities, incoherences, and instabilities of pre-critical perception. Ford especially values radical experiences of dislocation — Tietjens and Valentine in a car-crash, the confusion of life in the trenches, Dowell suddenly dispossessed of years of ignorance — because they reveal with particular vividness a bafflement in the face of the world which is, in his view, our ordinary, fundamental state of mind. The epistemology of Ford's impressionism simultaneously asserts and denies the rights of consciousness. His aesthetic of the mind insists that the novel render the workings of consciousness because they are the home of meaning — but the priority he assigns to unreflective experience suggests that consciousness is not fully in control of what happens in its own house.

Notes

1. Ford Madox Ford, "On Impressionism" (1913) in *Critical Writings of Ford Madox Ford*, ed. Frank MacShane (Lincoln: Univ. of Nebraska Press, 1964), p. 48.

2. Ford Madox Ford, *Joseph Conrad: A Personal Remembrance* (Boston: Little, Brown, and Company, 1924), p. 192.

3. Ford's claims to the contrary, however, he and Conrad do not agree in all matters of epistemology and aesthetics. For a comparison of their different impressionisms, see my essay "The Hermeneutics of Literary Impressionism: Interpretation and Reality in James, Conrad, and Ford," *The Centennial Review*, 27 (1983):244–69.

4. Ford Madox Ford, *The Good Soldier: A Tale of Passion* (1915: rpt. New York: Vintage, 1951), p. 183.

5. For a further explanation of this position, see my essay "The Epistemology of *The Good Soldier*: A Phenomenological Reconsideration," *Criticism*, 22 (1980):230–51. Important recent defenses of Dowell's credibility are Thomas C. Moser, *The Life in the Fiction of Ford Madox Ford* (Princeton: Princeton Univ. Press, 1980), pp. 154–85, and Ann Barr Snitow, *Ford Madox Ford and the Voice of Uncertainty* (Baton Rouge: Louisiana State Univ. Press, 1984), pp. 165–89.

6. See Carol Ohmann, *Ford Madox Ford: From Apprentice to Craftsman* (Middletown, Conn.: Wesleyan Univ. Press, 1964), pp. 71–111. Dowell's recent detractors include Frank Kermode, "Novels: Recognition and Deception," *Critical Inquiry*, 1 (1974), 108ff., and Carol Jacobs, "The (Too) Good Soldier: 'A Real Story' " in *Glyph 3*, ed. Samuel Weber and Henry Sussman (Baltimore: The Johns Hopkins Univ. Press, 1978), pp. 32–51.

7. Ford Madox Ford, *Some Do Not . . .* (1924) in *Parade's End* (1924–28; rpt. New York: Knopf, 1950), p. 139.

8. Ford's understanding of pre-critical perception has much in common with Husserl's notion of "passive genesis" and Merleau-Ponty's concept of "operative intentionality." The following analysis is indebted to Edmund Husserl, *Cartesian Meditations*, trans. Dorion Cairns (The Hague, Martinus Nijhoff, 1970), pp. 77–81, and Maurice Merleau-Ponty, *Phenomenology of Perception*, trans. Colin Smith (London: Routledge and Kegan Paul, 1962), pp. x–xi, xviii, 177, 337, 347, 401–04.

9. I would not disagree, however, with Richard A. Cassell's perceptive description of the paradox of the impressionist's program — namely, that "the form of his novels must give the effect of the formlessness and fragmentary nature of life as it meets the individual consciousness" (Cassell, *Ford Madox Ford: A Study of his Novels* [Baltimore: The Johns Hopkins Univ. Press, 1961], p. 50). I would only rephrase the paradox. It is not that the artist must reconcile formlessness and form but that he must render low-level perceptual structures in a medium from which we expect a high level of organization and complexity. This is one reason why *Parade's End* is frequently criticized for looseness and wordiness.

10. Moser, *The Life in the Fiction of Ford*, p. 131.

Going beyond Modernism
[Review of *The Rash Act*]   Cornelia Cook*

"The rash act . . . seems to have been inspired by a number of motives, not least amongst which was the prevailing dissoluteness and consequent depression that are now world wide." Capitalize "Rash Act" and this is a wholly plausible critical comment on Ford Madox Ford's twenty-seventh novel, the first in a series "meant," Ford wrote, "to do for the post-war world and the crisis what the Tietjens tetralogy did for the war." *The Rash Act* was published in 1933 and has happily been reissued by Carcanet with an introduction by C. H. Sisson. Its sequel, *Henry for Hugh*, which Ford called "by far the best written and the best constructed of all my books" appeared in New York in 1934, has never been published in this country, and remains sadly inaccessible to readers here. The reissue of that book is much to be desired.

In these novels of the Great Depression the "hero," an insufficiently suicidal American ex-millionaire renews acquaintance with and adopts the posthumous identity of an amply suicidal English millionaire who bears his own features, initials and surname. The theme of the double, familiar territory in Ford's fictions (as in those of his mentors James and Conrad) is taken to the favourite idealized and idyllic Provence of Ford's late works and allowed to govern a masterfully planned, (as Ford puts it) "elaborately time-shifted" fiction informed by socio-political criticism,

*From *English* 33, no. 146 (1984):159–67. Reprinted by permission of The English Association.

nostalgia and farce. In their "modernist" form, their patchwork language of cosmopolitan talk and literary echoes, and their uneasy comedy, these novels are eloquent beyond setting or subject of their historical moment.

The words quoted at the outset are those of no literary critic; they are the coroner's comment on a suicide reported in the *Times* Law Report of July 14, 1931, and selected by Ford for his novel's epigraph. The doubleness of reference detectable in the epigraph is thoroughly characteristic of this novel which deals in doubleness throughout. It deals its reader a double sense by looking janus-faced outward to the circumstantial world of "public events," human utterances, and material objects — the familiar "world" of an historical realism — and inward to its own artefactual existence as a "handling" of words and images, a pattern not of an "historic" reality but of its own "constructed" self. It fixes on doubleness as the subject of its comic plot, and formally, summoning a sequel to complete this comic development of the change-of-identity story which announces the divisions and desires inevitably displayed within the text of the realist author who must both become his creation for the purposes of imaginative verisimilitude and deny, by the exercise of his authority, its reality.

A species of doubling creates the circular progress of *The Rash Act* and *Henry for Hugh*. Ford reported of his "sympathetic nonentity" of a hero that "whatever he does — whatever feeble action he commits himself to — he always finds himself in exactly the same situation." The periods of Henry Martin Smith's existence which surface in the reported stream of impression and recollection to compose a chronology outside the narrative's shifting interior time, emerge as a series of repetitions, of episodes which so resemble each other that the present appears not to step away from the past, or to grow from it, but to mirror it. The emergent "character" of Henry Martin is therefore a static one; accumulated information fails to deepen it or enlarge our knowledge of it. This peculiarity persists in his experience upon "becoming" Hugh Monkton; the enforced passivity which overtakes Smith in this phase becomes an image for a character caught in a decreed condition not of consistency, but of sameness.

It is for this reason unfortunate that Sisson dismisses *Henry for Hugh* on the grounds that *The Rash Act* is a "rounded work" and "complete in itself." The terms have on the one hand an old-fashioned inadequacy and on the other a provoking relevance to the significant structure of the novels which rather demands the accessibility of *Henry for Hugh* than otherwise.

Arguing against the exclusion of *Last Post* from *Parade's End*, Sisson says "the twentieth-century conventions which require a novel to end 'with no absolute certainties about the past . . . or about the future' are not self-evidently superior to the conventions of the happy ending, and are now as worn." *Henry for Hugh* importantly complements *The Rash Act* precisely by supplying a ludicrously happy ending in which (while affording "no

absolute certainties about the past . . . or about the future") Henry Martin
has his identity returned to him, gets the girl, and disappears into a
Riviera sunset on his way to a final permutation of "exactly the same
situation." It is noticeable that in this train of events he behaves exactly as a
conventional "hero" should.

Ford's work in the 'thirties displays a movement away from the early
modernist modes which Ford called "Impressionist" and with which he,
along with the elder James and Conrad, is readily associated. A clue to the
tendencies — and conflicts — visible in Ford's attitudes and works of the
'thirties may be discovered in remarks found in *The English Novel* (1930),
the critical polemic with which Ford opened the decade: "From [seeing
that "such a thing as a hero does not exist"] to seeing that it is not
individuals but enterprises or groups that succeed or fail is a very small
step to take . . . it is not the mere death and still less the mere marriage of
an individual that brings an end either to a group or an enterprise . . .
when a seemingly indispensible individual disappears for one reason or
another from an enterprise, that adventure proceeds with equanimity and
very little shock." It is a perception Ford associates with the modern
moment — a culmination of historical development expressed by a literary
form (the modernist novel), as Ford argues in *The English Novel*'s opening
chapter (which bears its own sense of history in the Arnoldian title "The
function of the novel in the modern world"). The perception, however,
takes Ford's contemporary practice away from the realist basis of "impressionist" modernism. A strong sense of historic fatality unconsoled by a
vision of progress translates itself into an imposed primacy of plot. The
individual dilemma (consistently at issue in the fiction of James and
Conrad) as the centre of the fictional "affair" is rendered ironically in
fictions which emphasize the linguistic basis and the arbitrariness of
"character." The "aloof" author in Ford's later novels is not effaced within
the fiction; his God-like posture, however impersonal, is a self-advertising
one, executing a rigid determinism through which desire, intention and
value in the world of the fictions are mocked, and choice eliminated. The
irrelevance of the individual to the "adventure's" proceeding becomes a
kind of joke in Ford's late novels in which rewards and misfortunes occur
independently of merit or of effort, and fictional form masters its
"subject."

It has been suggested (by MacShane and Green) that the later fiction
reflects the hankering Ford confessed after an expressionist and musical art
such as he found in the "absolute imaginative literature" of the Trouba-
dours. The aloofness aimed at here, and detected by Ford in the Joyce of
Work in Progress turned radically away not only from realism but from the
communicative "significance" of words.

It seems that away from England in his Provençal retreat Ford was
inclined to relinquish those aspects of his once-revolutionary literary
practice that were most "Tory" — its thoughtful accommodation of histori-

cism and its altruist impulse. Though Ford continued to call his impulse "historic," these books offer a typifying image of a contemporary society so absurd as to mock realist projects of benefitting by revealing human affairs. The "outside" world of business, finance, the arts, recalled by Henry Martin is as grotesque as the improbable events and ludicrous situations of the "inside" world of the novel. That world is naturalized for us through Henry Martin's acceptance; we are tempted with him to accept its inconsistencies, its self-generated values, to turn our backs on the problems of survival, responsibility and value in the real world.

Ford called Henry Martin's experience (with a view to winning his publisher's indulgence) "a tragedy of these (crisis) years." Smith's "tragedy" is that, as representative of an unheroic, drifting, compromised culture, he is incapable of making a tragic end. That Hugh Monkton Smith, another last English Tory, should accomplish *his* suicide is entirely appropriate to the allegorical dimension of the story. Monkton Smith — impotent since the great War — whose continued existence is essential to the national economy and who therefore dare not threaten that existence by action, has ceased to live long since. Henry Martin, through the exchange of identity, inherits these disabilities and disabling responsibilities. Thus is set up an absurd concatenation of events, memories and speculations which make up the "affair" of this work and overshadow its historical-allegorical dimension, and in which "a tragedy of these (crisis) years" becomes a formal comedy, even a burlesque.

The Rash Act reads as something periously like a pastiche modernist novel. What Sisson takes for "an act of contemplation" in which Ford moves "through his own past — seen under various disguises — with great sureness of touch" seems to me less a sublime meditation than a self-aware joke. The narrative calls attention to its own "staged tragedy" which turns to "parody"; posturing as "destiny," the invisible author throws fish at his hero and allows the narrative to question the "meaning" of this, and to criticise its "execrable taste." Allusion in these novels to Ford's past — his literary career, methods, influences does not enrich the texture of the fictional "affair" but underlies the affair's fictionality; "subject" exists to throw the focus onto treatment.

The Rash Act effectively takes for its motto the Provencal epitaph *Saltavit, Placuit, Mortuus Est*. The reader's interest discovers itself in the deception, the charade, the double-act and its successful outcome — in the technical performance which constitutes the book's "dance" and yields its pleasure. Yet the Crisis is not, as Sisson insists, "of no more than incidental importance" to these novels. Like the Great War which preceded it (and which remains a crucial element in the history of both Smiths *in* the novels) the Great Depression enforced the recognition that "not individuals but enterprises . . . succeed or fail," that there *is* no "indispensible individual," that the great events of realist comedy and tragedy, marriage and death, and all they culminate are the constructed boundaries of a notion of character that is as outmoded in the Crisis world as Hugh Monkton Smith's cavalry sabre. Hugh Monkton Smith is not only a character, but an *idea* of character effectively killed off by *The Rash Act* — narrowly that of earlier Ford heroes, broadly that of the humanist basis of realist fiction. *That* Hugh Monkton Smith is a fiction within the novel, largely the creation of the admiring, escapist Henry Martin. Of consequence to the public world within the novel is Hugh Monkton, presider over the family firm, a nexus of industrial and financial activity. The visible public image of Monkton stability and prosperity, "he" is necessary to preserve both in the midst of global financial collapse. *This* aspect of character is what can be as easily occupied by the look-alike Henry Martin Aluin Smith. On that recognition the novel's plot, its subtle questioning of the primacy of the subjective self, and its valediction to the commitments of an earlier humanist modernism are built.

History in these novels is not problematic. It is not a source of values, but of fictions. History is made into instant myths (by Smith, his father, throughout a small-town new world, by gossip, and by a worldwide capitalist economy which needs not Hugh Monkton Allard Smith, but *a* Hugh Monkton Allard Smith). The past as a source of value here has been rendered a-historical, lodged in a sense of place, mythologized as a timeless moment of aesthetic pleasure-giving.

The creation of fictions itself becomes central in the novel with the change of identity. A fictional character is compelled to invent a new fictional self. Needless to say, it can't be done. Henry Martin must await the information his author will — and entertainingly does — provide, through the other "characters" who conspire with their creator to sustain the fiction, and through memories and observations which remain inaccessible to Henry Martin until verbalized for him. We are not allowed to forget that, however, "sympathetic," Henry Martin is a "nonentity" — a blank until words that are involuntarily his cohere to form a past for him; an object who takes his identity from description by others (by Hugh Monkton, a policeman, a hotel-waiter, an estate agent, a would-be-mistress, and scheming lover), who is defined by a series of likenesses or possibilities (including his relationships with Hugh Smith, with his father, with the chance-met red-nosed Smith who predicts his financial nemesis, and with his own proliferating selves, Pisto-Brittle Smith, White Man Smith of Magdalen, and the conflicting subjects he labels Henry Martin I, II and III). The frantic and sustained making of the "maker" (Smith, once Faber) is but one aspect of the comedy of self-consciousness in this work.

Henry Martin Smith sounds like another Dowell. "He began to think that he knew nothing in the world about anything — or at least about life. People's lives. How did they live . . . Even where?" But *The Good Soldier* creates, in the tensions between what is unknown and what can be learned, between what is commented on and what informs our moral understanding, a space in which the reader must actively know and judge or confront his own limitations in these areas. In *The Rash Act* and its sequel ontological lacunae are of a different order. Henry Martin tardily piecing together in *The Rash Act* the truth of the past deceptions which have deprived him of mistresses, wife, fortune and occupation, fails comprehensively to notice the crucial communication made to him by the desperate Hugh Monkton. The event may be seen as a pathetic sign of the inhumane times and as a comic instance of Smith's incapacity as an independent cognizant or active agent. Ford mocks his character's help-lessness (which is not shared by the reader) through another character's exclamation which the reader's position endorses: "opportunities [to see] . . . you have them. And you don't see what's as near to you as your moron's face to your moron's nose." The sharer of Henry Martin's story does not wait for the next discovery of a Proustian narrator; he waits to see what the character will be allowed to know. *Henry for Hugh* intensifies this awareness, for here Henry Martin lacks the "memory," the information necessary to "be" his new self. The informing activity here is visibly performed by others who tactfully fill Henry in on what he "knows."

In *Henry for Hugh* Henry Martin knows little about the life he must enact but his limitations are irrelevant; what his memory and intuition fail to supply, the desirable and omnicompetent Eudoxie supplies in impossible abundance so that there is no possibility of Henry's "not knowing." Eudoxie knows everything; she manages our hero as completely as if she were the author of his fate. Our attention fixes on the unravelling and re-constitution of the past in the present, on the suspense inherent not (as in *The Good Soldier* or *Last Post*) in the causes of the present state, but in the present deception and the outcome of the plottings surrounding and enveloping the hero. Ford concluded his comments on modernism in *The March of Literature* with the remark that "even the 'time shift' device which in the early days of the century drove the established critics to utter paeans of fury . . . has been perforce adopted by every writer who has since sat down to concoct a detective story." *The Rash Act* and *Henry for Hugh* together approximate to that form; curiosity is satisfied in the completion of plot. Further, language is all-sufficient to the book's concerns (how radically different from the sombre obscurities of *Heart of Darkness*, the blatant ambivalences of *The Good Soldier*, the interplay of relatives and absolute in *Nostromo* or *A Man Could Stand Up*); "impres-sionism," like the sun on the sea in *The Rash Act's* opening paragraph, gives a depth-denying "life" to an infinitely variable surface.

"Grotesque" is a word which repeatedly invades Henry Smith's consciousness and largely suits his predicament. It is through this aspect of his novel that Ford weds comment on his time with comment on his art, for if Smith has no "entity" as a character we must ask what is reflected in him. "A grotesque . . . message from Destiny opened the ball." "That would be grotesque . . . But why should you not be grotesque?" Smith is a man of some physical and sexual prowess condemned to inactivity in both areas. What condemns him is a promiscuity not simply sexual but profoundly moral. Unsuccessful in realizing an identity through repeated litanies of self-description ("free, male and twenty-one," "six-foot tall in his stockings") and through efforts of recollection, his desire to be another, to displace himself for his own eyes to see, and to *use* others is as promiscuous as his desire to *know* others is slight and largely affected. A Lothario Dowell may be seen as a leap from Edwardian innocence (however pernicious) to post-war decadence; it may also be seen as a leap from conservative modernist fiction to bitter parody. Such a book implicates reader and writer in positions which question the motivation of the very acts of reading and writing. Smith's double—his childish ideal self and absurdly thwarted secret sharer—is similarly, a grotesque version of the Marwoodian Ford hero, no longer the repository of tradition, morality, and communal values. The world they inhabit is grotesque, not as Western Europe in the 'thirties was made so by the menaces of economic depression, moral desperation and the opportunism of political power, but as, in the enforced "theatre" of Henry Martin's self-preoccupation, it is presented (in a way characteristic of much 'thirties fiction) through caricature and burlesque. Whereas Dowell glimpsed a madhouse, Smith surrenders himself to a world entrapped in farce. In *Henry for Hugh* the novel again calls attention to its own uneasy comedy through Smith's embarrassed self-reflection "And yet there was something *louche* . . . He imagined that what he most feared was ridicule."

Antony Burgess said upon reading the reprinted *Rash Act*, "This is modernism, which died in 1939, along with Ford Madox Ford." *The Rash Act* suggests that Ford, as sensitive to the time as ever, has himself gone beyond modernism, to register his distaste for and despair of the modern moment in a literature of futility and self-absorption. Burgess says "*The Rash Act* is so patently what fictional modernism is, or was"—it may be so as patently as patent leather is leather. The novel executes a perfect modernist exercise in form; lambent passages of description remind us that this is the Ford who, Pound said, "knew about WRITING." It indulges the senses with abundant immediate detail, to make "luminous" a vacant or self-denigrating content.

In such a subtle questioning of the fictional enterprise, in so thoroughly obstructing the ostensible realism of his text and its subjective centre, the novel which Ford called so "correct in handling" of its modernist form suggests an uneasy groping in the direction of post-modernist awareness. It might better be said that this is the execution of modernism by Ford Madox Ford, amounting to a death: indeed a rash act, and a radical one.

Poet, Memoirist, Social Critic

Mr. Hueffer and the Prose Tradition in Verse [Review of *Collected Poems*, 1914]

Ezra Pound*

In a country in love with amateurs, in a country where the incompetent have such beautiful manners, and personalities so fragile and charming, that one can not bear to injure their feelings by the introduction of competent criticism, it is well that one man should have a vision of perfection and that he should be sick to the death and disconsolate because he can not attain it.

Mr. Yeats wrote years ago that the highest poetry is so precious that one should be willing to search many a dull tome to find and gather the fragments. As touching poetry this was, perhaps, no new feeling. Yet where nearly everyone else is still dominated by an eighteenth-century verbalism, Mr. Hueffer has had this instinct for prose. It is he who has insisted, in the face of a still Victorian press, upon the importance of good writing as opposed to the opalescent word, the rhetorical tradition. Stendhal had said, and Flaubert, De Maupassant and Turgenev had proved, that "prose was the higher act" — at least their prose.

Of course it is impossible to talk about perfection without getting yourself very much disliked. It is even more difficult in a capital where everybody's Aunt Lucy or Uncle George has written something or other, and where the victory of any standard save that of mediocrity would at once banish so many nice people from the temple of immortality. So it comes about that Mr. Hueffer is the best critic in England, one might say the only critic of any importance. What he says today the press, the reviewers, who hate him and who disparage his books, will say in about nine years' time, or possibly sooner. Shelley, Yeats, Swinburne, with their "unacknowledged legislators," with "Nothing affects these people except our conversation," with "The rest live under us;" Rémy De Gourmont, when he says that most men think only husks and shells of the thoughts that have been already lived over by others, have shown their very just appreciation of the system of echoes, of the general vacuity of public

*From Ezra Pound, *Literary Essays of Ezra Pound*. Copyright 1935 by Ezra Pound. Originally appeared in *Poetry* 4 (1914):111–20. Reprinted by permission of New Directions Publishing Corporation and of the Editor of *Poetry*.

opinion. America is like England, America is very much what England would be with the two hundred most interesting people removed. One's life is the score of this two hundred with whom one happens to have made friends. I do not see that we need to say the rest live under them, but it is certain that what these people say comes to pass. They live in their mutual credence, and thus they live things over and fashion them before the rest of the world is aware. I dare say it is a Cassandra-like and useless faculty, at least from the world's point of view. Mr. Hueffer has possessed the peculiar faculty of "foresight," or of constructive criticism, in a pre-eminent degree. Real power will run any machine. Mr. Hueffer said fifteen years ago that a certain unknown Bonar Law would lead the conservative party. Five years ago he said with equal impartiality that Mr. D. H. Lawrence would write notable prose, that Mr. De la Mare could write verses, and that *Chance* would make Conrad popular.

Of course if you think things ten or fifteen or twenty years before anyone else thinks them you will be considered absurd and ridiculous. Mr. Allen Upward, thinking with great lucidity along very different lines, is still considered absurd. Some professor feels that if certain ideas gain ground he will have to rewrite his lectures, some parson feels that if certain other ideas are accepted he will have to throw up his position. They search for the forecaster's weak points.

Mr. Hueffer is still underestimated for another reason also: namely, that we have not yet learned that prose is as precious and as much to be sought after as verse, even its shreds and patches. So that, if one of the finest chapters in English is hidden in a claptrap novel, we cannot weigh the vision which made it against the weariness or the confusion which dragged down the rest of the work. Yet we would do this readily with a poem. If a novel have a form as distinct as that of a sonnet, and if its workmanship be as fine as that of some Pleiade rondel, we complain of the slightness of the motive. Yet we would not deny praise to the rondel. So it remains for a prose craftsman like Mr. Arnold Bennett to speak well of Mr. Hueffer's prose, and for a verse-craftsman like myself to speak well of his verses. And the general public will have little or none of him because he does not put on pontifical robes, because he does not take up the megaphone of some known and accepted pose, and because he makes enemies among the stupid by his rather engaging frankness.

We may as well begin reviewing the *Collected Poems* with the knowledge that Mr. Hueffer is a keen critic and a skilled writer of prose, and we may add that he is not wholly unsuccessful as a composer, and that he has given us, in "On Heaven," the best poem yet written in the "twentieth-century fashion."

I drag in these apparently extraneous matters in order to focus attention on certain phases of significance, which might otherwise escape the hurried reader in a volume where the actual achievement is uneven. Coleridge has spoken of "the miracle that might be wrought simply by one man's feeling a thing more clearly or more poignantly than anyone had felt it before." The last century showed us a fair example when Swinburne awoke to the fact that poetry was an art, not merely a vehicle for the propagation of doctrine. England and Germany are still showing the effects of his perception. I can not belittle my belief that Mr. Hueffer's realization that poetry should be written at least as well as prose will have as wide a result. He himself will tell you that it is "all Christina Rossetti," and that "it was not Wordsworth, for Wordsworth was so busied about the ordinary word that he never found time to think about *le mot juste*."

As for Christina, Mr. Hueffer is a better critic than I am, and I would be the last to deny that a certain limpidity and precision are the ultimate qualities of style; yet I can not accept his opinion. Christina had these qualities, it is true—in places, but they are to be found also in Browning and even in Swinburne at rare moments. Christina very often sets my teeth on edge, — and so for that matter does Mr. Hueffer. But it is the function of criticism to find what a given work is, not what it is not. It is also the faculty of a capital or of high civilization to value a man for some rare ability, to make use of him and not hinder him or itself by asking of him faculties which he does not possess.

Mr. Hueffer may have found certain properties of style first, for himself, in Christina, but others have found them elsewhere, notably in Arnaut Daniel and in Guido and in Dante, where Christina herself would have found them. Still there is no denying that there is less of the *ore rotundo* in Christina's work than in that of her contemporaries, and that there is also in Hueffer's writing a clear descent from such passages as:

> I listened to their honest chat:
>   Said one: "Tomorrow we shall be
> Plod plod along the featureless sands
>   And coasting miles and miles of sea."
> Said one: "Before the turn of tide
>   We will achieve the eyrie-seat."
> Said one: "To-morrow shall be like
>   To-day, but much more sweet."

We find the qualities of what some people are calling "the modern cadence" in this strophe, also in "A Dirge," in "Up Hill," in—

> Somewhere or other there must surely be
> The face not seen, the voice not heard,

and in—

> Sometimes I said: "It is an empty name
>   I long for; to a name why should I give
> The peace of all the days I have to live?"—
>   Yet gave it all the same.

Mr. Hueffer brings to his work a prose training such as Christina never had, and it is absolutely the devil to try to quote snippets from a man whose poems are gracious impressions, leisurely, low-toned. One would quote "The Starling," but one would have to give the whole three pages of it. And one would like to quote patches out of the curious medley, "To All the Dead," — save that the picturesque patches aren't the whole or the feel of it; or Süssmund's capricious "Address," a sort of "Inferno" to the "Heaven" which we are printing for the first time in another part of this issue. But that also is too long, so I content myself with the opening of an earlier poem, "Finchley Road."

> As we come up at Baker Street
> Where tubes and trains and 'buses meet
> There's a touch of fog and a touch of sleet;
> And we go on up Hampstead way
> Toward the closing in of day. . . .
>
> You should be a queen or a duchess rather,
> Reigning, instead of a warlike father,
> In peaceful times o'er a tiny town,
> Where all the roads wind up and down
> From your little palace — a small, old place
> Where every soul should know your face
> And bless your coming.

I quote again, from a still earlier poem ["Views"] where the quiet of his manner is less marked:

> Being in Rome I wonder will you go
>   Up to the Hill. But I forget the name . . .
> Aventine? Pincio? No: I do not know
>   I was there yesterday and watched. You came.

(I give the opening only to "place" the second portion of the poem.)

> Though you're in Rome you will not go, my You,
> Up to that Hill . . . but I forget the name.
> Aventine? Pincio? No, I never knew . . .
> I was there yesterday. You never came.
>
> I have that Rome; and you, you have a Me,
> You have a Rome, and I, I have my You;
> My Rome is not your Rome; my You, not you.
>   . . . . . . For, if man knew woman
> I should have plumbed your heart; if woman, man,
> Your Me should be true I . . . If in your day —
> You who have mingled with my soul in dreams,
> You who have given my life an aim and purpose,
> A heart, an imaged form — if in your dreams
> You have imagined unfamiliar cities

And me among them, I shall never stand
Beneath your pillars or your poplar groves, . . .
Images, simulacra, towns of dreams
That never march upon each other's borders,
And bring no comfort to each other's hearts!

I present this passage, not because it is an example of Mr. Hueffer's no longer reminiscent style, but because, like much that appeared four years ago in *Songs from London*, or earlier still in *From Inland*, it hangs in my memory. And so little modern work does hang in one's memory, and these books created so little excitement when they appeared. One took them as a matter of course, and they're not a matter of course, and still less is the later work a matter of course. Oh well, you all remember the preface to the collected poems with its passage about the Shepherd's Bush exhibition, for it appeared first as a pair of essays in *Poetry*, so there is no need for me to speak further of Mr. Hueffer's aims or of his prose, or of his power to render an impression.

There is in his work another phase that depends somewhat upon his knowledge of instrumental music. Dante has defined a poem as a composition of words set to music, and the intelligent critic will demand that either the composition of words or the music shall possess a certain interest, or that there be some aptitude in their jointure together. It is true that since Dante's day—and indeed his day and Cassella's saw a re-beginning of it—"music" and "poetry" have drifted apart, and we have had a third thing which is called "word music." I mean we have poems which are read or even, in a fashion, intoned, and are "musical" in some sort of complete or inclusive sense that makes it impossible or inadvisable to "set them to music." I mean obviously such poems as the First Chorus of *Atalanta* or many of Mr. Yeats' lyrics. The words have a music of their own, and a second "musician's" music is an impertinence or an intrusion.

There still remains the song to sing: to be "set to music," and of this sort of poem Mr. Hueffer has given us notable examples in his rendering of Von der Vogelweide's "Tandaradei" and, in lighter measure, in his own "The Three-Ten":

When in the prime and May-day time dead lovers went a-walking,
How bright the grass in lads' eyes was, how easy poet's talking!
Here were green hills and daffodils, and copses to contain them:
Daisies for floors did front their doors agog for maids to chain
    them.
So when the ray of rising day did pierce the eastern heaven
Maids did arise to make the skies seem brighter far by seven.
Now here's a street where 'bus routes meet, and 'twixt the wheels
    and paving
Standeth a lout who doth hold out flowers not worth the
    having.

But see, but see! The clock strikes three above the Kilburn
*   Station.*
Those maids, thank God, are 'neath the sod and all their
*   generation.*

What she shall wear who'll soon appear, it is not hood nor
    wimple,
But by the powers there are no flowers so stately or so simple.
And paper shops and full 'bus tops confront the sun so brightly,
That, come three-ten, no lovers then had hearts that beat so lightly
As ours or loved more truly,
Or found green shades or flowered glades to fit their loves more
    duly.
And see, and see! 'Tis ten past three above the Kilburn Station,
Those maids, thank God! are 'neath the sod and all their
*   generation.*

Oh well, there are very few song writers in England, and it's a simple old-fashioned song with a note of futurism in its very lyric refrain; and I dare say you will pay as little attention to it as I did five years ago. And if you sing it aloud, once over, to yourself, I dare say you'll be just as incapable of getting it out of your head, which is perhaps one test of a lyric.

It is not, however, for Mr. Hueffer's gift of song-writing that I have reviewed him at such length; this gift is rare but not novel. I find him significant and revolutionary because of his insistence upon clarity and precision, upon the prose tradition; in brief, upon efficient writing — even in verse.

    Note

Mr. Hueffer is not an *imagiste*, but an impressionist. Confusion has arisen because of my inclusion of one of his poems in the *Anthologie des Imagistes*.

The Function of Rhythm [Review of *On Heaven and Poems Written on Active Service*, 1918]

Conrad Aiken*

In the Preface to his new book of poems, *On Heaven*, Mr. Ford Madox Hueffer remarks: "The greater part of the book is, I notice on putting it together, in either *vers libre* or rhymed *vers libre*. I am not going

*From *Collected Criticism of Conrad Aiken*, Oxford University Press. Copyright 1935, 1939, 1940, 1942, 1951, 1958 by Conrad Aiken. Reprinted by permission of Brandt & Brandt Literary Agents, Inc. Originally appeared in *Dial* 65 (1918):417–18.

to apologize for this or to defend *vers libre* as such. It is because I simply can't help it. *Vers libre* is the only medium in which I can convey any more intimate moods. *Vers libre* is a very jolly medium in which to write and to read, if it be read conversationally and quietly. And anyhow, symmetrical or rhymed verse is for me a cramped and difficult medium — or an easy and uninteresting one." One recollects, further, that Mr. Hueffer has in the past been also insistent, in theory and in practice, on the point that poetry should be at least as well written as prose — that, in other words, it must be good prose before it can be good poetry. Taken together, these ideas singularly echo a preface written one hundred and twenty odd years ago — Wordsworth's preface to the Lyrical Ballads. In the appendix to that volume Wordsworth, it will be recalled, remarked that in works of imagination the ideas, in proportion as they are valuable, whether in prose or verse, "require and exact one and the same language." And throughout he insisted on doing away with all merely decorative language and on using the speech of daily life.

On the matter of meter or rhythm, however, the two poets are not so entirely in agreement as they might appear to be. They are in agreement, it might be said, just in so far as they both seem inclined to regard the question of rhythm as only of minor or incidental importance. "Metre," said Wordsworth, "is only adventitious to composition." Mr. Hueffer, as is seen above, candidly admits that he avoids the strictest symmetrical forms because to use them well is too difficult. Do both poets perhaps underestimate the value of rhythm? In the light of the widespread vogue of free verse at present, it is a question interesting to speculate upon. And Mr. Hueffer's poems, which are excellent, afford us a pleasant opportunity.

Wordsworth's theory as to the function of rhythm was peculiar. He believed that as poetry consists usually in a finer distillation of the emotions than is found in prose, some check must be used lest the excitation arising therefrom, whether pleasurable or painful, exceed desired bounds. Rhythm is to act as a narcotic. "The co-expression of something regular, something to which the mind has been accustomed . . . in a less excited state cannot but have great efficacy in tempering . . . the passion by an admixture of ordinary feeling. . . ." Only by way of incidental emendation did Wordsworth suggest that in some cases meter might "contribute to impart passion to the words." This is perhaps to put the cart before the horse. Mr. Hueffer, on the other hand, while equally regarding or appearing to regard meter as a subsidiary element, raises a different and subtler objection to it. In common with a good many champions of free verse he feels that free verse is better than symmetrical verse for the conveyance of more intimate moods. This is a plausible and intriguing theory. At first glance it seems only natural that in a freer and more discursive medium the poet should find himself better able to fix upon the more impalpable nuances of feeling. But a steadier inspection leaves one not quite so sure. If one can convey subtler moods in free verse than in symmetrical verse, might one not logically argue that prose could be subtler still than either? And we should have reached the conclusion that poetry should employ, to reach its maximum efficiency, not only the language but also the rhythms of prose — in other words, that it should *be* prose.

The logic is perhaps not impeccable; but it is sufficiently strong to suggest the presence of some error. If prose could convey subtler emotional moods and impressions than poetry, why write poetry? We suspect however that the reverse is true, and that it is poetry which possesses the greater and subtler power of evocation. But the language is, largely speaking, the same in both. And consequently we must assume that this superior quality of evocativeness or magic which we associate with poetry has something to do with the fact that, more artfully than in prose, the language is *arranged*. And this arrangement is, obviously, in great part a matter of rhythm.

This brings us back, accordingly, to the afterthought in Wordsworth's appendix to the *Lyrical Ballads* — the idea that meter may impart "passion" to words. The truth of this seems irrefragable. When a poet, therefore, discards rhythm he is discarding perhaps the most powerful single *artifice* of poetry which is at his disposal — the particular artifice, moreover, which more than any other enables the poet to obtain a psychic control over his reader, to exert a sort of hypnosis over him. Rhythm is persuasive; it is the very stuff of life. It is not surprising therefore that things can be said in rhythm which otherwise cannot be said at all; paraphrase a fine passage of poetry into prose and in the dishevelment the ghost will have escaped. A good many champions of free verse would perhaps dispute this. They would fall back on the theory that, at any rate, certain moods more colloquial and less intense than those of the highest type of poetry, and less colloquial and more intense than those of the highest type of prose, could find their aptest expression in this form which lies halfway between. But even here their position will not be altogether secure, at least in theory. Is any contemporary poetry more colloquial or intimate than that of T. S. Eliot, who is predominantly a metrical poet? It is doubtful. Metrical verse, in other words, can accomplish anything that free verse can, and can do it more powerfully. What we inevitably come to is simply the fact that for some poets free verse is an easier medium than metrical verse, and consequently allows them greater efficiency. It is desirable therefore that such poets should employ free verse. They only transgress when they argue from this that free verse is the finer form. This it is not.

The reasons for this would take us beyond the mere question of rhythm. When Wordsworth remarked that one could re-read with greater pleasure a painful or tragic passage of poetry than a similar passage of prose, although he mistakenly ascribed this as altogether due to the presence of meter, he nevertheless touched closely upon the real principle at issue. For compared with the pleasure derived from the reading of prose, the pleasure of reading poetry is two-natured: in addition to the pleasure afforded by the ideas presented, or the material (a pleasure which prose equally affords), there is also the more purely esthetic delight of the art itself, a delight which might be described as the sense of perfection in complexity, or the sense of arrangement. This arrangement is not solely a question of rhythm. It is also concerned with the selection of elements in the language more vividly sensuous and with the more adroit combination of ideas with a view to setting them off to sharper advantage. Given two poems in which the theme is equally delightful and effective on the first reading, that poem of the two which develops the theme with the richer and more perfect complexity of technique will longer afford pleasure in re-reading. It is, in other words, of more permanent value.

Mr. Hueffer confesses in advance that he prefers a less to a more complex form of art. As a matter of fact Mr. Hueffer is too modest. When he speaks of free verse he does not mean, to the extent in which it is usually meant, verse without rhythm. At his freest he is not far from a genuinely rhythmic method; and in many respects his sense of rhythm is both acute and individual. Three poems in his book would alone make it worth printing: "Antwerp," which is one of the three or four brilliant poems inspired by the war; "Footsloggers," which though not so good, is none the less very readable; and "On Heaven," the poem which gives the volume its name. It is true that in all three of these poems Mr. Hueffer very often employs a rhythm which is almost as dispersed as that of prose; but the point to be emphatically remarked is that he does so only by way of variation on the given norm of movement, which is essentially and predominantly rhythmic. Variation of this sort is no more or less than good artistry; and Mr. Hueffer is a very competent artist, in whose hands even the most captious reader feels instinctively and at once secure. Does he at times overdo the dispersal of rhythm? Perhaps. There are moments, in "Antwerp" and in "On Heaven," when the relief of the reader on coming to a forcefully rhythmic passage is so marked as to make him suspect that the rhythm of the passage just left was not forceful enough. Mr. Hueffer is of a discursive temperament, viewed from whatever angle, and this leads him inevitably to over-inclusiveness and moments of let-down. One feels that a certain amount of cutting would improve both "Antwerp" and "On Heaven."

Yet one would hesitate to set about it oneself. Both poems are delightful. Mr. Hueffer writes with gusto and imagination, and—what is perhaps rarer among contemporary poets—with tenderness. "On Heaven" may not be the very highest type of poetry—it is clearly of the more colloquial sort, delightfully expatiative, skilful in its use of the more subdued tones of prose—but it takes hold of one, and that is enough. One accepts it for what it is, not demanding of it what the author never intended to give it—that higher degree of perfection in intricacy, that more intense and all-fusing synthesis, which would have bestowed on it the sort of beauty that more permanently endures.

The Poems of Ford Madox Ford
[Review of *Collected Poems*, 1936]   John Peale Bishop*

Though the *Collected Poems* of Ford Madox Ford now appear for the first time in an American edition, it is not the first volume of that title to be published. A *Preface to Collected Poems*, dated 1911, is here reprinted, with some apology for the frivolity of its tone, none for its opinions. This is as it should be. For if it is hard not to resent the patronizing attitude which Mr. Ford then took toward William Butler Yeats, it must be allowed him that, while his own poetic art shows a sure consistent gain down through the war period, there is, from first to last, no essential change in his point of view. In 1914 there was an English edition of *Collected Poems* which was reissued in 1916. The present volume gathers together all that Mr. Ford has written in verse, from "The Wind's Quest," his first poem, printed in 1891, through *Buckshee: Last Poems*, finished in Paris only last year. His famous "On Heaven," which first appeared in *Poetry* in 1914, has here its pride of place, and is followed by the equally unforgettable "Antwerp." From these two poems we are led, in the familiar Ford manner, back and forth through time until we have covered a career of forty-five years.

Mr. Ford's position as a poet has been somewhat over-topped by his place as a writer of prose. For it has been his fortune — and it is this that has won him, in so many cities and in more than one country, the esteem and affection of many writers younger than he — to insist upon the professional attitude. He has done it by precept and, more importantly, by example. The novelist might, as he so often told us, practice a *métier du chien*. It was still a *métier*. And nothing less than a complete consciousness of the craft would do. Of course, he was not alone among his contemporaries in holding that the French had a far finer and fuller sense of what it meant to construct a novel than the English; around the turn of the century there were not a few who spoke and wrote his language and like him followed the cult of conscience, ready at any instant to call upon Flaubert as their only saint. But of them none survive who has proved more constant to that faith; none was ever more devout than Ford Madox Ford.

His approach to the novel is in the French manner. But when it comes to poetry, Mr. Ford would have us believe that he is a man of England. It is

*From *Poetry* 50 (1937):336–41. Reprinted by permission of Jonathan Bishop.

a country where, as a living French poet has observed, poems grow like grass, — that is to say with apparent ease and an incomparable freshness, secretly sustained by centuries of care. Ford Madox Ford disclaims too profound a concern with poetry, either his own, or others'. If, when he starts a novel, he knows from beginning to the end just how each word is to be placed, he knows — or so he says — practically nothing of how his poems are made. They come to him — a little tune in the head, then words, and then more words, on paper. How should he say if they are good or bad? He has read so little poetry. When he opens the morning paper, it is to turn first to the cricket scores.

This need not really deceive us. Like Congreve, who told Voltaire he did not wish to be visited as a dramatist, Mr. Ford, the poet, prefers to be thought of as among the country gentlemen. Their class, it might be remembered, has made no small contribution to English literature.

Before the War came, Mr. Ford was able to bring to the writing of verse not only the skill and scrupulousness which have distinguished his best novels, but also a good many tricks of his conscious trade. There are, from first to last in his work, poems which have the April spontaneity of grass; but they are not his best poems. At his best, he will be found almost invariably not to have departed too far from his methods in prose. This discourse which is a record of his own emotions and is meant, too, to record the contemporary world; which is so realistic on the surface, so romantic in its depths; which is never so pleased as when adding one discordant passage to another; which slides as smoothly as a *Wagon-Lit* from place to place, and at dead of night from a known country to one that is strange; which is careless with the years and indifferent to the clock as memory is: where have we encountered it before? The verse has a strong insistent, uneven beat; the rhymes arrive unexpectedly. But this cosmopolitan speech, whose English slips so readily into a French or a German phrase, which pauses scarcely an instant and with only a touch of superiority before it turns to slang: where did it come from — if not from the prose of Ford Madox Ford? When he began writing verse, it was under those influences which a young Englishman of independent tastes might have been expected to feel just before the close of the century. They were soon discarded. Mr. Ford's own manner seems to have been rather easily come by; it has been worn since with comfortable assurance, like an old country-coat of good cut and the best tweed. If at times something in a poem reminds us of one of his contemporaries, that is only because his aim and theirs happen to coincide.

Mr. Ford's contribution to the poetry of his time was to assist in bringing it nearer to the art of prose. It was, when he did it, a necessary thing to do. There were others: Ezra Pound also knew that if poetry was to live and not die in a living and dying world, it must, in his own phrase, catch up with prose; but none of the others knew so much about prose as Ford Madox Ford did.

It is thus that poetry has always been renewed. Jules Romains, in his recent *Preface à l'Homme Blanc*, reminds us that it was so in France, for as late as his own boyhood the charge he constantly heard levelled against Victor Hugo was one of *prosaïsme*, while in the *lycées* Baudelaire was still referred to as a *prosaïeur froid et alambique*. When the Muse's sandal is bound too strictly, there is nothing for her to do but loosen it and for a time go barefoot. When too much that he sees about him in the world is forbidden to the poet there is nothing he can do but lay violent hands on the immense matter of prose and seize whatever he thinks he can appropriate.

So little is now forbidden, that it is not altogether easy for us to conceive how difficult this was for an English poet in the decade before the War. Mr. Ford could conclude a poem on the death of Queen Victoria with these straightforward lines:

> A shock,
> A change in the beat of the clock,
> And the ultimate change that we fear feels
> a little less far.

But he had to go through no small amount of rather facile poetizing—

> Keep your brooding sorrows for dewy misty hollows,
> Here's blue sky and lark song, drink the air—

before he could come to

> This is Charing Cross:
> It is midnight;
> There is a great crowd
> And no light.

And it is precisely because there were difficulties to be surmounted that there remains so much that is tough and enduring in these poems, despite their constant use of not too particular sentiment.

> They await the lost.
> They await the lost that shall never leave the dock;
> They await the lost that shall never come again
>   by the train
> To the embraces of all these women with dead faces;
> They await the lost who lie dead in trench and
>   barrier and foss,
> In the dark of the night.
> This is Charing Cross; it is past one of the clock;
> There is very little light.
>
> There is so much pain.

This gives, as does no other poem, the feel of a great London in the midst of the war. And more than that, "Antwerp" remains one of the distinguished poems of our time.

The Landowner in Revolt
[Review of *Great Trade Route*]

Graham Greene*

Great Trade Route—that is Mr. Ford's personal dream of a past golden age, a huge oval belt extending from Cathay east and west of the fortieth parallel north through Europe up to the southern coast of England, a place of perfect peace and culture. "The Sacred Merchants were at once civilizers, gift bringers, educators and the trainers of priesthoods." It is never clear at what period this dream existed in fact; but that doesn't really matter, for to Mr. Ford the Great Trade Route means "a frame of mind to which, unless we return, our Occidental civilization is doomed."

Mr. Ford's genius has always been aristocratic. His flirtation with the Fabians was of the briefest; his real heroes were Tories and landowners, Tietjens and the Good Soldier. Perhaps that is why Mr. Ford, so incontestably our finest living novelist and perhaps the only novelist since Henry James to contribute much technically to his art, is not very widely read. The world, absorbed in the Communist-Fascist dog-fight, is ill prepared to listen to this Tory philosopher who finds the Conservative politician as little to his taste as any other. And yet men of Mr. Ford's character have much to offer: there is something disagreeably easy in the notion that only two political philosophies can exist and that we must choose between them. Mr. Ford is a Catholic, though he has seldom been in sympathy with his Church, and it is no coincidence that the subject of *Great Trade Route* is similar to that of the recent Pastoral Letter issued by the Catholic Bishops in this country. There must always seem something a little parvenu in the fierce self-absorption of the two new political creeds: an atmosphere of popular science, "how wonderful this wireless, this electricity, this radium, this twentieth century," to members of an international organization which has existed for nearly two thousand years.

Mr. Ford's solution, like that of the Catholic Bishops, is the Small Producer, as against the big individual capitalist and the small communist cog. He would have every man a part-time agriculturalist, because such a man is free in a sense unrecognized by either Fascist or Communist, free from the State ideal. "I want to belong to a nation of small producers, with some local, but no national feeling at all."

*From *London Mercury* 35 (February 1937):422–24. Reprinted by permission of Laurence Pollinger Limited.

The inhabitants of the Great Trade Route to-day "never taste vegetables fresh from the beds, fruit fresh from the trees, bread from wheat not manured by chemicals, meats not rendered unassimilable by refrigeration and again by chemicals. . . . So their brains are for ever starved of good blood, their minds are incapable of reflection, courage or stability. . . . And, carrying on its back a screaming Mass Production the bronze bull that is the Machine Age charges the brazen wall called Crisis."

Mr. Ford defines the Small Producer: "He is a man who with a certain knowledge of various crafts can set his hand to most kinds of work that go to the maintenance of humble existences. He can mend or make a rough chest of drawers; he will make shift to sole a shoe or make a passable pair of sandals; he will contrive or repair hurdles, platters, scythe-handles, styes, shingle roofs, harrows. But above all, he can produce and teach his family to produce good food according to the seasons." It is not a low ideal; it is the ideal of a country gentleman who knows his job; it is in the tradition behind Tietjens, and during this long and rambling journey, while Mr. Ford spots the villain Mass Production (little cellophane packets of corn sold at a high price on land where it had once been cheap as air), some readers will find their chief reward in vivid and dramatic asides which recall the novelist of the Tietjens series: Bismarck "whom I remember to have seen walking along the Poppelsdorfer Allee after his fall, his head dejected and his great hound dejected also, following him, his immense dewlaps almost touching his master's heel;" the bourgeoisie of Flemington: "extraordinarily silent men with harsh, hanging hands and Abraham-Lincoln-like faces who sat for hours without moving or speaking in rooms all shining linoleum, bentwood furniture, and tombstone-like sewing-machine cases."

Their chief reward, because not unexpectedly the landowner with his appeal for "a change of heart" is less practical than the ecclesiastic, who has the technique at hand for "changing hearts." He is a romantic. The enemy of the Great Trade Route was the barbarous North, and Mr. Ford still questionably stages his conflict in the terms of North and South, Yankee against Southerner, Lancashire against Kent. "A clear, cold, tinny note of regions where food is not touched by the human hand—the note of grim peoples now and then trying to be cheerful in creditable circumstances—of regions where honesty is only a policy on a par with the other policy which leads septentrionals to recommend their raiding generals to leave invaded peoples only their eyes to weep with." There may be truth in this picture of the barbarian North, but to its threat Mr. Ford presents only an unequivocal pacifism: he won't fight even for his small holdings, and he never answers satisfactorily the thoughts in all our minds, that Hitler is a southern Teuton and that it was Italy who first broke the peace in Europe.

Impressions of the "Impressionists"
[Review of *Mightier Than the Sword*]

V. S. Pritchett*

The effect of the Great War upon English life is only just being felt in literature, for we are only now beginning to see the work of a generation that was untouched by any serious pre-war memory. How very different that other world was a glance at Mr. Ford Madox Ford's portraits of men like Turgenev, Hardy, Hudson, Conrad, Stephen Crane, Henry James, Galsworthy and Lawrence will show. Impressionist, Mr. Ford calls his time. Rebellious, he says, against the moral purpose of the "Victorian eunuchs and the elderly widow," romantic but with due stress on the sinister side of things even in Mr. Wells. For if you are neither a Christian nor a reformer, original sin is released from its doctrinal bonds to grow and flower in the imagination in spectacular, hot-house fashion. Hardy has his stage Fates, James his unmentionable whispers of corruption, as obvious to him as Blake's angels of darkness were to Blake, Galsworthy his haunting guilts, Wells his anti-human vapours, Conrad his impalpable betrayals. Even a writer appearing among this group, as late as Lawrence did, finds an exotic Satan in the mind of civilization itself.

They did not much care (not even Henry James) for civilization, except in so far as its corruption fascinated them. Losing Christianity, they believed in a kind of cultivated witchcraft, in which evil was still a principle, but unorthodox and relatively picturesque. Our psychological or economic theories of individual or social mechanism were despised, if at all known, when these men heard of them. Very properly they understood that art was not explanation; very naturally, thrown back upon themselves, they were content to elaborate imaginative personal theories which came to look more and more like a lot of words for luxurious private sensations that were not common coinage; like Byronism, something indeed dramatic but also to us somehow false. So it seems now that the far more spectacular and concrete evil of the war stands between us and has left us with the feeling that, for the moment, we have our hands full in preserving or reconstructing society and little time for thinking about the more grandiose but nevertheless speculative wilfulness of the cosmos. But if the "little man, what now?" theme has been shoved aside, Mr. Ford's book is a valuable reminder that what matters is less the atmosphere of an age than the honesty of the work that was done in it. To this the judgment of posterity and even the kiss of fashion, sooner or later return.

Somehow Mr. Ford escaped the peculiar seriousness of his seniors in the period, and I imagine this is why his own mark has not been as strong

*From *London Mercury* 37 (March 1938):550–51. Reprinted by permission of A D Peters & Co. Ltd.

as his talents warranted. It is always exciting to read Mr. Ford. He has that kind of quality which is easily underrated by the soulful world of English letters: a hard and brilliant originality, full of laughter, gusto, theories, digressions and asides. He is a festive and gregarious mind but not a heart. Stunned by a volubility in which every word strikes and starts a dozen echoes which distract him to further effects like a boy shouting under an archway, one sways giddily but enlivened. Before everything else a personality, he excels at recreating an impression of the personality of people like Turgenev, Hardy or James, by gathering together the least expected fragments. Bizarre as they may be, they are kept in place by an unusual common sense. The defence of Turgenev, for example, from the charges of expatriate rootlessness which are made against him strikes one as being very sound and shrewd. Turgenev was, indeed, working when all that educated Russia did was to talk.

The Hardy portrait, too, besides its irony, has several sound things in it: the observation, for example, that, whereas Hardy would alter a plot to suit any editor, he would not alter a syllable of his verse for anyone—with its obvious conclusion. There is a nice story of Mrs. Hardy begging the Garnetts to make her husband tear up the MS. of *Jude*, and another one of a visit to Max Gate where poetry was read at tea—Mrs. Hardy's poetry. But most delightful of all is the portrait of Henry James. This is a masterpiece of reminiscence and criticism. It is a model of Mr. Ford's method which is to plant an incident and then watch with glee its ramifications grow. A violent disillusion turned the later James into a man of infinite precautions, disastrous to his prose (unless it is read aloud) and yet an oblique stimulus to the immense patience and thoroughness of his investigation of any subject he was working on. Such, anyway, is Mr. Ford's theory, and with great wit he expounds it. The surviving impressionist of the Impressionists—and it is a typical effrontery, if I have not misunderstood him, that he can lump Turgenev, Wells, Galsworthy and Dreiser together under this egoistic term, with Hudson and Conrad—has brought the essence of them all to life in a manner which, outside his own earlier efforts, has not been equalled by any other writer.

Overviews

Ford Madox Ford — A Neglected Contemporary

Granville Hicks*

It would not, I imagine, please Mr. Ford to be called neglected. He has written more than sixty books, and he has seen the Shelleys of the last half-century very plain indeed. When he was in his twenties he was called the most perfect stylist in the English language; Joseph Conrad sought him as a collaborator; and more recently, his war tetralogy has led to his being compared with Proust. He has not, obviously, been neglected in any ordinary sense. This is not a tale of a lonely genius, left to starve in the conventional garret, bequeathing to the world a slender manuscript of exquisite verse or a few pages of miraculous prose. It is a much more puzzling story, the story of a man who has been in the thick of every literary fray and yet is ignored by the literary historians, a man whose individual books have, as they appeared, been greeted as unusual achievements but whose work as a whole has made little impression on the contemporary mind. In several rather detailed studies of modern literature his name is not even mentioned, and no one, so far as I know, has ever made an effort to estimate his importance. Everyone knows he exists — it would be rather hard, all things considered, to ignore the fact — but there are few people who could accurately tell you what he has done.

. . .

There Ford stands, with one trusts, considerable of a career before him, but certainly with enough behind him to warrant the attention of the critic. Perhaps it is because there is so much of a career behind Ford — so many books and in such a variety of forms — that critics have hesitated to try to define his position among his contemporaries. The task is not, however, so difficult as it appears; examination of his work shows that we may legitimately confine our attention to his novels. Even in his non-fiction Ford is primarily the novelist and should be so judged. His books about France, England, and America have the merits of a novelist's note-

*From New York *Bookman* 72 (December 1930):364–70. Reprinted by permission of Russell and Volkening, Inc. as agents for the author. Copyright 1930, renewed 1958 by Granville Hicks. An omitted section, indicated by an ellipsis, summarizes Ford's literary career until 1930 and is more descriptive than critical.

165

books; quickness and accuracy of observation, an interest in the precise rendering of physical and mental qualities, a sense of the dramatic possibilities of situations that are only hastily and fragmentarily seen. His criticism also, though Ford lacks the patience to rear that structure of hypothesis and generalization towards which the judicial critic aims, does show the sensitiveness and discrimination of a thoughtful novelist to whom no phase of his craft can be uninteresting.

One might even, without extravagance, go on to say that Ford's poetry discloses his talents as a master of prose fiction. He has said that the conventional forms of verse are either too easy or too difficult to be worth bothering with, and certainly his own experiments in these forms are little more than the exercise of a bright student. In "vers libre" his performances are more individual, but even here the level of intensity is usually low and the diction often careless. The imagery is fresh, but is involved and leisurely; usually it could be transferred to a page of prose without the reader's being conscious of any incongruity. Ford probably does not lack the qualities of imagination that are essential to poetry, but he has never made the effort to master poetic expression. The writing of verse seems to be for him a kind of recreation, whereas the writing of fiction is a matter of careful artistry.

Ford has, in short, tried his hand at all sorts of things, and his brilliant resourcefulness has always stood in the way of complete failure; but there is only one literary form that he has taken the trouble to master, and that is the novel. Only the novel has been sufficiently attractive to persuade him to subject his facility to a thorough discipline, and, though his work in other fields is never discreditable, it is his novels alone that entitle him to serious consideration. Perhaps, indeed, the best one can say is that in whatever he undertakes there are evidences of a first-rate talent for the novel.

In examining the novels we come first upon the historical romances. Whether Ford's disparagement of this type of fiction is purely "ex post facto" we cannot tell, but we are not likely to disagree with his judgment. The historical novel seldom permits the full expression of a rich mind or a scrupulous technique, and it may even be that some of the qualities we think of as necessary for the creation of first-rate fiction are for the historical novelist only handicaps. The historical novel should have a clear and fast-moving plot; it should contain plenty of incident; its characters should be boldly presented. In Ford's *Henry VIII* series these qualities are not to be found. The author's interest, on the contrary, is centered in the presentation of states of mind and the rendering of sequences that are largely psychological. Lacking the animation, the pageantry and the simplicity of the true romance, they derive their interest almost altogether from virtues not ordinarily discoverable in works of their kind. Conrad was not far wrong in calling the series the swan song of historical romance; the "genre" cannot flourish long in an atmosphere of sophistication, analysis and artifice. What Ford was clearly working toward was the psychological novel. Difficult as it is to accept his statement that, while waiting for the crucial fortieth year to arrive, he consciously devoted himself to the writing of "divertissements," one cannot deny that his earlier work was, though not in any obvious way, a suitable preparation for the tasks assigned to his maturity.

On his fortieth birthday Ford began writing *The Good Soldier*. The subject on which he chose to "extend himself" was one that, he says, had been hatching for a decade and to this period of gestation the novel doubtless owes both sureness of conception and strength of construction. The aim is to present a situation in the lives of five persons, and for method Ford selected one that, though it had certain great advantages, offered towering obstacles. The narrator is one of the major participants in the story. During the several years in which the situation was developing he was completely ignorant of what was going on; and yet at the moment he tells the story he is, of course, aware of all the facts. Since he is conceived as a naive person, he could not be allowed to withhold facts for the sake of effect; and since he is supposed to be telling the story as it recreates itself in his mind, he could not be allowed to develop the narrative in simple chronological order. He must present the characters at first in one light and afterwards in a quite different light, but he must not do this consciously. Ford's problem was to maintain the consistency of his narrator and at the same time reveal the situation with complete accuracy and with careful consideration of climactic effect.

To test Ford's success all that is necessary is to read the novel a second time. Though you know how the story ends, though you have seen the characters as they really are, you cannot find a phrase that is misleading nor can you discover any withholding of facts that the narrator could justly be expected to give. On the other hand, you discover in the early chapters references and allusions that carefully prepare the reader for his final impression. It comes close to being a flawless book, remarkable for its sustained inventiveness and its sound, unfaltering progress. There was justice in calling it "the finest French novel in the English language."

With all its technical virtuosity, however, *The Good Soldier* is not merely a "tour de force." There is no disproportion between the technical skill and the solidity of the work. As a revelation of life the book is worthy of the technique, and every formal subtlety adds to the accuracy and force of that revelation. With the utmost tenderness Ford pushes deeper and deeper into the minds of his characters, disclosing realms of passion and agony and meanness. Conrad never attempted to present so complex a situation, and James never ventured to explore emotion so intense and volcanic. When the book reaches its terrifying close, one realizes that only such formal perfection as Ford exhibits could bear the weight of this tragedy.

If Ford had kept his vow of literary nonparticipation, *The Good*

Soldier would have been a magnificent climax to a not undistinguished career, but, standing, so far above its predecessors, it would have had something of the appearance of a happy accident. Fortunately the vow was not kept, and we have the war tetralogy to set beside *The Good Soldier*. This group of novels has suffered because of its subject. There are, it appears, special standards by which war books are judged, and according to those standards [*Some Do Not . . .*] and its sequels fall short. But this is patently unfair, for they are only incidentally war books and are primarily psychological novels, to be judged precisely as one judges *The Good Soldier*.

Considered in this way, they show the originality and clarity with which Ford can create characters and the force and logic with which he can present situations. How faithfully Tietjens is modelled upon Arthur Marwood we cannot know, and it does not matter. He is, with his omniscience and his strange suggestion of being Christ, one of the most unusual figures in recent fiction, and at the same time one of the most credible. Sylvia, quite as far removed from the commonplace of life and literature, is equally real. None of the other characters—Valentine, Duchemin, Macmaster, Campion, Mark Tietjens—is ordinary and none is implausible. These strongly individualized characters Ford takes and marshals into such amazing scenes as the Duchemin breakfast, the celebration of the Armistice in Tietjens's room, or the descent of Sylvia upon the Tietjens *ménage* the day Mark dies. Only a strong grasp of structural principles could control such inventiveness as Ford displays in these works.

The style in which the tetralogy is written is a kind of diluted stream-of-consciousness method, a report in indirect discourse of the thoughts and impressions of the various characters. At times the method becomes a little monotonous, and there are moments, especially in *The Last Post*, when the reader feels that Ford can go on this way indefinitely and fears that he has taken it into his head to do so. On the whole, however, the method serves to reveal precisely those mental states that it is necessary for the reader to understand in order to catch the dramatic values of the climactic situation. Like Conrad, Ford takes the reader forward and backward, hither and yon, but in the end the reader finds that he has progressed to the goal the author has appointed for him.

If all four of the Tietjens books seem to have been a little hastily written, and if none of them attains to the formal perfection of *The Good Soldier*, their cumulative effect, the greater vitality of certain sections, the brilliance and especially the variety of character portrayal, and the intimations they offer of a changing social order, all demonstrate that Ford's creative powers have not weakened. They definitely show that he has a place in what he is fond of calling the main stream of European literature.

It is chiefly with the five novels just discussed that any attempt to evaluate Ford's work must be concerned. In thus limiting the Fordian canon we are following the method that would have to be pursued by the serious critic of Wells, Galsworthy, or Bennett; few of Ford's contemporaries have "extended" themselves in all their books. In these five books Ford reveals himself as the principal psychological novelist in England, the chief contemporary representative of the school of Henry James, and Joseph Conrad. In the twentieth century the English novel has been predominantly in the Fielding tradition; the aim has been to give a cross-section of English life and the method has been biographical. In the latter decades of the nineteenth century James broke away from that tradition, occupying himself with situations rather than social orders and imitating the compact organization of the French novel instead of adopting the sprawling leisureliness of the English. James left few followers. His greatest disciple, Conrad, was so much more than a disciple that his indebtedness was obscured. Other novelists—Joyce, Mrs. Woolf, Miss Richardson, for example—triumphantly carried the novel into new fields and devised new methods. The characteristic Jamesian approach—as formulated, for example, in Percy Lubbock's *The Craft of Fiction*—has, for the most part, been neglected. Fortunately there has been Ford. He has not departed in any fundamental way from James's aims and methods, yet he has done certain sorts of things that James could never have done and would not have attempted. Thus he has demonstrated the vitality of the Jamesian novel in our day.

It is, among other things, including the temperamental eccentricities to which I have alluded, the distance that separated Ford from his contemporaries that has led to his comparative neglect. His books have neither the sociological interest of the novels of Wells and his associates nor the experimental interest of the works of Joyce and his followers. However, as the sociological novel continues to decline in favor, and as the experimental novel reveals its limitations, Ford's work may receive more attention. The past few years have brought an increased interest in problems of form, but there still exists, especially in the United States, an unhealthy dichotomy. For the most part we have life and passion on one side, with formal perfection and sound writing on the other. If one must choose between the two, one would, surely, prefer the strength of *Look Homeward, Angel* to the symmetry of *The Woman of Andros*. But the choice is unnecessary. Ford's work not only shows that formal excellence may be combined with vitality and vigor; it reminds us that the sole justification of formal excellence is its effect in enhancing the vitality of the work in question.

The burst of novelistic energy released by the publication of *Ulysses* seems, at the moment, to have dissipated. Many of the more talented young writers content themselves with sleek and plausible imitations of the successful novels of the last hundred years. As a result, almost the only novelists one can watch with any pretense of interest are the few radical experimenters. Dos Passos, for example, one studies eagerly—but also with a certain amount of trepidation. He may, of course, succeed; but even if he does, it will still be true that not many novelists are capable of such an enterprise as he has begun in the *42nd Parallel* and that not all worthy subjects could be treated by such a method. It seems clear that there must be some kind of novel less amorphous and less fully exploited than the sociological novel, at the same time less perilously difficult than the experimental novel, whether of the Joyce or the Dos Passos type. Perhaps the Jamesian novel offers the best solution of the dilemma. But the Jamesian novel, if it is to serve our purposes, must break away from the limitations of subject matter that James himself submitted to, and it must develop the ability to portray more aspects of human character than he was interested in. That it can transcend the original limits Ford has already demonstrated; he has shown that it has greater possibilities than James attempted to exploit; it remains for other novelists to indicate how great these possibilities are. No one can predict the course that the novel will take, but at this moment of uncertainty, we can afford to neglect no method that offers promise for the future. It would at any time be a pleasure to call attention to the excellence of certain of Ford's books; at the present time there may also be some importance in indicating their possible significance for the development of the novel.

[Ford Madox Ford: Obituary]   Ezra Pound*

There passed from us this June a very gallant combatant for those things of the mind and of letters which have been in our time too little prized. There passed a man who took in his time more punishment of one sort and another than I have seen meted to anyone else. For the ten years before I got to England there would seem to have been no one but Ford who held that French clarity and simplicity in the writing of English verse and prose were of immense importance as in contrast to the use of a stilted traditional dialect, a "language of verse" unused in the actual talk of the people, even of "the best people," for the expression of reality and emotion.

In 1908 London was full of "gargoyles," of poets, that is, with high reputation, most of whose work has gone since into the discard. At that time, and in the few years preceding, there appeared without notice various fasciculae which one can still, surprisingly, read and they were not designed for mouthing, for the "rolling out" of "ohs." They weren't what

*From *Pound / Ford: A Story of a Literary Friendship.* © 1982 by the Trustees of the Ezra Pound Literary Property Trust. Reprinted by permission of New Directions Publishing Corporation. Originally appeared in *Nineteenth Century and After* 126 (August 1939):178–81.

people were looking for as the prolongation of Victoria's glory. They weren't, that is, "intense" in the then sense of the word.

The justification or programme of such writing was finally (about 1913) set down in one of the best essays (preface) that Ford ever wrote.

It advocated the prose value of verse-writing, and it, along with his verse, had more in it for my generation than all the retchings (most worthily) after "quantity" (i.e., quantitative metric) of the late Laureate Robert Bridges or the useful, but monotonous, in their day unduly neglected, as more recently unduly touted, metrical labours of G. Manley Hopkins.

I have put it down as personal debt to my forerunners that I have had five, and only five, useful criticisms of my writing in my lifetime, one from Yeats, one from Bridges, one from Thomas Hardy, a recent one from a Roman Archbishop and one from Ford, and that last the most vital, or at any rate on par with Hardy's.

That Ford was almost an *halluciné* few of his intimates can doubt. He felt until it paralysed his efficient action, he saw quite distinctly the Venus immortal crossing the tram tracks. He inveighed against Yeats' lack of emotion as, for him, proved by Yeats' so great competence in making literary use of emotion.

And he felt the errors of contemporary style to the point of rolling (physically, and if you look at it as mere superficial snob, ridiculously) on the floor of his temporary quarters in Giessen when my third volume displayed me trapped, fly-papered, gummed and strapped down in a jejune provincial effort to learn, mehercule, the stilted language that then passed for "good English" in the arthritic milieu that held control of the respected British critical circles, Newbolt, the backwash of Lionel Johnson, Fred Manning, the Quarterlies and the rest of 'em.

And that roll saved me at least two years, perhaps more. It sent me back to my own proper effort, namely, toward using the living tongue (with younger men after me), though none of us has found a more natural language than Ford did.

This is a dimension of poetry. It is, magari, an Homeric dimension, for of Homer there are at least two dimensions apart from the surge and thunder. Apart from narrative sense and the main constructive, there is this to be said of Homer, that never can you read half a page without finding melodic invention, still fresh, and that you can hear the actual voices, as of the old men speaking in the surge of the phrases.

It is for this latter quality that Ford's poetry is of high importance, both in itself and for its effect on all the best subsequent work of his time. Let no young snob forget this.

I propose to bury him in the order of merits as I think he himself understood them, first for an actual example in the writing of poetry; secondly, for those same merits more fully shown in his prose, and thirdly, for the critical acumen which was implicit in his finding these merits.

As to his prose, you can apply to it a good deal that he wrote in praise of Hudson (rightly) and of Conrad, I think with a bias toward generosity that in parts defeats its critical applicability. It lay so natural on the page that one didn't notice it. I read an historical novel at sea in 1906 without noting the name of the author. A scene at Henry VIIIth's court stayed depicted in my memory and I found years later that Ford had written it.

I wanted for private purposes to make a note on a point raised in *Ancient Lights;* I thought it would go on the back of an envelope, and found to my young surprise that I couldn't make the note in fewer words than those on Ford's actual page. That set me thinking. I did not in those days care about prose. If "prose" meant anything to me, it meant Tacitus (as seen by Mackail), a damned dangerous model for a young man in those days or these days in England, though I don't regret it; one never knows enough about anything. Start with Tacitus and be cured by Flaubert via Ford, or start with Ford or Maupassant and be girt up by Tacitus, after fifty it is kif, kif, all one. But a man is a pig not to be grateful to both sides.

Until the arrival of such "uncomfortables" as Wyndham Lewis, the distressful D. H. Lawrence, D. Goldring, G. Cannan, etc., I think Ford had no one to play with. The elder generation loathed him, or at any rate such cross-section of it as I encountered. He disturbed 'em, he took Dagon by the beard, publicly. And he founded the greatest Little Review or pre-Little Review of our time. From 1908 to 1910 he gathered into one fasciculus the work of Hardy, H. James, Hudson, Conrad, C. Graham, Anatole France, the great old-stagers, the most competent of that wholly unpleasant decade, Bennett, Wells, and I think, even Galsworthy.

And he got all the first-rate and high second-raters of my own decade, W. Lewis, D. H. Lawrence (made by Ford, dug out of a board school in Croydon), Cannan, Walpole, etc. (Eliot was not yet on the scene).

The inner story of that review and the treatment of Ford by its obtainers is a blot on London's history that time will not remove, though, of course, it will become invisible in the perspective of years.

As critic he was perhaps wrecked by his wholly unpolitic generosity. In fact, if he merits an epithet above all others, it would be "The Unpolitic." Despite all his own interests, despite all the hard-boiled and half-baked vanities of all the various lots of us, he kept on discovering merit with monotonous regularity.

His own best prose was probably lost, as isolated chapters in un-achieved and too-quickly-issued novels. He persisted in discovering capaci-ties in similar crannies. In one weekly after another he found and indicated the capacities of Mary, Jenny, Willard, Jemimah, Horatio, etc., despite the fact that they all of 'em loathed each other, and could by no stretch of imagination be erected into a compact troop of Fordites supporting each other and moving on the citadels of publication.

And that career I saw him drag through three countries. He took up the fight for free letters in Paris, he took it up again in New York, where I saw him a fortnight before his death, still talking of meritorious novels, still pitching the tale of unknown men who had written the *histoire morale contemporaine* truthfully and without trumpets, told this or that phase of American as seen from the farm or the boiler-works, as he had before wanted young England to see young England from London, from Sussex.

And of all the durable pages he wrote (for despite the fluff, despite the apparently aimless meander of many of 'em, he did write durable pages) there is nothing that more registers the fact of our day than the two portraits in the, alas, never-finished *Women and Men* (Three Mountains Press, 1923), Meary Walker and 'T.'

Ford Madox Ford [Obituary]   Graham Greene*

The death of Ford Madox Ford was like the obscure death of a veteran — an impossibly Napoleonic veteran, say, whose immense memory spanned the period from Jena to Sedan: he belonged to the heroic age of English fiction and outlived it — yet he was only sixty-six. In one of his many volumes of reminiscence — those magnificent books where in an atmosphere of casual talk outrageous story jostles outrageous story — he quoted Mr Wells as saying some years ago that in the southern counties a number of foreigners were conspiring against the form of the English novel. There was James at Lamb House, Crane at Brede Manor, Conrad at The Pent, and he might have added his own name, Hueffer at Aldington, for he was a quarter German (and just before the first world war made an odd extravagant effort to naturalize himself as a citizen of his grandfather's country). The conspiracy, of course, failed: the big loose middlebrow novel goes on its happy way unconscious of James's "point of view": Conrad is regarded again as the writer of romantic sea stories and purple passages: nobody reads Crane, and Ford — well, an anonymous writer in *The Times Literary Supplement* remarked in an obituary notice that his novels began to date twenty years ago. Conservatism among English critics is extraordinarily tenacious, and they hasten, on a man's death, to wipe out any disturbance he has caused.

The son of Francis Hueffer, the musical critic of *The Times*, and grandson, on his mother's side, of Ford Madox Brown, "Fordie" Hueffer emerges into history at the age of three offering a chair to Turgenev, and again, a little later, dressed in a suit of yellow velveteen with gold buttons, wearing one red stocking and one green one, and with long golden hair, having his chair stolen from him at a concert by the Abbé Liszt. I say

*From *Collected Essays*, 159–62. Copyright 1951, © 1966, 1968, 1969 by Graham Greene. © renewed 1979 by Graham Greene. Reprinted by permission of Viking Penguin Inc. Originally appeared in *Spectator* 72 (7 July 1939):11.

emerges into history, but it is never possible to say where history ends and the hilarious imagination begins. He was always an atmospheric writer, whether he was describing the confused Armistice night when Tietjens found himself back with his mistress, Valentine Wannop, among a horde of grotesque and inexplicable strangers, or just recounting a literary anecdote of dubious origin—the drunk writer who thought himself a Bengal tiger trying to tear out the throat of the blind poet Marston, or Henry James getting hopelessly entangled in the long lead of his dachshund Maximilian. Nobody ever wrote more about himself than Ford, but the figure he presented was just as dubious as his anecdotes—the figure of a Tory country gentleman who liked to grow his own food and had sturdy independent views on politics: it all seems a long way from the yellow velveteen. He even, at the end of his life, a little plump and a little pink, looked the part—and all the while he had been turning out the immense number of books which stand to his name: memoirs, criticism, poetry, sociology, novels. And in between, if one can so put it, he found time to be the best literary editor England has ever had: what Masefield, Hudson, Conrad, even Hardy owed to the *English Review* is well known, and after the war in *The Transatlantic Review* he bridged the great gap, publishing the early Hemingway, Cocteau, Stein, Pound, the music of Antheil, and the drawings of Braque.

He had the advantage—or the disadvantage—of being brought up in pre-Raphaelite circles, and although he made a tentative effort to break away into the Indian Civil Service, he was pushed steadily by his father towards art—any kind of art was better than any kind of profession. He published his first book at the age of sixteen, and his first novel, *The Shifting of the Fire*, in 1892, when he was only nineteen—three years before Conrad had published anything and only two years after the serial appearance of *The Tragic Muse*, long before James had matured his method and his style. It wasn't, of course, a good book, but neither was it an "arty" book—there was nothing of the 'nineties about it except its elegant period binding, and it already bore the unmistakable Hueffer stamp—the outrageous fancy, the pessimistic high spirits, and an abominable hero called Kasker-Ryves. Human nature in his books was usually phosphorescent—varying from the daemonic malice of Sylvia Tietjens to the painstaking, rather hopeless will-to-be-good of Captain Ashburnham, "the good soldier." The little virtue that existed only attracted evil. But to Mr Ford, a Catholic in theory though not for long in practice, this was neither surprising nor depressing: it was just what one expected.

The long roll of novels ended with *Vive le Roy* in 1937. A few deserve to be forgotten, but I doubt whether the accusation of dating can be brought against even such minor work as *Mr Apollo, The Marsden Case, When the Wicked Man*: there were the historical novels, too, with their enormous vigour and authenticity—*The Fifth Queen* and its sequels: but the novels which stand as high as any fiction written since the death of

James are *The Good Soldier* with its magnificent claim in the first line, "This is the saddest story I have ever heard"—the study of an averagely good man of a conventional class driven, divided and destroyed by unconventional passion—and the Tietjens series, that appalling examination of how private malice goes on during public disaster—no escape even in the trenches from the secret gossip and the lawyers' papers. It is dangerous in this country to talk about technique or a long essay could be written on his method in these later books, the method Conrad followed more stiffly and less skilfully, having learnt it perhaps from Ford when they collaborated on *Romance*: James's point of view was carried a step further, so that a book took place not only from the point of view but in the brain of a character and events were remembered not in chronological order, but as free association brought them to mind.

When Ford died he had passed through a period of neglect and was re-emerging. His latest books were not his best, but they were hailed as if they were. The first war had ruined him. He had volunteered, though he was over military age and was fighting a country he loved; his health was broken, and he came back to a new literary world which had carefully eliminated him. For some of his later work he could not even find a publisher in England. No wonder he preferred to live abroad—in Provence or New York. But I don't suppose failure disturbed him much: he had never really believed in human happiness, his middle life had been made miserable by passion, and he had come through—with his humour intact, his stock of unreliable anecdotes, the kind of enemies a man ought to have, and a half-belief in a posterity which would care for good writing.

The King over the Water: Notes on the Novels of F. M. Hueffer
R. P. Blackmur*

It would seem now, after re-reading some seven or eight of his novels, that Ford Madox Hueffer belonged to that race of novelists whose facility for the mere act of writing is so great that their minds never quite catch up with the job under way, and whose writing seldom stops on the difficulties that make the job worth doing. If you have the ease of too much talent you cannot benefit from the hardships of genius. Twenty years ago and more, when these novels were first read, nothing of this sort could have been said by the present writer. Let us see along what lines it has become possible now.

Ford Madox Hueffer—or Ford Madox Ford; to me he remains Hueffer—wrote a great many novels, publishing the first at the age of

*Reprinted from *Princeton University Library Chronicle* 9, no. 3 (1948):123–27. Reprinted by permission of the journal.

nineteen, and between 1920 and 1928 I read as many as I could lay hands on, without ever a twinge of reaction which might lead to judgment until it was asked for in the present circumstance. The twinge will appear later, but I do not think it will reach judgment; I do not think Hueffer was the kind of writer who takes to being judged much, because he did not display the materials, or the order of materials, suitable to our means of judgment; the twinge is enough.

Meanwhile, there is the memory of reading, and how it came about. Joseph Conrad just then, in 1920, had come to the height of his reputation with *The Rescue,* and in reading Conrad one found that he had twice collaborated with Hueffer, in *Romance* and in *The Inheritors.* These being read and indiscriminately admired, one went on and read *The Good Soldier* out of curiosity to see what Hueffer was like all by himself, and came out with an admiration out of all proportion. Hueffer at the time seemed to belong to a group: he belonged to Conrad, W. H. Hudson, Stephen Crane; but that was only part of it, for he belonged also to Henry James, Ezra Pound, and T. S. Eliot; he belonged to two generations and to the bridge that over-arched them. He occupied, mysteriously but evidently, all the interstices between all the members of both groups, and somehow contributed an atmosphere in which all of them were able to breathe. He had something to do with the *life,* the genuineness, of the literature written between *Lord Jim* and *The Waste Land,* between *The Dynasts* and *Ulysses.* All this was actual enough at the time; *The English Review,* dug up and read in old numbers, and *the transatlantic review,* both of which Hueffer edited, make the history stand. Yet to think of Hueffer in this way involved a view of him which has little of the truth in it that goes beyond history, the kind of truth which must somehow be our subject here. Atmospheres do not last, and can be re-created only in the living memory. Ford Madox Hueffer bore no real relation to Conrad and Hudson except the editorial relation; he had in his own writing, what corresponds there to the editorial, he had the relation of the chameleon-response to them. When his work was in the felt presence of their work, the skin of his writing changed color accordingly. What he responded with was partly the stock baggage of English literature and partly his own sensibility. I do not see how anybody who had not read Conrad and James could see what Hueffer was up to by way of form and style in their separable senses, or for that matter how anybody not knowing Conrad and James could feel the impact of Hueffer's sensibility attempting to articulate itself in terms of what it had absorbed of theirs. Without that knowledge, Hueffer's novels seem stock and even hack on the formal side and freakish or eccentric on the side of sensibility.

All this is summary description of the sensibility articulated in *The Good Soldier,* and in the four novels of which Christopher Tietjens is the central character, *Some Do Not, No More Parades, A Man Could Stand Up,* and *Last Post.* The first was published in 1915, the Tietjens novels in the early twenties. Aside from *Romance*, written in collaboration with Conrad, I take it that these novels are what we mean when we speak of Hueffer as a novelist. If they stand, we have to put beside them at least one Utopian fantasy, *Ladies Whose Bright Eyes* (1911) and perhaps the late Napoleonic romance, *A Little Less than Gods* (1928); because his serious novels lie always between fantasy and romance. *Ladies Whose Bright Eyes* is gay, light, tender: the fantasy of a commercially-minded London publisher (himself a fantasy rather than a caricature of the type) transported in a traumatic dream to the England of 1326; in terms of which, when he wakes, he undergoes a kind of backwards conversion, and unearths a corner of fourteenth-century Utopia in modern England. *A Little Less than Gods* is the historical romance of an Englishman who finds himself, a kind of chivalrous traitor, in the service of Napoleon between Elba and Waterloo; it is pompous, stuffy, and sloppy both as romance and as history; but is written, so the dedicatory letter says, in the belief that it is—or means to be—a true sight of history. Each of these books has something to do with the glory of an arbitrary prestige resting on values asserted but not found in the actual world: values which when felt critically deform rather than enlighten action in that world, so that the action ends in the destruction of the values themselves. Like the idea of Napoleon, such values have all the greatness possible without virtue, and like the Napoleonic and the medieval ideas, they have a genuine and universal popularity. Many people—or parts of many people—find life tolerable only because they think it is like that; other people find literature tolerable only if it furnishes such ideas for getting back at life. In writing light novels—more or less unconscious pot-boilers—in the exemplification of such ideas, Hueffer was certainly on the track of what people want in a light and preoccupied way.

In his serious novels, *The Good Soldier* and the novels about Tietjens listed above, what makes them serious is that these same ideas are treated seriously, with all the fanaticism that goes with fresh conversion or the sore point of fixed prejudice. Edward Ashburnham, the hero of *The Good Soldier*, is an extravagant princely sensualist, a wrecker of lives in the pursuit of life; he is also a soldier and he is seen by the narrator as a model of glory—a glory which is brought to a climax when, because his manners make it impossible to accept the body of a young girl brought up in his house, he cuts his throat and drives the young girl mad. Edward is feudal and Protestant; what modern Protestant feudalism cannot do to ruin him through his sensuality is done for him by his wife's Roman Catholicism. Feudalism, sensuality, Roman Catholicism, are, all three, forces which prevent the people in this book from coping with the real world and which exacerbate their relations to it.

In the Tietjens novels Toryism replaces feudalism, as it is the modern form of it, and as Tietjens is a Tory public servant in a world of 1914, or Lloyd George, liberalism; the sensuality is given to the wife rather than to the husband; the wife, being both Roman Catholic and sensualist, is thus more exacerbated than the wife in *The Good Soldier*. Otherwise the ideas are much the same. The virtues of the deprived Tory and the deprived Catholic are seen as the living forms of damnation. The Tory becomes the object of undeserved scandal, leading to disinheritance and his father's suicide, and thus, as a result *only* of his held beliefs as to the proper relations between father, son, and brother in a Tory family, to his own ruin. For her part, the Catholic sensualist becomes a bitch *manquée*, that is to say, an unmotivated destroyer of her own goods. There is not a person of account in the four volumes who is not animated by principle so high as to be a vocation from his or her point of view; but there is not a decent, frank, or satisfying relation between any two of them till the very end; principles get in the way by determining rather than formulating or judging values in conflict. Yet these principles are shown as admirable and exemplary in Christopher Tietjens, and exemplary if not wholly admirable in his wife Sylvia. Indeed the world is shown as in conspiracy against these principles—with the war of 1914–1918 as a particularly foul part of the conspiracy. The war, in presented fact, is only a kind of international Whiggery and interested scandal-mongering—all but those aspects of it which permit Christopher Tietjens to follow the Lord and behave like a princely Yorkshire Tory gentleman. Surely, if we want an easy name for this sort of thing, it is romanticism in reverse; it is the Faustian spirit of mastery turned suicidal on contact with classical clichés; it is also to say that these serious novels are only an intensified form of whatever happens when you put together the ideas of the medieval fantasy and the Napoleonic romance.

What intensifies them is, what we began by saying, the relation they bear to the work of his two immediate masters. And this is to say that Hueffer is a minor novelist in the sense that his novels would have little existence without the direct aid and the indirect momentum of the major writers upon whom he depended. He dealt with loyalty and the conflict of loyalties like Conrad, he dealt with fine consciences and hideously brooked sensualities like James. But all the loyalty he did not find heightened by Conrad was obstinacy, and all the conscience and sensuality he did not find created by James were priggery and moral suicide. Adding this to what has already been said of the chief novels, makes a terrible simplification: it says that Hueffer supplied only the excesses of his characters' vices and virtues, and only the excesses of their situations; and it suggests that his sensibility was unmoored, or was moored only in the sense that a sensibility may be moored to lost causes known to be lost.

Known to be lost. If there is an image upon which Hueffer's sensibility can be seen to declare its own force it is in an image of devotion to lost causes known to be lost; that is what his more serious novels dramatize, that is what his characters bring to their conflicts and situations, otherwise viable, to make them irremediable—for the law is already gone that could provide a remedy. In politics and philosophy we call this the cultivation of ancestral Utopias; in literature, since we can recognize these cultivations with the pang of actuality, they make a legitimate, though necessarily always subordinate, subject matter. They are real, these causes known to be lost—as real as the King over the Water—but they depend for their reality on their relation to causes not lost, much as history depends on the present which it disturbs, not for its truth but for its validity. So it is with Hueffer's novels; the validity of his dramatizations of men and women devoted to causes known to be lost depends on our sense of these same causes in the forms in which they are still to be struggled for. To the purposes of his obsession he chose the right masters in Conrad and James. His lost English Catholic women, his lost English Tories, his lost medievalists and his strange inventions of lost Americans, depend on Conrad's sailors and James's ladies and gentlemen (since they are not men and women) of the world—in whom only the milieu, the ambience of positive sensibility, is strange or lost. The difference is that where the people in Conrad and James are beaten by the life to which they are committed and by the great society of which they believe themselves to be at the heart, in Hueffer the people are beaten because they believe themselves animated by loyalties and consciences utterly alien to the life and the society in which they find themselves. Not only their fate, but also their ideals are intolerable to them. They make of their *noblesse oblige* the substance as well as the instrument of their damnation. They are ourselves beside ourselves the wrong way; and they are so because the sensibility of the novels is identical with that of the characters; there is no foil or relief, whether of aspiration or of form; only that terrible facility with the medium which goes with causes known to be lost.

That is the twinge of reaction that comes in re-reading Hueffer's novels; that as an artist as well as a man he knew his causes to be lost: which is why he had to be facile, and why he could not supply his novels with the materials for judgment. You cannot judge the King over the Water, however you may feel a twinge at the toast proposed.

The Shape of an Achievement   Robert Green*

Despite the publication of several critical studies since 1961, as well as a massive biography, the stature of Ford Madox Ford remains disputable. On the one hand, his two best novels, *The Good Soldier* and *Parade's End*, now command substantial academic respect as works that have helped

*From *Ford Madox Ford: Politics and Prose* (Cambridge: Cambridge University Press, 1981), 182–95. Reprinted by permission of Cambridge University Press.

shape the way in which we perceive English culture in the first quarter of the century. On the other hand, though, their creator only merits passing references in a recent encyclopaedic survey of "Modernism," a volume that includes quite full discussions of Joyce, Woolf and Conrad.[1] In an earlier generation it was perhaps the unevenness of Ford's private life, the personal and literary enmities he aroused, that worked against him. Now that these ripples have stilled maybe it's the unevenness of his *oeuvre* that prevents the establishment of an assured reputation as a major modern novelist. Certainly the two outstanding works are surrounded by more than seventy texts, the majority long out of print. The importance of Ford's few successful novels, together with the innovative theories that, in the shadow of Gustave Flaubert and in the company of Joseph Conrad, he advanced at the turn of the century, have been decisively outweighed by the large undistinguished mass of his canon.

The cumulative effect of recent studies of the Ford-Conrad collaboration has been to question the older view that the partnership was grossly unequal; that Ford was merely valuable as an amanuensis to the great novelist and an improver of Conrad's broken English. Demonstrably Ford brought more to the collaboration than his skills as secretary and translator. Moreover, his kind of impressionism, which sought to render visual phenomena as a modern man would see them, was very different from Conrad's devotion to a symbolic, iconographical representation. One critic has even argued that in terms of their impact on modern fiction it is Ford, rather than the more celebrated Conrad, "who must be seen as the more influential writer."[2] Ford certainly had little interest in a slavishly literal rendering of the external world, the liberties he took with facts being the source of much of the hostility he aroused, and even when writing in non-fictional genres his approach was "novelistic." "In a fundamental and consistent way, everything he wrote was fiction."[3] Ford's impressionism, his determination to render the impression made by fact on the mind rather than the literal truth, is as potent in the memoirs, essays and criticism as in the novels.

This recognition of Ford's importance as a theorist of modern fiction, as a harbinger of many later subjectivist experimentations, still leaves unsolved the curious problem of his unsettled reputation. If his theories were so boldly innovative and his practice in five texts so assured, why doesn't he now stand alongside the modern masters? Ford himself patently aspired to be affiliated with them, with James, Conrad and the modernists, and in these writers he invested a lifetime's admiration and affection. Yet the regularity with which he betrayed their austere ideals for fiction by publishing work that appeared to ignore both the theories he shared and had helped formulate, and the practice (*Nostromo, What Maisie Knew*) he had publicly applauded surely distinguishes Ford as a fundamentally different breed of novelist. His canon has been aptly described as "the incessant outpourings of a polygraph,"[4] and polygraphy was deeply

antipathetic to the chaste prudential ideals of modernism. The economic
pressures on Ford to publish incessantly were doubtless sharp enough —
Mizener has documented them — but the argument that these forced him
to produce too many "pot-boilers" doesn't quite dispel the suspicion that
his prolificacy had causes deeper than financial embarrassment. Economy
and thrift were tenets central to the aesthetics of James and Conrad, and
these Ford practised outstandingly in *The Good Soldier*. Nevertheless, the
nature of his canon, the sheer bulk of his published work, the variety of
topics to which he addressed himself and the plurality of modes adopted —
the memoir, art-criticism, travelogue, children's books, the founded journals, as well as poetry and fiction — all this heterogeneity hints that Ford's
creative energies were basically centrifugal. It suggests too that he might
have written in this same manner, diffusely and prodigally, even had he
been blessed with economic independence. The notion that all these books
"are in reality one gigantic book," each one a variation on the central
theme, "the problems of getting the modern world into focus, of acquiring
historical perspective in a quickly changing world," is doubtless both
attractive and useful in equipping the reader with a map to guide him
through the maze of streets and side-streets that constitute Ford's
legacy to us.[5] However, we still need to think about why Ford's preoccupation with continuity and tradition necessitated so many
reworkings.

In a very early book, the biography of his grandfather the painter,
Ford had begun to try to establish his place at the end of a long line of
family innovators, traced back as far as Dr John Brown, a radical
physician and contemporary of Austen and Scott. Thus even before his
first meeting with Conrad in 1898 Ford was bent on marking himself as a
potential revolutionary. Yet the record of his published work is curiously
contradictory, for it suggests that his true affinities lay more with the
prolific polemical authors of an earlier generation, with Ruskin or
Carlyle, than with those radical contemporaries, James or Conrad, who
above all valued introspection and self-denial, specialisation and reticence. Ford's attitude to the great Victorians was indeed always ambivalent, for, although they discomforted him, he never lost an acute sense that
it was to the nineteenth century that he really belonged. Perhaps Ford was
trying to combine two incompatible aesthetics — a modernist view of *art*
committing him to self-effacement and withdrawal away from the text,
alongside a Victorian notion of the *artist*'s duty as seer, prophet, teacher,
commentator, The former belief helped him produce *Parade's End* and
The Good Soldier, whereas the Victorian allegiance would account for the
plurality and breadth of his *oeuvre*.

The centrality of self in all Ford's work, irrespective of subject
matter — that is, our inability ever quite to forget the presence of Ford the
individual — distinguishes him from Conrad or James, and aligns him with
Ruskin or Carlyle, Dickens or George Eliot. We can read the whole of

Nostromo without being pressed to think about the relations between the text and the personality of the author whom we've met in the biographies of Karl or Baines. Conrad's own beliefs are diffused and refracted by the text. The "Author's Note" and Conrad's comment there that "My principal authority for the history of Costaguana is, of course, my venerated friend, the late Don José Avellanos" is the first of many attempts at authorial dissociation, the displacement of "authority" away from Conrad himself.

Nostromo, then, lacks that compelling personal dimension always close to the surface of a Ford text. Graham Greene remarked upon our "sense of Ford's involvement" in *The Good Soldier*. Here and in *Parade's End* Ford's presence behind or alongside Dowell, Ashburnham or Tietjens never departs from the text. Ford had no real ambition to withdraw, no sense of *literary* privacy, and, though he frequently acknowledged his debt to Flaubert, no ability to replicate the latter's self-abnegation. Ford certainly endorsed Flaubert's theory that the work was paramount, the author unimportant, but he never managed to practise the "discipline," the "perpetual sacrifice" that, as Flaubert wrote to George Sand, were necessary to authorial withdrawal. He couldn't match Flaubert's radical modesty, the consistent suppression of self. Ford's memoirs demonstrate that his rarefied upbringing among artists and musicians had implanted a very early self-consciousness. He was uncomfortably aware of having been born into "a dynasty of highly-gifted celebrities" and his work suggests that he could never forget this pedigree.[6] As a result of this premature self-consciousness Ford always strikes us as a theatrical figure, a man ever aware of himself and the reverberations he "produces" on those around him.

This is a trait of Christopher's character which, as we have seen, Ford caught very well in *Parade's End*. . . . Ford was always successful in his portrayals of acute, studied self-consciousness, and the devices it employed to attract and maintain the observer's attention. Tietjens carrying a riding-whip and placing himself next to the stuffed animal-head is in this context exactly right, for he had been "ridden" nearly to death by his wife's persecution. The novelist equipped Tietjens with his own theatrical sense of the perfect "blocking" of a scene.

Similarly effective is Ford's account in *Return to Yesterday* of the casualness he affected in 1898 for his first encounter with Joseph Conrad: "Conrad came round the corner of the house. I was doing something at the open fireplace in the house-end. He was in advance of Mr Garnett who had gone inside, I suppose, to find me. Conrad stood looking at the view. His hands were in the pockets of his reefer-coat, the thumbs sticking out. His black, torpedo beard pointed at the horizon. He placed a monocle in his eye. Then he caught sight of me. I was very untidy, in my working clothes. He started back a little. I said: 'I'm Hueffer.' He had taken me for the gardener."[7] There's a strong impression here of artifice, of choreography, and all the novelist's heroes — Katharine Howard, Ashburnham, as well as Tietjens — were also fine actors, masters of gesture, pose and timing, through whom Ford demonstrated an understanding of the nature of theatricality and self-consciousness.

His own life, likewise, is a record of gestures struck and positions taken up. Even in his privacy and unguardedness he was prepared to meet a camera or an interviewer. His eccentricity was part of the public figure's sense of occasion, and observers noted these traits in Ford when he was still young and unknown. Olive Garnett recorded in her diary how her mother had called one day on Ford Madox Brown to see his latest painting. Ford, his grandson, would have been eighteen at this time. The visitor had asked the old man if he were going to begin another cartoon: "Mr Brown said 'Yes, I see no reason why I should not begin, but my grandson Ford says that I must design a frontispiece for his novel & that he can't wait, so I suppose I had better begin sketching it out tonight.' The frame of the picture is of wood covered with gilt Japanese paper so the people who did not know what to say admired it, which amused Ford immensely. He . . . *stood like an iceberg in the middle of the room & behaved with great ceremony.*"[8] Olive Garnett's view of the young novelist pre-empting the centre of the stage and compelling notice anticipates Ford's portrait of Tietjens' theatricality in the novel written thirty years later. Neither James nor Conrad was the epitome of modesty, but their conceits don't impinge upon their fiction as Ford's constantly did. Like the iceberg in the drawing-room, Ford is always a felt presence in his fiction. This determination to dominate, the preoccupation with establishing his own character, with "making an impression," the inability to displace or camouflage his private obsessions, is closely connected with the prolixity and plurality of his output. It was as if he had to "have his say" on everything.

Such egoism, which perhaps hid a deep unconfidence, the unease of an immigrant's son, is now only of concern in so far as it affected the novels. In the fictional techniques employed, *The Good Soldier* and *Parade's End* may be two, very different, monuments of modernism. They represent, respectively, the aggressive and the assimilative strains in the movement. Yet they are successful not because Ford there managed any Flaubertian self-effacement, but rather because he found a way of expressing through them the tensions of his own life and times. Modernism, as variously defined by Hulme, Eliot and Joyce, isn't exemplified at its purest in *The Good Soldier* or the Tietjens novels, since Ford's private torments lie so close to their surface. Significantly, much of the critical attention paid the novels has revolved round issues of characterisation: "how honest is Dowell?" "how credible is Tietjens?" Behind such questions stands the larger issue of Ford's relations with these characters. He didn't dissociate himself from Dowell or Tietjens as radically as Flaubert and Joyce separated themselves from Emma and Stephen. The "heuristic" quality of the texts, Ford's use of them as vehicles for self-discovery and expression, would, then, move them closer to the work of the metonymic realists—Wells, Bennett and Galsworthy.

Heterogeneity, unevenness, inconsistency and the absence of a modernist authorial displacement are all qualities that might make Ford's work seem rather traditional and orthodox. Like Wells and Bennett, Ford indeed dispersed his energies away from the centralising drives of Conrad. (The *oeuvre* includes a sixpenny suffragist pamphlet, *This Monstrous Regiment of Women*.) However, in other notable respects, Ford is most unlike Wells or Bennett. Nowhere, for instance, does he interest himself in the portrayal of childhood, adolescence, or, in the broader sense, "education." Neither is Ford centrally concerned with parenthood, with the relations between work and private life, or with the effects of environment, as Wells' suburbia or Bennett's provinces, on the sensibility. (There are no schools or shops in Ford.) These are all constituents of the realism of his contemporaries that Ford virtually ignores. Instead we discover a fascination with isolation, rather than community. Even those late texts most concerned with communal values, *Provence* and *Great Trade Route*, are strangely lonely private documents, quite unlike, say, Sturt's *The Wheelwright's Shop* or Blythe's *Akenfield*. At the heart of Ford's work is a struggle between retrospective idealism and the gritty unsympathetic materialism Ford saw around him. By contrast, Wells and Bennett were materialists, fascinated by the quotidian, the texture of daily life, by growth and process.

Ford has been distinguished from these realist contemporaries, because he didn't write "from a fairly central concern with English life and manners. Compared with these, the half-German Ford does seem exotic."[9] Ford's German father loved and wrote on Provençal literature, and this cosmopolitan upbringing ensured that he was raised a "European" rather than an "Englishman." Thus there is no equivalent in Ford's work of the dense particularised "Sawston" of early Forster or Bennett's "Five Towns." Groby and Branshaw, the "seats" of Tietjens and Ashburnham, function not as metonyms but as metaphors, symbols of the traditional and landed. Like Forster's Schlegels in *Howard's End*, the Hueffers were recent émigrés from Germany—Ford's father had left in 1869—and the lack of deep English roots on this side of his family accounts for much of the externality of Ford's view of his adopted homeland.

In his immigrant status Ford was similarly placed to several of the period's leading writers: the Polish Conrad; James, Eliot and Pound from America; and Yeats and Joyce from Ireland. He's unlike them, however, in that Germany evidently provided him with no models or pressures in the way that Poland, America and Ireland made themselves variously felt for his contemporaries. To Ford, Germany only represented a dystopia— before the war, a nightmare of Bismarckian bureaucratisation; afterwards a hell to be set against the heaven of the Mediterranean littoral. Terry

Eagleton has argued that the other exiles all had alternative cultures and traditions with which to counter the social erosion they perceived in England, "broader frameworks against which, in a highly creative tension, the erosion of contemporary order could be situated and partially understood."[10] Germany didn't offer itself to Ford in this way: hated, feared and absolutely rejected, it could provide no vantage-point from which to survey and grasp English social change. Indeed Ford felt that Germany was only a more advanced and noxious example of dissolution. Eagleton's thesis is that it was possible for the "aliens" to achieve a controlled evaluation of English society in transition during and soon after the First World War because of "an awareness that the declining culture they confronted was in no full sense their own." Their major art was produced "not from the simple availability of an alternative [culture], but from the subtle and involuted tensions between the remembered and the real, the potential and the actual, integration and dispossession, exile and involvement."[11] Ford differs, decisively, from this celebrated group in that he was not born, reared and educated outside England. He couldn't, therefore, call upon these linguistic and cultural vestiges that, for Conrad, were stored in Podolia and Cracow.

Instead Ford manufactured for himself an "alternative tradition," a matrix of social and cultural experiences, some real, many invented, that functioned rather like Conrad's "Poland," James' "Boston" or Eliot's "St. Louis." His German ancestry couldn't supply him with what Joyce gleaned from Dublin, but equally his English upbringing as a "poor relation" of the Rossettis, a life that was nomadic and rootless, didn't give him that purchase upon indigenous reality which was the heritage of Wells and Bennett. (Wells' father was a cricket professional, Bennett's a provincial solicitor.) So, in these circumstances, Ford had to invent his own life, and the purpose of the various volumes of memoir and autobiography was to give substance to the fabrication. His inveterate myth-making can best be seen as a continuing attempt to furnish himself with a base from which to survey and understand a country never fully apprehended as "native." Ford turned everything into fiction, though his best works will survive because they can be grasped as metaphors of the facts of English history — social and sexual upheaval.

Although the myth he built for himself was inchoate and inconsistent, its central element was Ford's desire to be viewed as a member of the English establishment, the product of ancient public school and university, and a gentleman burdened with the onerous "traditions of responsibilities, duties, privileges, and no rights."[12] Ford's incorporation here of the trappings of *noblesse oblige*, in its self-pity and melancholia so unlike the manner adopted by any authentic member of this class in thinking about himself at the opening of the century, came to possess for the novelist the same veracity as Conrad's Polish roots. In his grandfather Ford had seen the neglected, traduced artist. He adopts Brown's aesthetic of patience and self-sacrifice, reproducing it now, though, in terms of class and caste. Ford becomes the neglected gentleman, surrounded by opportunistic "Macmasters," fixers and climbers. Only he preserves, unadulterated and pristine, the dogmas and standards of the gentleman. In reality a descendant of the German bourgeoisie, Ford advanced the audacious claim to be the sole survivor of a race now extinct, the only Englishman faithful to the "exploded traditions" of an earlier age. The conditions of exile and dispossession in which Conrad, James and the others worked were real and spatial, but because Germany was so hated, Ford had to manufacture an alienation essentially temporal and historical. He proceeded to invent himself as an anachronism. While the other modernist aliens were finding creative substance in the memory of another country, Ford located his ideals in another, and imaginary, age. Reminiscence, often indeed sheer invention, was truly "the characteristic mode of Ford's thought."[13] The modernists' impulse towards authorial displacement was, with Ford, rather a matter of authorial invention. As a fiction, his life rivalled his best novels.

In these novels Ford's central preoccupation was with the dissociation of power from principle. His most permanent works depict the conflict between physical dominance and moral integrity. Authority, as personified by Henry VIII in the Tudor trilogy, by Leonora in *The Good Soldier*, and by *Parade's End*'s General Campion, is pragmatic, relativist, essentially without scruple. Ford's heroes, opponents of the dominant power— Katharine, Ashburnham, Tietjens—embody different values, absolutist, idealist, and unfashionable. During the same period, between about 1910 and 1927, Forster and Lawrence were also active in criticising the sexual and economic hegemony, yet they differed essentially from Ford in being able to draw sustaining values from outside the dominant culture—from the Schlegel sisters or from Birkin. Ford, though, employed parodistic versions of the ruling class itself as a means of delineating the moral inertia of the powerful.

This method is exemplified in the conversation between General Campion and Sylvia Tietjens in *No More Parades*, where Campion is interrogating the dishonoured wife about her husband's principles:

". . . But what, then, is it that Christopher has said? . . . Hang it all: what *is* at the bottom of that fellow's mind? . . ."

"He desires," Sylvia said, and she had no idea when she said it, "to model himself upon Our Lord . . ."

The general leant back in the sofa. He said almost indulgently:
"Who's that . . . Our *Lord*?"

Sylvia said:
"Upon Our Lord Jesus Christ . . ."

He sprang to his feet as if she had stabbed him with a hat-pin.
"Our . . ." he exclaimed. "Good God! . . . I always knew he had a screw loose . . . But . . ." He said briskly: "Give all his goods to the

poor! . . . But He wasn't a . . . not a socialist! What was it He said:
Render unto Caesar . . . It wouldn't be necessary to drum Him out of
the army . . ." He said: "Good Lord! . . . Good Lord! . . . Of course his
poor dear mother was a little . . . But, hang it! . . . The Wannop
girl . . ." Extreme discomfort overcame him . . . Tietjens was half-way
across from the inner room, coming towards them.[14]

This episode, a scene of magnificent high comedy, demonstrates that the
values of a Christian civilisation, which Campion purports to be defending against German "barbarism," really reside in Christopher, the
pariah of the establishment. Ford's tactics, then, were hyperbolic: he drew
stylised, exaggerated pictures of the dominant class in order to portray its
moral bankruptcy. As Walter Benjamin remarked of Baudelaire, Ford was
a "secret agent" of the social and political order — a "mole" — destroying
from within, rather than, as Forster and Lawrence did, from without.[15]
By overstating the chivalric disinterestedness of his harried heroes Ford
recorded the self-interest of the rulers.

Ford's style of perception and notation is, then, frankly non-mimetic,
metaphorical. His methods of characterisation — of himself and of his
fictional creations — are close to those of the caricaturist. His novels
weren't intended as precise renderings of the external world of the realists.
Ford's memoirs, too, portray the past as he himself saw it, in preference to
any objective photographic version. His weakest novels are ineffective just
because they seem so private, quirky and lacking in any public reverberations. We have no means of "naturalizing" *Mr Apollo* or *The New
Humpty-Dumpty* because we can't discern how these two texts might be
set against any real world.[16] Here Ford had invested so heavily in the
depiction of extreme and violent mental states that when these failed to
resonate, the reader has nothing else on which to fall back. On the other
hand, his indubitably major work, *The Good Soldier* and *Parade's End*,
succeeds because the embattled mental conditions there presented epi-
tomised certain sectional or national neuroses of the time. It was, in other
words, no accident that *The Good Soldier* coincided with a period of acute
pre-war crisis for a particular class, nor that the Tietjens cycle, likewise,
depicted an abnormally dangerous national emergency. In both instances,
Ford's eccentric, highly subjective vision overlapped more widely held
structures of feeling and experience.

The relative infrequency with which Ford managed to create novels
of such permanence — though most novelists of any age would be content
to have written *The Good Soldier* or *Parade's End* — may, then, be
attributed to the kind of *novelist* he was, rather than to the personal
vicissitudes of his life, to the marital entanglements and persistent insol-
vency documented by Mizener. Ford in truth was an "expressionist" artist
in his revulsion from science — the single subject of which he invariably
claimed ignorance — and the triumphs of the bourgeois state. He saw the
Germany created by Bismarck as a nightmare of the modern world, and

feared England was rushing down a parallel slope, propelled by the Fabians and Social Imperialists satirised in *The Inheritors*. In revulsion Ford turned inwards and made his own feelings — particularly the notion of a pristine honour defending itself against intrigue, calumny and pragmatism — the true subject-matter of his work. His cavalier attitude towards facts and history was a part of this movement inwards, away from the external world. Such expressionist subjectivity, however, often ran counter to the deepest impulses and conventions of Ford's preferred form, for, of all genres the novel is most closely affiliated with the history Ford was rejecting: "the notions of narrative, of character, and of formal unity in fiction are all congruent with the system of concepts making up the Western idea of history."[17] Ford's unsuccessful novels disturbed fiction's intimacy with history, while his handful of major works resulted from an ability to project his inner visions and link them with historical developments. Thus the nightmares of Ashburnham in 1914 and of Tietjens between 1912 and 1920 were expressive of the widespread convulsions of that era. German expressionism was deeply implicated in war, revolution and cultural crisis. Similarly it was no coincidence that Ford's lasting achievements as an expressionist novelist were also the product of a decade of acute public upheaval. His best work required historical crises to validate the novelist's inner disjunctions.

Notes

1. Malcolm Bradbury and James McFarlane, eds., *Pelican Guides to European Literature: Modernism 1890–1930* (Harmondsworth, 1976).

2. Lawrence Thornton, "Deux bonshommes distinct: Conrad, Ford, and the Visual Arts," *Conradiana*, VIII (1976), 11.

3. Sondra Stang, *Ford Madox Ford* (New York, 1977), p. 130.

4. M. D. Zabel, *Craft and Character in Modern Fiction* (London, 1957), p. 259.

5. Stang, pp. 6, 44.

6. Douglas Goldring, *The Last Pre-Raphaelite: A Record of the Life and Writings of Ford Madox Ford* (London, 1948), p. 18.

7. Ford Madox Ford, *Return to Yesterday* (New York, 1932), p. 58.

8. Thomas C. Moser, "From Olive Garnett's Diary: Impressions of Ford Madox Ford and his Friends, 1890–1906," *Texas Studies in Literature and Language*, XVI, iii (Fall, 1974), 516 (italics added).

9. Bernard Bergonzi, *The Turn of a Century: Essays on Victorian and Modern English Literature* (London, 1973), p. 145.

10. Terry Eagleton, *Exiles and Emigrés: Studies in Modern Literature* (London, 1970), p. 15.

11. *Ibid.*, p. 18.

12. "Literary Portraits — LV: Trimalchio," *Outlook*, XXXIV (26 September 1914), 399–400, cited in David Dow Harvey, *Ford Madox Ford 1873–1939: A Bibliography of Works and Criticism* (Princeton, 1962), p. 202.

13. Richard W. Lid, *Ford Madox Ford: The Essence of His Art* (Berkeley, 1964), p. 14.

14. Ford Madox Ford, *No More Parades* (New York, 1964), p. 417.

15. Walter Benjamin, *Charles Baudelaire: A Lyric Poet in the Era of High Capitalism* (London, 1973), p. 104, fn. 1.

16. I take the concept of "naturalization" from Jonathan Culler, *Structualist Poetics* (London, 1975), ch. VII.

17. J. Hillis Miller, "Narrative and History," *English Literary History*, XLI, iii (Fall 1974), 461.

INDEX

12/97 3